FEATURING FEMALES

PSYCHOLOGY OF WOMEN
BOOK SERIES

CHERYL BROWN TRAVIS, Series Editor

FEATURING FEMALES

Feminist Analyses
of Media

Edited by
Ellen Cole and Jessica Henderson Daniel

American Psychological Association
Washington, DC

Published by
American Psychological Association
750 First Street, NE
Washington, DC 20002
www.apa.org

To order
APA Order Department
P.O. Box 92984
Washington, DC 20090-2984
Tel: (800) 374-2721; Direct: (202) 336-5510
Fax: (202) 336-5502; TDD/TTY: (202) 336-6123
Online: www.apa.org/books/
E-mail: order@apa.org

In the U.K., Europe, Africa, and the Middle East, copies may be ordered from
American Psychological Association
3 Henrietta Street
Covent Garden, London
WC2E 8LU England

Typeset in Goudy by Stephen McDougal, Mechanicsville, MD

Printer: VictorGraphics, Baltimore, MD
Cover Designer: Naylor Design, Washington, DC
Technical/Production Editors: Harriet Kaplan and Gail Munroe

The opinions and statements published are the responsibility of the authors, and such opinions and statements do not necessarily represent the policies of the American Psychological Association.

Library of Congress Cataloging-in-Publication Data

Featuring females : feminist analyses of media / edited by Ellen Cole and Jessica Henderson Daniel. — 1st ed.
    p. cm.
Includes bibliographical references and index.
ISBN 1-59147-278-4
1. Women in mass media. I. Cole, Ellen. II. Daniel, Jessica Henderson.

P94.5.W65F43 2005
302.23'082—dc22   2005004592

British Library Cataloguing-in-Publication Data
A CIP record is available from the British Library.

Printed in the United States of America
First Edition

CONTENTS

PREFACE

The junction where media, psychology, and feminism meet—the focus of this volume—is obviously complex. For clear access to the multilayered scenarios that emerge from such an intersection, a lens capable of close-ups, wide angles, and various filters is needed. Print, electronic, and cinematic media are multifaceted: Print alone includes news stories, advertisements, cartoons, features, and editorials. The more than 50 divisions of the American Psychological Association testify to the complexity of the discipline and its topics and areas of expertise. Feminism, although not a monolithic concept, is a term to be explored and discussed. The authors' hope is that the broad-based discourse in this volume will spark a lively exchange about media and its impacts among psychologists in the realms of practice, science, public interest, and education. Media matter.

This volume is the product of the Task Force on Media, Women, and Girls of the Society for the Psychology of Women, Division 35, of the American Psychological Association. The chapter authors represent a range of psychologists as well as one communications scholar. Included are practitioners who provide clinical and counseling services and have consequently explored media as part of a client's social context; scientists who have conducted research about the contents and the effects of media; public policy advocates who have focused on media as it impacts policy and practice at the macro level; and educators who have provided both instruction and training about how the media interact with practice, science, and public policy.

In highlighting critical issues feminist psychologists raise about media, a certain breadth of the discipline is necessary. For example, gender issues in the construction of media and the use of media are viewed in this volume as tools of socialization. The authors have taken a deliberately feminist view of the subject, a female gaze rather than the male gaze that has so often reflected an ignorance of or apathy toward women's stature. In addition, the text includes perspectives on race and class consciousness.

In the 1995 edited book *Gender, Race, and Class in Media*,[1] the authors focused on specific television programs featuring women as main characters. Pop icon Madonna, soap opera roles, advertising, modalities of sexual representation, daytime and nighttime programming, and pornography provided material for exploration. It is noteworthy that pornography is absent from this current volume for the simple reason that mainstream culture and pornography appear to have met and merged. In the earlier volume, analyses of advertising to increase consumption and create images were included. In this volume, the authors examine images that are detrimental to girls and women, including, perhaps surprisingly, ads featuring women employed in traditionally male jobs. Finally, popular culture, primarily hiphop culture in the form of music videos and rap culture, was treated in the earlier volume in terms of racial and gender issues and the appropriation of Black culture. At this point, much of Black culture has become part of the mainstream, accepted especially by adolescents. In this volume, racial stereotypes are explored as present in contemporary advertisements and film.

Part I begins with the mandate to examine the impact of media images on girls as they pertain to gender roles, body image, and sexuality. Research psychologists Ward and Harrison provide a comprehensive literature review (chap. 1). Their conclusion is that such media are sources of socialization regarding both sexual and gender identity. In addition, resulting processes appear to be more restrictive for girls rather than being growth promoting. Sorsoli, Porche, and Tolman, who conduct research at the meeting place of television consumption and sexual behavior, conclude that media literacy for both girls and boys, based on an understanding of ideologies of both genders, can potentially generate an effective intervention strategy (chap. 2). Both genders can benefit from higher levels of awareness. Gilbert, Keery, and Thompson examine the current preoccupation with attaining body images that are most difficult or likely impossible to achieve (chap. 3). Effects for girls and women may include eating disorders that manifest as psychiatric and physical illnesses. Part I contains information for researchers of media, educators who may focus on media literacy, practitioners who provide services to females, and public policy advocates monitoring women's issues in the media.

In Part II, Defining Reality, Zuckerman and Dubowitz (chap. 4) begin with a history of women in television programs, presenting discrepancies between television preferences of mothers and daughters as one source of a generational rift within the family. Brown recounts a personal experience as resident psychologist for a reality TV show and reveals that the reality show

---

[1]Dines, G., & Humez, J. M. (Eds.). (1995). *Gender, race and class in media: A text reader*. Thousand Oaks, CA: Sage.

is no more real than television's usual fare (chap. 5). In doing so, she notes who is visible and who is either invisible or in the shadows. In the next chapter (chap. 6), the reality of living in a technologically driven society is explored in the context of women in related advertisements. Burlingame-Lee and Canetto note that women are either absent or cast in passive roles in computer advertisements. The limited number of ads in women-oriented publications is noted along with a masculine orientation in the messages. Such ads do not appear to welcome female applications. Finally, Schultz provides a gendered analysis of cinematic portrayals of psychologists and psychiatrists (chap. 7). Stereotypical women psychotherapists violate boundaries and engage in violence, in sharp contrast to data that attribute such behaviors primarily to male psychotherapists. The author seeks to provide explanations for the discrepancy between these cinematic images and actual research data. Part II suggests that television programming, even in the reality shows, films, and advertisements, often falls short of providing positive images of women diverse in age, sexual orientation, and race or ethnicity. For educators and practitioners seeking to address image options for girls and women, it is hoped that this volume will create a heightened awareness of harmful portrayals of women in media so that we may begin to counter negative images when and where we find them.

Authors included in Part III, Aggression and Violence, approach the topic by focusing on the news, film, television, and video games. Although video games are often depicted as harmless entertainment, their contents suggest otherwise. As Dill and her colleagues note (chap. 8), the level of violence, including gratuitous violence, may be particularly harmful, as the games typically fail to generate guilt or shame. Paulson (chap. 9) focuses on film images of and issues around violence and motherhood to explore cultural mythology about women's nature and its relationship to an understanding and treatment of women's violence toward their children. Carll (chap. 10) examines film portrayals and news coverage of women as both perpetrators and victims. In particular, differences in media coverage of domestic violence and rape as well as gender differences in the perpetrators are delineated. Feshbach (chap. 11) raises an important distinction between direct and indirect aggression, noting that women in the media are more likely to be portrayed engaging in the latter approach. One noteworthy finding is the high level of indirect aggression in comedy shows. Violence comes in a variety of forms, including a game show or a comedy. The identification of violence in unlikely contexts is important in the provision of services as well as the conduct of research. As a result, public policy advocates have the opportunity to raise public awareness of the manifestations of violence from a feminist perspective.

When gender intersects with race and age, the results tend to be bold stereotypes. In Part IV, Bryant-Davis (chap. 12) examines the roles of Black women in Spike Lee films, noting his varied story lines and yet typecast representations of Black women. Sanchez-Hucles and her coauthors (chap. 13), in an empirically based chapter, find that although advertisements in majority and ethnic magazines have tended to include more women of color in recent years, the range of depictions is limited, and they conclude that negative bias toward women of color remains unchanged. Finally, Kjaersgaard (chap. 14) provides information pointing to the continued absence of women in the media as they age and the implied significance of that message in the lives of girls and women. Media literacy could and should counter cinematic and print images of women of color and differentially gendered treatment of aging that continues to stigmatize the older woman.

Today most media are mass media that can be accessed by millions on a daily basis. Moreover, media in various forms continue to evolve. Analyses of content and implications of images provide the basis for the creation of media literacy programs for both girls and women. Such awareness informs the male population regarding potential problems caused by traditional masculine perspectives. Equally as important, the chapters document a paucity of story lines and images related to girls and women that in a better informed world would contribute to women's feelings of worth and life's options. Women being demeaned and dismissed in the media is but one option. Other options, if made available, could contribute to women's empowerment. Women making choices regarding their bodies as well as society's appreciation of their intelligence would be a major step in the right direction.

Media as entertainment convey messages that potentially inform and influence attitudes and behaviors. Deconstructing the messages is warranted. Many lenses—close-up and wide-angle—and various filters that analyze voice–silence, appearance–absence, stereotypes–everyday images, and high-profile–marginalized women on the basis of age, class, sexual orientation, race or ethnicity, and disability status are critical tools. In exploring these issues, the many voices here provide multiple tools and perspectives. These points and more are made compellingly in the chapters of this volume.

Authors were asked to begin their chapters with a short vignette. The vignettes provide uniformity in an otherwise disparate collection of styles and topics. Moreover, when viewed as a cumulative whole, they create a vivid portrayal of girls and women depicted and affected by multiple forms of media in existence today.

I

BEGINNING WITH GIRLS: GENDER ROLES, BODY IMAGE, AND SEX

1

THE IMPACT OF MEDIA USE ON GIRLS' BELIEFS ABOUT GENDER ROLES, THEIR BODIES, AND SEXUAL RELATIONSHIPS: A RESEARCH SYNTHESIS

L. MONIQUE WARD AND KRISTEN HARRISON

We are educated by the entertainment media, even if unintended by the source and unnoticed by the audience.
—A. Singhal and E. M. Rogers (1999, p. 8)

Evidence from several decades of research indicates that media portrayals typically construct rather narrow and stereotypical portraits of women and of femininity (Signorielli, 2001; Ward & Caruthers, 2001). For female characters, the focus is on physical appearance, sexual appeal, and romantic success, with women appearing most often as housewives, mothers, or objects of desire. As subordinates and nurturers, female characters are frequently depicted with stereotypical attributes (e.g., as emotional) and exhibiting stereotypical behaviors (e.g., deferring). Women's bodies are habitually presented as objects for others' viewing pleasure, objects used to beautify and adorn. Although showing a woman as a loving mother or as a sexual being is not inherently problematic, it becomes a problem if they are almost always shown this way, which normalizes objectification and provides a limited perspective on women's humanity.

3

How, then, does repeated exposure to these portrayals affect girls' beliefs about themselves and the female role? With only a limited range of roles, looks, and behaviors presented and rewarded in the media, will girls' beliefs about femininity become equally constrained? Empirical attempts to address these questions have typically taken one of three approaches. One approach examines the impact of TV's gender role portrayals, testing whether frequent exposure to stereotypical images of women brings about more traditional gender-role beliefs or constrains young viewers' preferences and aspirations. A second approach examines the media's impact on body satisfaction and eating disorders. Here, the expectation is that exposure to and identification with thin-ideal media will decrease body satisfaction and encourage disordered eating. The third approach investigates how the media's portrayal of sexual relationships shapes young viewers' sexual attitudes and behaviors. Studies in this area typically examine whether the media's overemphasis on sex encourages sexual activity among teens or strengthens their acceptance of nonrelational sex. Although each literature has developed and moved along separate tracks, sometimes even drawing support from different theories, they are in fact highly interrelated, each addressing a specific aspect of society's expectations of women. Thus, if the goal is to investigate the extent to which the media teach and reinforce traditional definitions of femininity, examining any of the three literatures in isolation may lead to incomplete conclusions. Instead, by looking at the three together, one can begin to understand the full breadth of the media's impact on girls. This review represents a first attempt to do this.

Thus, to more fully address the media's influence on girls, in this chapter we unite and summarize evidence indicating a link between media use and girls' attitudes about gender roles, their bodies, and sexual relationships. These domains were chosen both because of their importance as part of society's definition of feminine success (Basow & Rubin, 1999) and because of growing evidence that media use affects girls more than boys in these areas (Ward & Caruthers, 2001). Focusing on TV and magazine content (media on which the three literatures are based), we examine the findings of 129 studies compiled using both electronic and ancestral search mechanisms that were as exhaustive as possible. Electronic searches were conducted with PsycINFO and the Web of Science with the following keywords: *gender roles, gender stereotyping, body image, sexuality,* and *sexual roles,* in combination with *media, television, advertising,* and *magazines.* We conducted ancestral searches by examining the reference section of each of the articles uncovered and all available review articles in these fields. To keep the review current, we limited it to articles published between 1975 and 2002 and included studies testing girls and boys, or girls only, in the United States or Canada. We divide the findings into correlational survey research, which examines the contributions of everyday exposure, and experimental studies, which test the impact of laboratory exposure to specific content. With this review, we do not offer a critique of each study or its methods. Instead, our goal is to synthesize findings from three domains that are typically viewed separately to better demonstrate the full impact of the media's influence on girls.

IMPACT ON GENDER-ROLE DEVELOPMENT

How does repeated exposure to the media's often stereotypical images affect girls' beliefs about gender? Over the past 30 years, dozens of works have attempted to answer this question, forming a substantial literature containing more than 42 published studies. Previous descriptive reviews (e.g., Signorielli, 2001) focused mainly on the contributions of television, concluding that moderate to weak links exist between TV exposure and gender stereotyping. Our goal is to extend these reviews by examining the impact of TV and magazine content; by including samples of children, teens, and undergraduates; and by looking at multiple gender-role outcomes. Drawing from a recent review of this field (Ward & Caruthers, 2001), we segment our discussion according to four gender-role outcomes commonly studied.

Impact on Gender-Role Stereotyping

The largest set of studies in this area examines the media's impact on people's gender stereotyping and flexibility. Here, the concern is that if the media present female characters with only a limited range of attributes, skills, and abilities, viewers will develop equally limited assumptions about the sexes. Drawn from the premises of cultivation theory (Gerbner, Gross, Morgan, & Signorielli, 1994), findings from correlational data validate these concerns. First, frequent TV viewing is associated with holding more stereotypical associations about masculine and feminine activities, traits, and occupations (Kimball, 1986; McGhee & Frueh, 1980; Morgan, 1987; Signorielli & Lears, 1992; Zuckerman, Singer, & Singer, 1980). Second, greater exposure to specific genres is associated with viewers' assumptions about the distribution of real-world roles (Buerkel-Rothfuss & Mayes, 1981; Carveth & Alexander, 1985; Potter & Chang, 1990). More specifically, greater exposure to action-adventure programs more specifically is associated with lower estimates of the numbers of professional women; conversely, greater exposure to soap operas is associated with higher estimates of the numbers of housewives and female professionals. Third, significant associations have been reported between regular exposure to educational TV or to programs with nontraditional characters and greater flexibility (Repetti, 1984; Rosenwasser, Lingenfelter, & Harrington, 1989). Finally, results from experimental studies support these survey data. Laboratory exposure to images of the sexes in stereotypical roles appears to reinforce girls' gender stereotyping (O'Bryant & Corder-Bolz,

1978a), whereas exposure to nontraditional images or to verbal critiques of traditional images appears to reduce it (Davidson, Yasuna, & Tower, 1979; Nathanson, Wilson, McGee, & Sebastian, 2002; O'Bryant & Corder-Bolz, 1978a; Vaughan & Fisher, 1981). Brief exposure to stereotypic content has also been found to prime sex-biased evaluations of women and men encountered subsequently (Hansen, 1989; Kilbourne, 1990; Lafky, Duffy, Steinmaus, & Berkowitz, 1996). Because null to minimal results have been reported in other studies (Durkin & Hutchins, 1984; McCauley, Thangavelu, & Rozin, 1988; Meyer, 1980; Miller & Reeves, 1976; O'Bryant & Corder-Bolz, 1978b; Perloff, 1977; Repetti, 1984), these connections are by no means absolute. However, it does appear as if media use can be associated with holding more stereotypical views about who the sexes are and what they typically do.

Impact on Gender-Role Attitudes

A second group of studies examines the media's impact on children's attitudes about gender, focusing on their beliefs about the appropriateness of women's place in the domestic and work arenas and the competencies of each sex. Survey data linking heavier TV use with more sexist attitudes have produced many significant outcomes (e.g., Morgan, 1982), although some studies report results only for girls (Gross & Jeffries-Fox, 1978; Ward & Rivadeneyra, 1999) or specific genres (Potter & Chang, 1990; see Wroblewski & Huston, 1987, for null results). In one of the strongest connections reported, Time 1 viewing amounts correlated with teens' sexism scores at Time 1 and 6 months later, and were stronger among those with fewer social affiliations (Morgan & Rothschild, 1983). Exposure to nontraditional models is related to greater acceptance of nontraditional roles, as well (Miller & Reeves, 1976).

Mixed findings emerge from experimental work in which participants are exposed to stereotypical, neutral, or counterstereotypical media stimuli and are then surveyed concerning their gender-role beliefs. The hypothesized outcomes have emerged in some instances, with those exposed to traditional images reporting more sexist attitudes and those exposed to egalitarian stimuli reporting less sexist attitudes (Johnston, 1982; Lanis & Covell, 1995; MacKay & Covell, 1997; Pingree, 1978). Yet the literature also reports one null result (Schwarz, Wagner, Bannert, & Mathes, 1987) and two countereffects (Kilbourne, 1984; Matteson, 1991) with the same paradigms. Causal connections between media use and viewers' gender-role attitudes are therefore unconfirmed, requiring further study of possible mediating factors.

Impact on Viewers' Preferences for Stereotypical Activities and Occupations

In addition to shaping students' attitudes and assumptions about the sexes, might media use play a role in guiding viewers' own preferences? Findings here are mixed. In one study, frequent viewers verbalized stronger preferences for traditional activities and occupations than did infrequent viewers (Frueh & McGhee, 1975), but another study reported null results (Meyer, 1980). When the traditionality of the viewing diet is examined, significant correlations emerge (Wroblewski & Huston, 1987). In addition, findings from experimental work support these connections. Laboratory exposure to nontraditional images has been found to highlight the importance of achievement in women's aspirations (Geis, Brown, Jennings, & Porter, 1984), to increase girls' preferences for stereotypically masculine jobs (O'Bryant & Corder-Bolz, 1978a, 1978b), and to heighten children's interest in nontraditional hobbies and activities (Johnston, 1982). In a similar manner, experimental exposure to traditional models has been linked with less interest in political participation (Schwarz et al., 1987), reduced interest in quantitative careers (Davies, Spencer, Quinn, & Gerhardstein, 2002), and a stronger preference for feminine toys (McArthur & Eisen, 1976). Thus, the limited number of findings in this area suggests that girls' interest in specific activities and careers may be influenced by the range of possibilities to which they are exposed.

Influence on Gender-Related Behavior

Because gender roles do not easily translate into an observable set of behaviors, studying the media's influence on gender-related behavior is difficult. One approach is to examine whether children more consistently imitate the actions of same-sex or gender-traditional media models, making the same toy and activity selections that they demonstrate. Results are mixed, with some findings supporting this notion (Bussey & Bandura, 1984, Study 1; Cobb, Stevens-Long, & Goldstein, 1982; McArthur & Eisen, 1976) and others countering it (Vaughan & Fisher, 1981). Follow-up research demonstrated that characteristics of the model and the child affect the degree of the exposure's impact (Bussey & Bandura, 1984), indicating for example that children are more likely to avoid cross-sex behavior if they have reached higher levels of gender constancy (Ruble, Balaban, & Cooper, 1981). Exposure to nontraditional models has also been found to enhance young women's self-confidence and independent judgments as assessed in experimental tasks (Jennings, Geis, & Brown, 1980). A second approach examines whether frequent TV viewing is associated with performing more stereotypical chores around the house. Results indicate no links between these two factors (Morgan, 1987; Signorielli & Lears, 1992). It can be argued, however, that this may not be a true test of the impact of TV exposure on behavior because chore selection is not always within a child's control. Perhaps future study of this issue could focus on behaviors that are more voluntary, such as the games children play regularly. A third approach, which uses the stereotype threat paradigm, has found that experimental exposure to gender-stereotypic commercials leads to lower performance on a math test and to avoidance of math test items in favor of verbal items (Davies et al., 2002). These provocative findings provide indication of the various ways in which exposure to stereotypical content may shape girls' actual behavior.

IMPACT ON BODY IMAGE, BODY SATISFACTION, AND EATING BEHAVIORS

The overwhelming bias toward thinness as the female beauty ideal on commercial television and in fashion and fitness magazines has not escaped the notice of researchers interested in media effects on girls and young women. As of 1990 there were only a few studies on the effects of thin-ideal media, but since that time researcher interest in the topic has blossomed. The chief concern is how repeated exposure to the thin ideal shapes young women's perceptions both of their own bodies and of the importance of thinness in general. Summarized here are findings from 52 studies examining this issue, most of which tested college students. We group our review of these studies according to four categories of outcome variables.

Body Dissatisfaction

One of the most commonly assessed issues is whether the media's emphasis on the value of physical appearance and an unrealistically thin ideal leads female viewers to become dissatisfied with their own bodies. Evidence reveals that this is generally the case, although the nature of the outcome varies by the type of media exposure assessed. Students' *overall* amounts of entertainment TV viewing or magazine reading have been inconsistent predictors of their body attitudes, sometimes associated with greater dissatisfaction (Anderson, Huston, Schmitt, Linebarger, & Wright, 2001; Harrison, 2001; Harrison & Cantor, 1997), but sometimes not (Botta, 1999, 2000; Cusumano & Thompson, 1997; Harrison, 2000b; Hofschire & Greenberg, 2001). More consistent connections have emerged when the focus is on the viewing of specific-sized TV characters or on viewers' comparing themselves with certain personae. Here, evidence indicates that stronger preferences for or exposure to programming with conspicuously thin (Harrison, 2000b, 2001) or conspicuously heavy characters (Harrison, 1997; Harrison & Cantor, 1997) is associated with greater body dissatisfaction. In addition, actively using (Levine, Smolak, & Hayden, 1994), idealizing (Hofschire & Greenberg, 2001), and drawing comparisons between media models and one's own body (Botta, 1999, 2000; Jones, 2001; Richins, 1991) are associated with greater body dissatisfaction.

Experimentation in this area has examined whether students exposed to images of attractive or model-thin women express greater body dissatisfaction than do students exposed to images of average, unattractive, or plus-sized women. This has indeed proven to be the case, with the consistency of the results varying by participant age. Strong support emerges in studies of undergraduate women, with laboratory exposure to the beauty ideal leading not only to increased body dissatisfaction (Cash, Cash, & Butters, 1983; Irving, 1990; Lavine, Sweeney, & Wagner, 1999; Lin & Kulik, 2002; Richins, 1991; Stice & Shaw, 1994; Turner, Hamilton, Jacobs, Angood, & Dwyer, 1997; for countereffects, see Mills, Polivy, Herman, & Tiggemann, 2002; Myers & Biocca, 1992) but also to decreased self-esteem (Thornton & Maurice, 1997); increased anger, depression, and negative mood (Cattarin, Williams, Thomas, & Thompson, 2000; Pinhas, Toner, Ali, Garfinkel, & Stuckless, 1999); and reduced confidence (Lin & Kulik, 2002). Among high school girls, findings are more inconsistent, often indicating null or conditional results (Champion & Furnham, 1999; Martin & Kennedy, 1993; Stice, Spangler, & Agras, 2001). Yet evidence does indicate that exposure to images of overweight women may lead female teens to see themselves as more attractive (Crouch & Degelman, 1998).

Because results frequently occur only for some women or for some stimuli, researchers have also investigated the factors that moderate or mediate these connections between media exposure and body dissatisfaction. One set of factors examines features of the viewing situation, demonstrating that both the nature of the self-comparison processes (Martin & Gentry, 1997) and the social context of the exposure (e.g., men present or not; Henderson-King, Henderson-King, & Hoffman, 2001) influence the degree of the stimuli's impact. A second set of factors focuses on aspects of the participants. Evidence indicates that laboratory exposure to the thin ideal produces more negative effects on body satisfaction among women who initially exhibit a more negative body image (Harrison, 2001; Heinberg & Thompson, 1995; Stice et al., 2001), have less social support (Stice et al., 2001), are more accepting of the thin ideal and the importance of appearance (Heinberg & Thompson, 1995; Henderson-King et al., 2001), are heavier (Henderson-King & Henderson-King, 1997), or are more responsive to personal cues (Wilcox & Laird, 2000). Also playing a role are participant race and gender, with fewer connections emerging for Black women than for White women (Makkar & Strube, 1995) and for men than for women (Anderson et al., 2001; Cusumano & Thompson, 2000; Harrison, 2000b; Hofschire & Greenberg, 2001).

Weight Concerns and Self-Consciousness

A small set of studies has examined connections between media use and girls' general concerns about their weight and self-consciousness about their bodies. Using survey (Borzekowski, Robinson, & Killen, 2000; Taylor et al., 1998; Thomsen, 2002) and experimental paradigms (e.g., Kalodner, 1997), researchers have found that exposure to the thin ideal is associated with greater self-consciousness and concern with one's weight. For example, women exposed to photographs of fashion models reported greater general and body self-consciousness than did women exposed to no images or neutral images (e.g., children playing; Thornton & Maurice, 1997; Wegner, Hartmann, & Geist, 2000). This outcome is especially likely to occur among women who already express body dissatisfaction (Posavac, Posavac, & Posavac, 1998) and among women rather than men (Kalodner, 1997).

Internalization of the Thin Ideal and Drive for Thinness

In addition to examining how media use affects girls' beliefs about their own bodies, much research in this area addresses girls' acceptance and internalization of the thin ideal in general, testing how strongly they value thinness for themselves and for others. Results here are somewhat mixed. Findings across several studies indicate that greater media use or, more often, greater exposure to specific genres such as fashion magazines, is associated with stronger awareness and endorsement of the thin ideal (Borzekowski et al., 2000; Field, Cheung, et al., 1999; Harrison, 2001; Harrison & Cantor, 1997; Levine et al., 1994; Stice, Schupak-Neuberg, Shaw, & Stein, 1994). Indeed, many girls report the media as exerting more pressure to be thin than do peers and family members. Yet results often vary according to the genre or gender in question (Harrison, 2000a; Hofschire & Greenberg, 2001; Morry & Staska, 2001), and null effects have been reported (Abramson & Valene, 1991; Botta, 1999, 2000; Cusumano & Thompson, 1997; Harrison, 1997, 2000b). Experimentation has yielded mixed results also, with some researchers finding that directed exposure to thin ideals increases women's preoccupation with thinness and perceived importance of appearance (Tan, 1979; Turner et al., 1997), but others not (Stice & Shaw, 1994; Stice et al., 2001).

Others studying this issue have focused on levels of viewer involvement. Here, students' interest in thin-ideal media (Harrison, 2000b), their drawing of comparisons between themselves and thin characters (Botta, 1999, 2000), and their interpersonal attraction to thin personalities (Harrison, 1997) have each been found to predict their endorsement of the thin ideal, often more so than exposure levels did. For example, Harrison (1997) reported that students' levels of exposure to multiple media genres did not predict their drive for thinness, yet their attraction to thin personalities did. Yet because women's level of attraction to thin celebrities is not a correlate in every study (Hofschire & Greenberg, 2001; Levine et al., 1994), further work is needed to explore links between exposure, character attraction, and the thin ideal.

Behaviors and Beliefs Related to Eating

A final concern in this area is whether the media's excessive depiction of a thin ideal will lead girls to try to attain it themselves through restrained eating, excessive exercise, or bingeing and purging. This concern appears to be valid. Findings from survey data indicate that greater exposure to thin-ideal media is associated with higher levels of dieting, exercising, and disordered eating symptomatology (Abramson & Valene, 1991; Field, Camargo, et al., 1999; Harrison, 2000a; Stice et al., 1994; Thomsen, Weber, & Brown, 2002). For example, Hofschire and Greenberg (2001) reported that music video and soap opera viewing predicted more frequent dieting, and that stronger identification with media characters predicted more frequent exercising to lose weight. Stronger links exist for Anglo women than for Black (Botta, 2000) or Cuban American women (Jane, Hunter, & Lozzi, 1999), and women with eating disorders exhibit stronger negative responses to thin-ideal media than do others (Pinhas et al., 1999; see Irving, 1990, for null results). In addition to these direct effects, other researchers found that the media's impact on eating behavior is mediated by women's ideal discrepancies (Harrison, 2001), gender-role endorsement (Stice et al., 1994), and internalization of beauty ideals (Morry & Staska, 2001). Level of involvement with media characters is also influential. Being interpersonally attracted to thin TV characters (Harrison, 1997), assigning greater importance to beauty and fitness information obtained from the media (Levine et al., 1994), and consciously comparing oneself with TV characters (Botta, 1999; Field, Camargo, et al., 1999) are each associated with more frequent dieting and exercise. Although null results are reported (Cusumano & Thompson, 1997; Fouts & Vaughan, 2002) and many findings are genre- or gender-specific (Harrison, 1997, 2000b; Harrison & Cantor, 1997), overall, it appears as if girls' media use is correlated with their eating behavior.

Experimentation in this area has been rare and has yielded mixed results. Young women exposed to media images of ideal bodies offered greater endorsement of dieting attitudes and behaviors in one study (Turner et al., 1997), but not in another (Thornton & Maurice, 1997). In two experiments that measured eating behavior as a dependent variable, high-restraint (dieting) women exposed to diet advertisements or to thin models ate more after exposure than did nondieting women or women exposed to full-figured models (Mills et al., 2002; Strauss, Doyle, & Kreipe, 1994). Finally, Stice et al. (2001) reported that receiving a 15-month subscription to *Seventeen* had no direct effect on girls' dieting behavior or bulimic symptoms; however, the eating and dieting behaviors of girls with little social support were affected.

IMPACT OF MEDIA PORTRAYALS ON ATTITUDES AND ASSUMPTIONS ABOUT SEXUAL RELATIONSHIPS

The prevalence of sexual content in the media has raised concern that heavy media use may encourage stereotypical or casual attitudes toward sexual relationships, distorted expectations, and irresponsible sexual decision making. Although research in this area began only in the early 1980s, more than 32 studies have been published examining links between mainstream media exposure and students' sexual attitudes, assumptions, and behaviors. Of this group, approximately 40% of the studies used experimental designs, more than half focused on undergraduates, and nearly all chose TV as the medium for investigation. Our discussion is segmented by the sexual outcome in question, of which there are three.

Sexual Attitudes

The largest block of studies in this area focuses on contributions of media use to students' attitudes about sexual relationships. Does regular exposure to the media's frequent portrayals of sex as recreational and risk-free encourage viewers to adopt similar perspectives? Results are typically in the affirmative, indicating that greater exposure to or involvement with sexually oriented genres, such as soap operas and music videos, is associated with stronger support of premarital sex and traditional sexual roles, especially among female viewers (Strouse & Buerkel-Rothfuss, 1987; Strouse, Buerkel-Rothfuss, & Long, 1995; Walsh-Childers & Brown, 1993; Ward, 2002; Ward & Rivadeneyra, 1999), with stronger endorsement of negative or dysfunctional beliefs about relationships (Haferkamp, 1999; Signorielli, 1991) and with a greater acceptance of sexual harassment (Strouse, Goodwin, & Roscoe, 1994). Viewing amounts have also been linked with students' attitudes about their own sexual status. Here, being a frequent TV viewer and perceiving media characters as sexually more competent than oneself are associated with holding negative attitudes toward remaining a virgin and with less satisfaction with one's own sexual experiences (Baran, 1976a, 1976b; Courtright & Baran, 1980). Although both null and counterintuitive outcomes have been reported (Davis & Mares, 1998; Fabes & Strouse, 1987; Olson, 1994; Potter & Chang, 1990), the dominant trends indicate that frequent exposure to certain TV genres is linked to attitudes that elicit displeasure with virginity and support both nonrelational sex and sexual stereotypes.

Attempts have been made to test the causality of these associations through experimental means and to examine whether students exposed to sexual content express different attitudes about sexuality than do students exposed to nonsexual content. Although the results obtained are sometimes conditional, evidence does suggest that laboratory exposure to the sexual content of music videos (Calfin, Carroll, & Shmidt, 1993; Greeson & Williams, 1986; Kalof, 1999), prime-time programs (Bryant & Rockwell, 1994; Ward, 2002; but see Greenberg, Linsangan, & Soderman, 1993, for null results), and magazine advertisements (Lanis & Covell, 1995; MacKay & Covell, 1997) is associated with stronger endorsement of stereotypical attitudes about sex. For example, Ward (2002) reported that regardless of their regular viewing levels, women (but not men) exposed to images depicting men as sex-driven, women as sex objects, or sex as recreation offered stronger support of these stereotypes than did women in control groups.

Sexual Expectations and Attributions

A second concern has been the extent to which media use shapes viewers' sense of social reality. Do the media's frequent depictions of specific sexual actions or outcomes (e.g., extramarital affairs) make them seem more prevalent? Does media use shape the way in which the sexual actions of real women and men are perceived? Studies addressing these questions frequently report strong associations. Greater exposure to sexually oriented genres is linked to viewers' assumptions about the prevalence of sex and of certain sexual actions frequently depicted on TV (Buerkel-Rothfuss & Mayes, 1981; Buerkel-Rothfuss & Strouse, 1993; Carveth & Alexander, 1985; Davis & Mares, 1998; Larson, 1996; Olson, 1994; Potter & Chang, 1990; Ward, 2002). For example, frequent soap opera viewers offer higher estimates than do less frequent viewers of the numbers of real people who divorce, have affairs, or bear illegitimate children (e.g., Carveth & Alexander, 1985). Levels of viewer involvement are influential as well, such that women who strongly identify with popular TV characters assume that greater percentages of their peers are sexually active (Ward & Rivadeneyra, 1999). Thus, frequent and more involved viewers are likely to cultivate expectations that sex is prevalent and that sexual relationships are casual and fleeting.

Experimental exposure to sexual content has also been shown to affect students' perceptions of other women and men, such that real people encountered after sexual content has been viewed seem to take on attributes of that content (e.g., Hansen & Krygowski, 1994), appearing more sexualized themselves (Hansen & Hansen, 1988; Sigal, Gibbs, Adams, & Derfler, 1988). For example, exposure to suggestive videos featuring Black female performers led White students to attribute fewer positive traits and more negative traits to Black women encountered subsequently (Gan, Zillmann, & Mitrook, 1997). Hence, by means of contrast and comparison, viewers draw from fictional content in developing expectations about real-world interactions.

Sexual Behavior

Of critical concern in this area is how repeated exposure to sexual references and to images of risk-free sex might influence viewers' sexual decision making. Although these are difficult links to establish because of the complexity of sexual behavior, tentative evidence is building that heavier media use is linked to more sexual experience. Although total TV viewing is not typically associated with viewers' sexual behavior (Alexander, 1985; Brown & Newcomer, 1991; Peterson, Moore, & Furstenberg, 1991; Strouse &

Buerkel-Rothfuss, 1987), stronger results emerge when exposure to specific genres is examined. Among women, frequent viewing of music videos is linked with a greater number of sexual partners (Strouse & Buerkel-Rothfuss, 1987) and with more sexual experience (Strouse et al., 1995). For men, frequent soap opera viewing is linked to having more sexual partners (Strouse & Buerkel-Rothfuss, 1987). For both sexes, including a higher proportion of sexual content in one's TV diet is associated with a greater likelihood of becoming sexually active (Brown & Newcomer, 1991). Finally, viewer involvement plays a role, such that expressing stronger personal connections with media models and sexual situations is associated with greater levels of sexual experience (Fabes & Strouse, 1987; Ward & Rivadeneyra, 1999).

DISCUSSION

With their ability to depict, define, and discount, the media serve as powerful agents of gender and sexual socialization. Reported here were results from 120 published, empirical investigations testing whether directed, more frequent, or more involved media use is associated with a greater acceptance of the traditional dictates of the female role. We found several significant associations. First, media use appears to affect girls' beliefs about what it means to be a woman. Evidence indicates that girls with greater media use are more likely to endorse traditional beliefs about women's roles, occupations, and behaviors, are more likely to endorse the thin ideal, and are more likely to endorse more stereotypical notions about sexual relationships. Second, media use affects girls' expectations about the real world, such that girls with heavier media use expect that greater numbers of people divorce and have affairs and that greater numbers of their peers are sexually active. Finally, media use appears to shape how girls perceive themselves and their futures. Thus, girls with more frequent media use are more likely to be dissatisfied with their bodies and with their virginity status, to be concerned about their weight, to exhibit disordered eating attitudes and behaviors, and to aspire to traditionally feminine careers.

The implications of these findings for young viewers are potentially far-reaching. If girls' gender belief systems are shaped by media use, the most immediate outcome is likely to be their striving to adhere to dictates of the traditional female role. Many researchers believe that efforts to meet its rigid standards contribute to the high incidence of low self-esteem, poor body image, and depression seen among adolescent girls (Basow & Rubin, 1999). Other, less direct outcomes are also likely. For example, if frequent media users place physical appearance at the center of their self-worth, as media portrayals encourage them to do, it follows that great effort would be spent focusing on this domain, perhaps with less time to devote to other areas (e.g., political action, schoolwork). Indeed, Fredrickson and Roberts (1997) argued that this habitual body monitoring interferes with mental concentration and reduces women's opportunities for peak motivational states. It is also possible that girls' acceptance of stereotypes framing women as sex *objects* may lead them to feel less comfortable acting as agentic, sexual *subjects*. In addition, might believing that men are sex-driven (e.g., "boys will be boys") encourage women to endure infidelities and disrespectful behavior? Although additional research is needed to address these specific questions, it is apparent that many potential consequences may fall from the media's overemphasis on sexual and gender-role stereotypes.

Although the findings produced thus far are powerful and provocative, they are by no means complete. As noted throughout this review, null and conditional results are also reported, and the small number of studies in some domains prohibits drawing firm conclusions. Further work is needed in several areas to obtain a broader understanding of how media use shapes girls' constructions of the female role. First, continuing the efforts begun here, research needs to examine how connections in one area relate to outcomes in others, testing simultaneously how media use affects girls' beliefs about gender roles, their bodies, and sexuality. Second, research needs to expand to include media other than TV programs and magazines. Study is needed concerning the impact both of other media, such as feature films and popular music, and of new TV genres, such as reality programs. Third, research needs to use assessments of media exposure that go beyond examining amounts consumed at one point in time. Because media use is broad and person-specific, research needs to address girls' overall media diets, consumption histories, and levels of viewer involvement. Fourth, diversification is needed in the participants investigated; research is needed that compares across large age spans, follows girls over time, and tests both White and minority youth. Also needed is investigation of specific mechanisms that may lead Latinas and African American women to be less affected than Anglo women by media exposure in some domains. Finally, research needs to explore other individual difference factors that either strengthen negative media effects or protect girls from them. Identified here as factors that might intensify negative media effects were having preexisting appearance vulnerabilities, having reached gender constancy, and having a smaller social support system. Other issues to explore are aspects of physical development, such as pubertal status, and whether adopting feminist beliefs works as a protective factor.

For girls working to develop an understanding of the female role, media images and models are virtually unavoidable. However, the messages they convey about femininity are often rigid and constricting, presenting only select examples of who women are, how they look, and how they behave in romantic relationships. In uniting research across several fields, we saw the sweeping effects that exposure to these images may be having on girls, shaping their notions about gender and about themselves. With future research uniting these fields, we can continue to examine how media use affects multiple aspects of girls' lives and can begin to determine which girls are most at risk.

REFERENCES

Abramson, E., & Valene, P. (1991). Media use, dietary restraint, bulimia, and attitudes toward obesity: A preliminary study. *British Review of Bulimia and Anorexia Nervosa, 5*, 73–76.

Alexander, A. (1985). Adolescents' soap opera viewing and relational perceptions. *Journal of Broadcasting and Electronic Media, 29*, 295–308.

Anderson, D., Huston, A., Schmitt, K., Linebarger, D., & Wright, J. (2001). Early childhood television viewing and adolescent behavior. *Monographs of the Society for Research in Child Development, 66*, 108–118.

Baran, S. J. (1976a). How TV and film portrayals affect sexual satisfaction in college students. *Journalism Quarterly, 53*, 468–473.

Baran, S. J. (1976b). Sex on TV and adolescent self-image. *Journal of Broadcasting, 20*, 61–68.

Basow, S. A., & Rubin, L. R. (1999). Gender influences on adolescent development. In N. G. Johnson, M. C. Roberts, & J. Worell (Eds.), *Beyond appearance: A new look at adolescent girls* (pp. 25–52). Washington, DC: American Psychological Association.

Borzekowski, D. L., Robinson, T. N., & Killen, J. D. (2000). Does the camera add 10 pounds? Media use, perceived importance of appearance, and weight concerns among teenage girls. *Journal of Adolescent Health, 26*, 36–41.

Botta, R. A. (1999). Television images and adolescent girls' body image disturbance. *Journal of Communication, 49*, 22–41.

Botta, R. A. (2000). The mirror of television: A comparison of Black and White adolescents' body image. *Journal of Communication, 50*, 144–159.

Brown, J. D., & Newcomer, S. F. (1991). Television viewing and adolescents' sexual behavior. *Journal of Homosexuality, 21*, 77–91.

Bryant, J., & Rockwell, S. C. (1994). Effects of massive exposure to sexually oriented prime-time television programming on adolescents' moral judgment. In D. Zillman, J. Bryant, & A. C. Huston (Eds.), *Media, children, and the family: Social scientific, psychodynamic, and clinical perspectives* (pp. 183–195). Hillsdale, NJ: Erlbaum.

Buerkel-Rothfuss, N. L., & Mayes, S. (1981). Soap opera viewing: The cultivation effect. *Journal of Communication, 31*, 108–115.

Buerkel-Rothfuss, N., & Strouse, J. (1993). Media exposure and perceptions of sexual behaviors: The cultivation hypothesis moves to the bedroom. In B. S. Greenberg, J. D. Brown, & N. L. Buerkel-Rothfuss (Eds.), *Media, sex, and the adolescent* (pp. 225–247). Creskill, NJ: Hampton Press.

Bussey, K., & Bandura, A. (1984). Influence of gender constancy and social power on sex-linked modeling. *Journal of Personality and Social Psychology, 47*, 1292–1302.

Calfin, M. S., Carroll, J. L., & Shmidt, J. (1993). Viewing music videotapes before taking a test of premarital sexual attitudes. *Psychological Reports, 72*, 475–481.

Carveth, R., & Alexander, A. (1985). Soap opera viewing motivation and the cultivation process. *Journal of Broadcasting and Electronic Media, 29,* 259–273.

Cash, T. F., Cash, D. W., & Butters, J. (1983). "Mirror, mirror on the wall . . . ?": Contrast effects and self-evaluations of physical attractiveness. *Personality and Social Psychology Bulletin, 9,* 351–358.

Cattarin, J., Williams, R., Thomas, C., & Thompson, J. (2000). Body image, mood, and televised images of attractiveness: The role of social comparison. *Journal of Social & Clinical Psychology, 19,* 220–239.

Champion, H., & Furnham, A. (1999). The effect of the media on body satisfaction in adolescent girls. *European Eating Disorders Review, 7,* 213–228.

Cobb, N. J., Stevens-Long, J., & Goldstein, S. (1982). The influence of televised models on toy preference in children. *Sex Roles, 8,* 773–784.

Courtright, J. A., & Baran, S. J. (1980). The acquisition of sexual information by young people. *Journalism Quarterly, 57,* 107–114.

Crouch, A., & Degelman, D. (1998). Influence of female body images in printed advertising on self-ratings of physical attractiveness by adolescent girls. *Perceptual and Motor Skills, 87,* 585–586.

Cusumano, D., & Thompson, J. (1997). Body image and body shape ideals in magazines: Exposure, awareness, and internalization. *Sex Roles, 37,* 701–721.

Cusumano, D. L., & Thompson, J. K. (2000). Media influence and body image in 8- to 11-year-old boys and girls: A preliminary report on the multidimensional media influence scale. *International Journal of Eating Disorders, 29,* 37–44.

Davidson, E. S., Yasuna, A., & Tower, A. (1979). The effects of television cartoons on sex-role stereotyping in young girls. *Child Development, 50,* 597–600.

Davies, P., Spencer, S., Quinn, D., & Gerhardstein, R. (2002). Consuming images: How television commercials that elicit stereotype threat can restrain women academically and professionally. *Personality and Social Psychology Bulletin, 28,* 1615–1628.

Davis, S., & Mares, M.-L. (1998). Effects of talk show viewing on adolescents. *Journal of Communication, 48,* 69–86.

Durkin, K., & Hutchins, G. (1984). Challenging traditional sex role in careers education broadcasts: The reactions of young secondary school pupils. *Journal of Educational Television, 10,* 25–33.

Fabes, R. A., & Strouse, J. (1987). Perceptions of responsible and irresponsible models of sexuality: A correlational study. *Journal of Sex Research, 23,* 70–84.

Field, A. E., Camargo, C. A., Taylor, C. B., Berkey, C., & Colditz, G. (1999). Relation of peer and media influences to the development of purging behaviors among preadolescent and adolescent girls. *Archives of Pediatric Adolescent Medicine, 11,* 1184–1189.

Field, A. E., Cheung, L., Wolf, A., Herzog, D., Gortmaker, S., & Colditz, G. (1999). Exposure to the mass media and weight concerns among girls. *Pediatrics, 103*(3), E36.

Fouts, G., & Vaughan, K. (2002). Locus of control, television viewing, and eating disorder symptomatology in young females. *Journal of Adolescence, 25,* 307–311.

Fredrickson, B. L., & Roberts, T. (1997). Objectification theory: Toward under-standing women's lived experiences and mental health risks. *Psychology of Women Quarterly, 21*, 173–206.

Frueh, T., & McGhee, P. E. (1975). Traditional sex role development and amount of time spent watching television. *Developmental Psychology, 11*, 109.

Gan, S-l, Zillmann, D., & Mitrook, M. (1997). Stereotyping effect of Black women's sexual rap on White audiences. *Basic and Applied Social Psychology, 19*, 381–399.

Geis, F. L., Brown, V., Jennings (Walstedt), J., & Porter, N. (1984). TV commercials as achievement scripts for women. *Sex Roles, 10*, 513–525.

Gerbner, G., Gross, L., Morgan, M., & Signorielli, N. (1994). Growing up with tele-vision: The cultivation perspective. In J. Bryant & D. Zillman (Eds.), *Media effects: Advances in theory and research* (pp. 17–41). Hillsdale, NJ: Erlbaum.

Greenberg, B. S., Linsangan, R., & Soderman, A. (1993). Adolescents' reactions to television sex. In B. S. Greenberg, J. D. Brown, & N. L. Buerkel-Rothfuss (Eds.), *Media, sex, and the adolescent* (pp. 196–224). Creskill, NJ: Hampton Press.

Greeson, L. E., & Williams, R. A. (1986). Social implications of music videos for youth: An analysis of the content and effects of MTV. *Youth and Society, 18*, 177–189.

Gross, L., & Jeffries-Fox, S. (1978). What do you want to be when you grow up, little girl? In G. Tuchman, A. K. Daniels, & J. Benet (Eds.), *Hearth and home: Images of women in the mass media* (pp. 240–265). New York: Oxford Press.

Haferkamp, C. J. (1999). Beliefs about relationships in relation to television view-ing, soap opera viewing, and self-monitoring. *Current Psychology, 18*, 193–204.

Hansen, C. H. (1989). Priming sex role stereotypic event schemas with rock music videos: Effects on impression favorability, trait inferences, and recall of a subse-quent male-female interaction. *Basic & Applied Social Psychology, 10*, 371–391.

Hansen, C. H., & Hansen, R. D. (1988). How rock music videos can change what is seen when boy meets girl: Priming stereotypic appraisal of social interactions. *Sex Roles, 19*, 287–316.

Hansen, C. H., & Krygowski, W. (1994). Arousal-augmented priming effects: Rock music videos and sex object schemas. *Communication Research, 21*, 24–47.

Harrison, K. (1997). Does interpersonal attraction to thin media personalities pro-mote eating disorders? *Journal of Broadcasting and Electronic Media, 41*, 478–500.

Harrison, K. (2000a). The body electric: Thin-ideal media and eating disorders in adolescents. *Journal of Communication, 50*, 119–143.

Harrison, K. (2000b). Television stereotyping, fat stereotyping, body shape stan-dards, and eating disorder symptomatology in grade school children. *Communi-cation Research, 27*, 617–640.

Harrison, K. (2001). Ourselves, our bodies: Thin-ideal media, self discrepancies, and eating disorder symptomatology in adolescents. *Journal of Social and Clinical Psy-chology, 20*, 289–323.

Harrison, K., & Cantor, J. (1997). The relationship between media consumption and eating disorders. *Journal of Communication, 47,* 40–67.

Heinberg, L., & Thompson, F. (1995). Body image and televised images of thinness and attractiveness: A controlled laboratory investigation. *Journal of Social and Clinical Psychology, 14,* 325–338.

Henderson-King, E., & Henderson-King, D. (1997). Media effects on women's body esteem: Social and individual difference factors. *Journal of Applied Social Psychology, 27,* 399–417.

Henderson-King, D., Henderson-King, E., & Hoffman, L. (2001). Media images and women's self evaluations: Social context and importance of attractiveness as moderators. *Personality & Social Psychology Bulletin, 27,* 1407–1416.

Hofschire, L. J., & Greenberg, B. S. (2001). Media's impact on adolescents' body dissatisfaction. In J. D. Brown & J. Steele (Eds.), *Sexual teens, sexual media* (pp. 125–149). Mahwah, NJ: Erlbaum.

Irving, L. (1990). Mirror image: Effects of the standard of beauty on the self- and body-esteem of women exhibiting varying levels of bulimic symptom. *Journal of Social & Clinical Psychology, 9,* 230–242.

Jane, D. M., Hunter, G., & Lozzi, B. (1999). Do Cuban American women suffer from eating disorders? Effects of media exposure and acculturation. *Hispanic Journal of Behavioral Science, 21,* 212–218.

Jennings, J., Geis, F. L., & Brown, V. (1980). Influence of television commercials on women's self-confidence and independent judgment. *Journal of Personality and Social Psychology, 38,* 203–210.

Johnston, J. (1982). Using television to change stereotypes. *Prevention in Human Services, 2,* 67–81.

Jones, D. C. (2001). Social comparison and body image: Attractiveness comparisons to models and peers among adolescent girls and boys. *Sex Roles, 45*(9/10), 645–664.

Kalodner, C. R. (1997). Media influences on male and female non-eating-disordered college students: A significant issue. *Eating Disorders: The Journal of Treatment & Prevention, 5,* 47–57.

Kalof, L. (1999). The effects of gender and music video imagery on sexual attitudes. *The Journal of Social Psychology, 139,* 378–385.

Kilbourne, W. E. (1984). An exploratory study of sex-roles in advertising and women's perceptions of managerial attributes in women. *Advances in Consumer Research, 11,* 84–87.

Kilbourne, W. E. (1990). Female stereotyping in advertising: An experiment on male-female perceptions of leadership. *Journalism Quarterly, 67,* 25–31.

Kimball, M. M. (1986). Television and sex-role attitudes. In T. M. Williams (Ed.), *The impact of television: A natural experiment in three communities* (pp. 265–301). New York: Academic Press.

Lafky, S., Duffy, M., Steinmaus, M., & Berkowitz, D. (1996). Looking through gendered lenses: Female stereotyping in advertisements and gender role expectations. *Journalism and Mass Communication Quarterly, 73,* 379–388.

Lanis, K., & Covell, K. (1995). Images of women in advertisements: Effects on attitudes related to sexual aggression. *Sex Roles, 32*, 639–649.

Larson, M. S. (1996). Sex roles and soap operas: What adolescents learn about single motherhood. *Sex Roles, 35*, 97–110.

Lavine, H., Sweeney, D., & Wagner, S. (1999). Depicting women as sex objects in television advertising: Effects on body dissatisfaction. *Personality and Social Psychology Bulletin, 25*, 1049–1058.

Levine, M. P., Smolak, L., & Hayden, H. (1994). The relation of sociocultural factors to eating attitudes and behaviors among middle school girls. *Journal of Early Adolescence, 14*, 471–490.

Lin, L., & Kulik, J. (2002). Social comparison and women's body satisfaction. *Basic and Applied Social Psychology, 24*, 115–123.

MacKay, N. J., & Covell, K. (1997). The impact of women in advertisements on attitudes toward women. *Sex Roles, 36*, 573–583.

Makkar, J. K., & Strube, M. J. (1995). Black women's self-perceptions of attractiveness following exposure to White versus Black beauty standards: The moderating role of racial identity and self-esteem. *Journal of Applied Social Psychology, 25*, 1547–1566.

Martin, M. C., & Gentry, J. W. (1997). Stuck in the model trap: The effects of beautiful models in ads on female pre-adolescents and adolescents. *Journal of Advertising, 26*, 19–33.

Martin, M. C., & Kennedy, P. F. (1993). Advertising and social comparison: Consequences for female preadolescents and adolescents. *Psychology and Marketing, 10*, 513–530.

Matteson, D. R. (1991). Attempting to change sex role attitudes in adolescents: Explorations of reverse effects. *Adolescence, 26*, 885–898.

McArthur, L. Z., & Eisen, S. V. (1976). Television and sex-role stereotyping. *Journal of Applied Social Psychology, 6*, 329–351.

McCauley, C., Thangavelu, K., & Rozin, P. (1988). Sex stereotyping of occupations in relation to television representations and census facts. *Basic & Applied Social Psychology, 9*, 197–212.

McGhee, P., & Frueh, T. (1980). TV viewing and the learning of sex-role stereotypes. *Sex Roles, 6*, 179–188.

Meyer, B. (1980). The development of girls' sex-role attitudes. *Child Development, 51*, 508–514.

Miller, M. M., & Reeves, B. (1976). Dramatic TV content and children's sex-role stereotypes. *Journal of Broadcasting, 20*, 35–50.

Mills, J., Polivy, J., Herman, C., & Tiggemann, M. (2002). Effects of thin media images: Evidence of self-enhancement among restrained eaters. *Personality and Social Psychology Bulletin, 28*, 1687–1699.

Morgan, M. (1982). Television and adolescents' sex-role stereotypes: A longitudinal study. *Journal of Personality and Social Psychology, 43*, 947–955.

Morgan, M. (1987). Television, sex-role attitudes, and sex-role behavior. *Journal of Early Adolescence, 7*, 269–282.

Morgan, M., & Rothschild, N. (1983). Impact of the new television technology: Cable TV, peers, and sex-role cultivation in the electronic environment. *Youth and Society, 15*, 33–50.

Morry, M., & Staska, S. (2001). Magazine exposure: Internalization, self-objectification, eating attitudes, and body satisfaction in male and female university students. *Canadian Journal of Behavioural Sciences, 33*, 269–279.

Myers, P. N., & Biocca, F. A. (1992). The elastic body image: The effect of television advertising and programming on body image distortions in young women. *Journal of Communication, 42*, 108–133.

Nathanson, A., Wilson, B., McGee, J., & Sebastian, M. (2002). Counteracting the effects of female stereotypes on television via active mediation. *Journal of Communication, 52*, 922–937.

O'Bryant, S. L., & Corder-Bolz, C. R. (1978a). The effects of television on children's stereotyping of women's work roles. *Journal of Vocational Behavior, 12*, 233–244.

O'Bryant, S. L., & Corder-Bolz, C. R. (1978b). Black children's learning of work roles from television commercials. *Psychological Reports, 42*, 227–230.

Olson, B. (1994). Soaps, sex, and cultivation. *Mass Communication Review, 21*, 106–113.

Perloff, R. (1977). Some antecedents of children's sex-role stereotypes. *Psychological Reports, 40*, 463–466.

Peterson, J. L., Moore, K. A., & Furstenberg, F. F., Jr. (1991). Television viewing and early initiation of sexual intercourse: Is there a link? *Journal of Homosexuality, 21*, 93–118.

Pingree, S. (1978). The effects of non-sexist television commercials and perceptions of reality on children's attitudes about women. *Psychology of Women Quarterly, 2*, 262–276.

Pinhas, L., Toner, B., Ali, A., Garfinkel, P., & Stuckless, P. (1999). The effects of the ideal of female beauty on mood and body satisfaction. *International Journal of Eating Disorders, 25*, 223–226.

Posavac, H., Posavac, S., & Posavac, E. (1998). Exposure to media images of female attractiveness and concern with body weight among young women. *Sex Roles, 38*, 187–201.

Potter, W. J., & Chang, I. C. (1990). Television exposure measures and the cultivation hypothesis. *Journal of Broadcasting & Electronic Media, 34*, 313–333.

Repetti, R. (1984). Determinants of children's sex stereotyping: Parental sex-role traits and television viewing. *Personality and Social Psychology Bulletin, 10*, 457–468.

Richins, M. L. (1991). Social comparison and the idealized images of advertising. *Journal of Consumer Research, 18*, 71–83.

Rosenwasser, S., Lingenfelter, M., & Harrington, A. (1989). Nontraditional gender role portrayals on TV and children's gender role perceptions. *Journal of Applied Developmental Psychology, 10*, 97–105.

Ruble, D., Balaban, T., & Cooper, J. (1981). Gender constancy and the effects of sex-typed televised toy commercials. *Child Development, 52*, 667–673.

Schwarz, N., Wagner, D., Bannert, M., & Mathes, L. (1987). Cognitive accessibility of sex role concepts and attitudes toward political participation: The impact of sexist ads. *Sex Roles, 17*, 593–601.

Sigal, J., Gibbs, M., Adams, B., & Derfler, R. (1988). The effect of romantic and nonromantic films on perception of female friendly and seductive behavior. *Sex Roles, 19*, 545–554.

Signorielli, N. (1991). Adolescents and ambivalence toward marriage: A cultivation analysis. *Youth and Society, 23*, 121–149.

Signorielli, N. (2001). Television's gender role images and contribution to stereotyping. In D. Singer & J. L. Singer (Eds.), *Handbook of children and the media* (pp. 341–358). Thousand Oaks, CA: Sage.

Signorielli, N., & Lears, M. (1992). Children, television, and conceptions about chores: Attitudes and behaviors. *Sex Roles, 27*, 157–170.

Singhal, A., & Rogers, E. M. (1999). *Entertainment-education: A communication strategy for social change.* Mahwah, NJ: Erlbaum.

Stice, E., Schupak-Neuberg, E., Shaw, H., & Stein, R. (1994). Relation of media exposure to eating disorder symptomatology: An examination of mediating mechanisms. *Journal of Abnormal Psychology, 103*, 836–840.

Stice, E., & Shaw, H. E. (1994). Adverse effects of the media portrayed thin-ideal on women and linkages to bulimic symptomatology. *Journal of Social and Clinical Psychology, 13*, 288–308.

Stice, E., Spangler, D., & Agras, W. (2001). Exposure to media-portrayed thin-ideal images adversely affects vulnerable girls: A longitudinal experiment. *Journal of Social and Clinical Psychology, 20*, 270–288.

Strauss, J., Doyle, A. E., & Kreipe, R. E. (1994). The paradoxical effect of diet commercials on reinhibition of dietary restraint. *Journal of Abnormal Psychology, 103*, 441–444.

Strouse, J. S., & Buerkel-Rothfuss, N. L. (1987). Media exposure and the sexual attitudes and behaviors of college students. *Journal of Sex Education and Therapy, 13*, 43–51.

Strouse, J., Buerkel-Rothfuss, N., & Long, E. (1995). Gender and family as moderators of the relationship between music video exposure and adolescent sexual permissiveness. *Adolescence, 30*, 505–521.

Strouse, J. S., Goodwin, M. P., & Roscoe, B. (1994). Correlates of attitudes toward sexual harassment among early adolescents. *Sex Roles, 31*, 559–577.

Tan, A. S. (1979). TV beauty ads and role expectations of adolescent female viewers. *Journalism Quarterly, 56*, 283–288.

Taylor, C. B., Sharpe, T., Shisslak, C., Bryson, S., Estes, L. S., Gray, N., McKnight, K., Crago, M., Kraemer, H., & Killen, J. (1998). Factors associated with weight concerns in adolescent girls. *International Journal of Eating Disorders, 24*, 31–42.

Thomsen, S. (2002). Health and beauty magazine reading and body shape concerns among a group of college women. *Journalism & Mass Communication Quarterly, 79*, 988–1007.

Thomsen, S., Weber, M., & Brown, L. (2002). The relationship between reading beauty and fashion magazines and the use of pathogenic dieting methods among adolescent females. *Adolescence, 37,* 1–18.

Thornton, B., & Maurice, J. (1997). Physique contrast effect: Adverse impact of idealized body images for women. *Sex Roles, 37,* 433–439.

Turner, S., Hamilton, H., Jacobs, M., Angood, L., & Dwyer, D. (1997). The influence of fashion magazines on the body image satisfaction of college women: An exploratory analysis. *Adolescence, 32,* 603–614.

Vaughan, J. E., & Fisher, V. L. (1981). The effect of traditional and cross-sex modeling on children's sex-role attitudes and behaviors. *Journal of Psychology, 107,* 253–260.

Walsh-Childers, K., & Brown, J. D. (1993). Adolescents' acceptance of sex-role stereotypes and television viewing. In B. S. Greenberg, J. D. Brown, & N. L. Buerkel-Rothfuss (Eds.), *Media, sex, and the adolescent* (pp. 117–133). Creskill, NJ: Hampton Press.

Ward, L. M. (2002). Does television exposure affect emerging adults' attitudes and assumptions about sexual relationships? Correlational and experimental confirmation. *Journal of Youth & Adolescence, 31,* 1–16.

Ward, L. M., & Caruthers, A. (2001). Media influences. In J. Worell (Ed.), *Encyclopedia of women and gender: Vol. 2.* (pp. 687–701). San Diego, CA: Academic Press.

Ward, L. M., & Rivadeneyra, R. (1999). Contributions of entertainment television to adolescents' sexual attitudes and expectations: The role of viewing amount versus viewer involvement. *The Journal of Sex Research, 36,* 237–249.

Wegner, B., Hartmann, A., & Geist, C. (2000). Effect of exposure to photographs of thin models on self-consciousness in female college students. *Psychological Reports, 86,* 1149–1154.

Wilcox, K., & Laird, J. (2000). The impact of media images of super-slender women on women's self-esteem: Identification, social comparison, and self-perception. *Journal of Research in Personality, 34,* 278–286.

Wroblewski, R., & Huston, A. C. (1987). Televised occupational stereotypes and their effects on early adolescents: Are they changing? *Journal of Early Adolescence, 7,* 283–297.

Zuckerman, D. M., Singer, D. G., & Singer, J. L. (1980). Children's television viewing, racial and sex-role attitudes. *Journal of Applied Social Psychology, 10,* 281–294.

2

"HE LEFT HER FOR THE ALIEN": GIRLS, TELEVISION, AND SEX

C. LYNN SORSOLI, MICHELLE V. PORCHE, AND DEBORAH L. TOLMAN

> Liz found out that Max had slept with another alien. It was very dra-
> matic, but I was upset Max cheated on Liz. He just left her for the alien.
> —10th-grade girl describing the most memorable episode of her
> favorite television show, *Roswell*

Sex and violence on television have long been assumed to influence the behaviors of viewers. The causal link between violent television programming and desensitization toward violence, in attitudes and in actions, is well documented (National Television Violence Study, 1996, 1997, 1998). However, although there is no lack of public discussion and debate about the effects of adolescents' consumption of television on their sexual behavior, choices, and beliefs, there is still little research dedicated to untangling whether and how such effects might occur (Brown & Newcomer, 1991; Moore, Miller, Glei, & Morrison, 1998; Peterson, Moore, & Furstenberg, 1991; Strasburger, 1995). In contrast to research linking violent television programming to violent behavior, conducting controlled experimental studies to investigate the relationship between television viewing and adolescent sexual behavior would be problematic; in addition, unlike becoming a violent person, becoming a sexual person in adolescence is quite normal. Thus it is not surprising that very few studies of whether and how television view-

Funding for this research was provided by the National Institute of Child Health and Human Development (Grant No. R01 HD38393-02).

ing influences sexual behavior among adolescents have been conducted—in spite of the reality that teenagers convey a strong sense of identification with characters and their romantic relationships, even when the sex is otherworldly, as illustrated by the 10th-grade girl quoted above.

Meanwhile, in the past few decades, the sexual content of media has increased substantially (Brown, Walsh-Childers, & Waszak, 1990; Greenberg, Lingsangan, et al., 1993) and adolescents continue to consume media in ever larger doses (Greenberg, Brown, & Buerkel-Rothfuss, 1993), which increases societal concern about its potential effects and the need for research. In recent years, new initiatives for exploring the potential associations between television viewing and early adolescent behavior have appeared (Brown, Steele, & Walsh-Childers, 2002), and it has become clearer that the relationship between television viewing and sexual behavior is likely to be quite complex, possibly involving several competing factors (Bryant & Zillman, 1994). The complexity of this relationship suggests that in addition to methodological care in terms of design and rigor, flexible and creative approaches to analysis are necessary. For example, the relationship between overall amount of television viewing and sexual behavior may not be immediately apparent, but may be observable only in certain circumstances, as when sexually oriented programming is examined more specifically or when viewer involvement is considered (see Ward & Rivadeneyra, 1999). In this chapter, we describe some approaches that we have taken to expand our repertoire of methods for investigating this relationship.

Television is the most pervasive form of media: 98% of homes have TV sets (Nielsen Media Research, 2000). It forms by far the largest proportion of younger adolescents' total media consumption (Nielsen Media Research, 1998), and adolescents exert increasing control over what they view as they mature (Brown et al., 1990). Though numerous studies have documented the presence of sex on television, these studies have tended to focus on the general population without targeting shows particularly popular with adolescents (Cope-Farrar & Kunkel, 2002). One strategy for expanding the exploration of the influence of television consumption on sexual behavior involves attending to what adolescents are actually watching. Further, rather than investigating television consumption as a whole, as if all adolescents watch the same television programs and all programs are alike in their sexual content, researchers may find it prudent to attend to differences in viewing preferences, as this factor will more accurately represent the reality of adolescent experiences.

A second potential factor in the association between television viewing and sexual behavior is the relational context of viewing—the people with whom adolescents watch and process television. Past studies have found that the presence of parents influences adolescents' interpretations of programming (Austin, Roberts, & Nass, 1990; Corder-Bolz, 1981), in particular their perceptions of sexual content (Gerbner, Gross, Morgan, & Signorelli, 1986; Morgan & Rothschild, 1983). However, as adolescents mature, the influence of peers may outstrip that of parents (Bronfenbrenner, 1970) and watching with peers and romantic partners has been shown to influence both the amount of television watched by adolescents and the sexual content of what is watched (Courtright & Baran, 1980; Greenberg, Lingsangan, et al., 1993). The relational context of viewing may thus play an interesting role in the relationship between television consumption and sexual behaviors.

A final potential but rarely examined factor involves adolescents' conceptions of gender and beliefs about the importance of compliance with gender norms. Gender is a fundamental organizing concept in our society, and the influence of gender roles and expectations is particularly apparent in adolescence, a time during which cognitive, relational, and emotional processes change and mature (Lerner, Petersen, & Brooks-Gunn, 1991; McCaffree, 1989; Paul & White, 1990; Piaget, 1972). Gender development has also been shown to be a fundamental aspect of sexuality development in adolescence (Simon & Gagnon, 1986), and previous research has shown associations between adolescents' gendered behaviors and television viewing (Morgan, 1987). Therefore, as we explore the relationship between television and sexual behavior, it seems critical to examine the potential role of gender ideology—one's beliefs about what constitutes being a good, normal, and appropriate woman (i.e., femininity ideology; Bartky, 1990; Tolman & Porche, 2000) and what constitutes being a good, normal, and appropriate man (i.e., masculinity ideology; Pleck, Sonenstein, & Ku, 1993).

The aim of this chapter is to begin to unpack the interplay between television viewing and adolescent sexual behaviors. Focusing on a variety of sexual outcomes (i.e., kissing, touching, or being touched) among girls, we consider the potential role of gender ideology in addition to what girls are watching on television and with whom. We also explore the relationships between these three factors. Finally, using small subsamples of adolescent girls favoring particular characters from two popular television shows, we further tease out some of the nuances existing in these relationships.

PART 1: SURVEY OF ADOLESCENT TELEVISION CONSUMPTION AND SEXUAL BEHAVIORS

This section details methods and findings resulting from the statistical analyses of survey data. In this section, we explore the relationships between sexual outcomes, gender ideology, and relational context of viewing for girls participating in the first wave of a longitudinal study designed to evaluate the effects of television consumption on adolescent sexuality.

Method

Participants

One hundred and thirty-six girls attending the eighth grade in a suburban centralized school district in the Northeast participated in this study. (Altogether, 272 students participated; the boys were set aside for this analysis.) The girls ranged in age from 11 to 15 years, with an average age of 13. The majority of these girls identified themselves as White (54%), whereas smaller proportions described themselves as Latina (30%), African American (3%), Asian (2%), other (2%), or bi- or multiracial (9%). Fourteen percent of the girls reported being born outside of the 50 states (i.e., Puerto Rico); most of these girls were native Spanish speakers. In this diverse low-income to lower middle-class sample, over half (51%) reported ever having received some form of public assistance, and 31% reported receiving assistance at the time of the data collection.

Procedure

Students responded to a two-part paper-and-pen survey designed to gather information about (a) television consumption (programming watched, how often, in what contexts) and viewing involvement (perceived realism and identification with characters) and (b) sexual attitudes and behaviors, gender ideologies, and demographic characteristics. Surveys were administered during a single 90-minute class period. Informed written consent was obtained from each student's parent or guardian. Participants provided assent prior to the survey administration and were reminded of confidentiality and of their freedom to discontinue participation at any time. All materials were available in Spanish, along with support from a Spanish-speaking researcher.

Measures

Estimated Hours per Day

Students were asked to estimate the number of hours they watched television per day in an open-ended response. Responses were requested for current habits during the school year, not distinguishing weekend from weekday.

Total Prime-Time Viewing

Students were given a list of 56 prime-time television shows popular with teen audiences to record frequency of television viewing and to enable future content analyses of programming viewed. Frequency response categories ranged from 0 to 4 on a 5-point scale, with viewing coded as never/not this season, a few times a month, once a week, a couple times a week, and almost daily. Shows on a weekly programming schedule could not have a score higher than 2 (*once a week*), whereas syndicated shows could receive a high score of 4 (*almost daily*). Sum scores for prime-time viewing were compiled by adding up frequency responses, which provided information about approximate hours of prime-time television viewing.

Prime-Time Drama Viewing and Prime-Time Sitcom Viewing

On the basis of a previous factor analysis of extensive pilot data (Porche, Rosen-Reynoso, & Sorsoli, 2002), two genre groupings—dramas and sitcoms—were suggested from among the programming adolescents reported watching. Although it is self-evident that the networks create these two television genres, factor analysis suggested that adolescents tended to favor one genre over another: Girls reported heavier consumption of dramas and boys watched more sitcoms. Sum scores of total frequency of drama viewing and total frequency of sitcom viewing were tallied to reflect the consumption of each of these genres.[1]

Adolescents' Viewing Involvement

Ward and Rivadeneyra (1999) investigated the degree to which adolescents identified with selected characters and perceived programming as real and relevant to their lives and developed an experimental approach to assess level of viewing involvement. Our measure of identification with characters was designed to gather information about how adolescents responded to this construct in the context of natural settings (i.e., reports of viewing involvement in their homes). For this analysis, we focus on one item in which students were asked to name a favorite female character in an open-ended response.

Relational Context of Television Consumption

Using a 5-point scale, adolescents reported how frequently they watched television (never, rarely, sometimes, usually, always) with various people in their lives (parents, siblings, friends, boyfriends or girlfriends). This yielded a single relational context score for each of the four categories of persons.

Sexual Behaviors

Adolescents' experiences with sexual behaviors were scored as 1 (*had ever experienced*) or 0 (*had never experienced*) for each of the following behaviors: holding hands, kissing on the mouth, touching another person (underneath that person's clothes or with no clothes on), being touched (underneath clothes or with no clothes on), and sexual intercourse.

---

[1]Dramas: *Angel, Charmed, Dark Angel, Dharma & Greg, Dawson's Creek, ER, Felicity, Friends, Gilmore Girls, Roswell, Sabrina the Teenage Witch, 7th Heaven, Smallville, 24* ($\alpha = .84$).
Sitcoms: *The Bernie Mac Show, Drew Carey, Everybody Loves Raymond, The Family Guy, Futurama, Just Shoot Me, King of the Hill, Malcolm in the Middle, The Simpsons, Scrubs, South Park, That '70s Show, Will & Grace* ($\alpha = .77$).

Gender Ideology

To measure femininity ideology, we used the Adolescent Femininity Ideology Scale (AFIS; Tolman & Porche, 2000) which is composed of two 10-item subscales: Inauthentic Self in Relationship (ISR), which measures internalization of beliefs about relationships, and Objectified Relationship to Body (ORB), which measures internalization of relating to one's body as an object. Respondents rate their agreement with statements on a 6-point scale, ranging from 1 (*strongly disagree*) to 6 (*strongly agree*). Higher mean scores reflect greater alignment with conventional and stereotypically feminine ideas about how girls should think and behave within the context of interpersonal relationships and in relation to their bodies. To measure masculinity ideology, we used the Adolescent Masculinity Ideology in Relationships Scale (AMIRS; Chu, Porche, & Tolman, in press), which is composed of 12 belief statements regarding male behaviors within the context of interpersonal relationships. Respondents indicate agreement on a 4-point scale, ranging from 1 (*disagree a lot*) to 4 (*agree a lot*). Higher mean scores reflect greater alignment with conventional and more stereotypically masculine ideas about the ways boys should feel and act in relationships with peers and romantic partners.

Demographic Control Variables

Several background measures known to be correlated with media and sexuality outcomes were also included in this analysis (e.g., Chilman, 1983; Comstock & Paik, 1991; Hayes, 1987; Strasburger, 1995). These included a socioeconomic indicator (student report of whether or not the family had ever received any public assistance, including free lunch), student-identified race or ethnicity, religiosity, and educational aspirations.

Results

All of the girls reported watching at least some television on a regular basis, ranging from one-half hour to 12 hours per day, with approximately 3½ hours of television consumption per day on average. Television viewing by genre indicated an average score of 17 for drama. Because dramas tend to be one-hour shows, we can interpret this score as reflecting a prototypical adolescent's regular weekly viewing of approximately eight different nonsyndicated programs. The average viewing score of 10 for sitcoms, which tend to be half-hour shows, similarly suggests regular viewing of 10 different nonsyndicated programs per week.

Girls indicated a wide variety of female television characters as their favorites. In all, over 30 different characters (or actresses) were named and thus no overwhelming standout existed among girls in this sample. Rather, there were many smaller groups of girls with common favorites. When results were tallied up, even the two largest of these groups were quite small: 9 girls named Buffy the Vampire Slayer as their favorite female character and 10 girls named Rachel from *Friends*. This result appeared to indicate a real diversity of female characters on television, reflecting a continuum of female gender roles.

The girls in the study also reported a range of sexual experiences. Though most of the girls either had already dated or were dating at the time of the survey, 25% reported that they had never been in a dating relationship. Of the girls who had dated, 84% reported having held hands; 66% had kissed on the mouth; 24% had touched someone else underneath that person's clothing or with no clothing on; and 35% had been touched under their clothing or with no clothing on. In an approximation of national trends (Singh & Darroch, 1999), sexual intercourse was an experience reported by 10% of these girls.

A full range of scores for each of the AFIS subscales were reported; mean scores tended to be in the middle of the 6-point scale. The girls' responses indicated slightly less conventional beliefs about masculinity ideology, as measured by the AMIRS. None of the control variables were associated with gender ideologies or reported sexual behaviors, however; the only consumption measure related to demographic indicators was the association between having ever been on welfare and lesser tendency to report watching television with parents ($r = -.21, p < .01$).

Relationships to Sexual Behaviors

As expected, correlations revealed that the traditional measure of television consumption—the reported number of hours of viewing per day—was not significantly related to sexual behaviors. However, when television watching was analyzed by separate genres, significant associations between genre and behavior were present (see Table 2.1). Frequency of watching sitcoms was positively associated with reports of the following sexual behaviors: touching, being touched, and sexual intercourse; however, frequency of watching drama was not associated with reported sexual behaviors. In regard to relational context, on average, girls reported watching with parents sometimes and watching with boyfriends rarely. Girls who reported watching television with a boyfriend also tended to report the full range of sexual behaviors, including holding hands, kissing, touching, being touched, and sexual intercourse. In contrast, reports of touching someone and having had sexual intercourse were negatively associated with watching television with parents. The context of watching with siblings was similar to that of watching with parents and negatively associated with reports of touching or being touched. Watching with friends was positively associated with reports of hand-holding but not other sexual behaviors.

In this sample, scores on only one of the two femininity ideology subscales were related to sexual behaviors (Table 2.1). Girls with lower scores

TABLE 2.1
Correlations Among Consumption, Ideology, and Sexual Behavior Variables (n = 131–136)

Measure	1	2	3	4	5	6	7	8	9	10	11	12	13	14
Television consumption														
1. Watching dramas	—													
2. Watching sitcoms	.49***	—												
3. Watching with parent(s)	-.04	.05	—											
4. Watching with boyfriend	.12	.30***	-.14	—										
5. Watching with sibling(s)	.06	-.17*	.15	-.05	—									
6. Watching with friend(s)	.10	.10	.04	.38***	-.10	—								
Sexual behaviors														
7. Holding hands	.12	.10	-.16†	.33***	-.16	.24*	—							
8. Kissing	.12	.11	-.13	.48***	-.13	.06	.48***	—						
9. Touching	.01	.19*	-.19*	.34***	-.27**	.04	.19*	.36***	—					
10. Being touched	.10	.20*	-.14	.32***	-.20*	.10	.23**	.39***	.58***	—				
11. Sexual intercourse	.13	.19*	-.32***	.24**	-.06	-.15	.14	.23**	.42***	.45***	—			
Gender ideology														
12. Femininity ideology (ISR)	.05	.04	-.04	-.06	-.07	.07	-.04	-.04	-.17*	-.20*	-.24**	—		
13. Femininity ideology (ORB)	.07	.09	-.29***	.17†	-.15	.10	.11	.03	.07	.02	.07	.40***	—	
14. Masculinity ideology (AMIRS)	.01	-.13	-.11	.04	-.17	.07	.07	.11	-.01	.01	.08	.16†	.26**	—
M	17.31	10.06	1.97	1.09	2.11	2.38	0.84	0.66	0.24	0.35	0.10	3.17	3.01	1.63
SD	10.88	8.24	0.95	1.22	1.30	1.09	0.36	0.47	0.43	0.48	0.30	0.69	0.86	0.46
α												.59	.74	.77

Note. AMIRS = Adolescent Masculinity Ideology in Relationships Scale; ISR = Inauthentic Self in Relationships Scale; ORB = Objectified Relationship to Body.
†p < .10. *p < .05. **p < .01. ***p < .001.

on the ISR subscale were significantly more likely to report touching, being touched, and having had sexual intercourse. Neither the ORB subscale nor masculinity ideology (AMIRS) was related to any sexual behaviors.

Relationships Among Variables

There were no significant relationships between gender ideologies and the separate genres of prime-time television watching (dramas and sitcoms). However, there was a trend for girls who reported having a more objectified relationship with their bodies (ORB) to report watching television more often with a boyfriend, and they were significantly less likely to watch with a parent. Finally, though watching with parents was not associated with either genre of prime-time television watching, girls who watched television with a boyfriend were more likely to report higher frequency of watching sitcoms.

PART 2: EXPLORATORY ANALYSIS OF POPULAR FEMALE TELEVISION CHARACTERS

This section details the methods and findings of an exploratory analysis of television characters popular with girls. The purpose of this analysis was to explore the ways the associations between gender ideology, sexual outcomes, and relational context of viewing might differ for girls identifying with different kinds of females characters.

Method

Procedure and Participants

In an effort to shed further light on the survey results, an exploratory analysis was conducted on the content of two television shows popular with this sample of eighth-grade girls. The shows *Friends* and *Buffy the Vampire Slayer* were selected for this analysis because these shows featured favorite characters of the largest subgroups of girls. The subsample thus included the 9 girls naming Buffy the Vampire Slayer as their favorite female character and the 10 girls naming Rachel from *Friends*. This exploratory analysis involved a content review of concurrent episodes of these shows, as well as a comparison of the two subgroups of girls naming these two characters as their favorite females on television.

Differences Between Shows

Episodes from *Friends* and *Buffy the Vampire Slayer* were recorded at the same time during the 2000–2001 season. Both shows are in syndication and appear on television at least once every day, as well as holding coveted 8:00 p.m. prime-time slots on Tuesday and Thursday evenings. The situation comedy *Friends* is a show about six friends living in New York who often meet to talk in a local coffee house. The character Rachel typically takes part in conventional activities, such as shopping; she works in the fashion industry and embodies a strong and overt interest in attracting a romantic partner. During one scene in this analysis, she and a friend discussed "date moves," which for her involved both manipulating a man emotionally and making herself into a sexual object. In contrast, *Buffy the Vampire Slayer* is a show in which the witty characters, led by Buffy, routinely save the world from demons, vampires, and other assorted evils. Buffy is aggressive and action-oriented, a master of martial arts, and very outspoken. One analyzed scene involved her physically fighting and subsequently defeating a much larger male character while screaming, "You killed my date!" However, a scene-by-scene analysis of episodes from these two shows revealed that these observable differences between Buffy and Rachel disappear during scenes involving potential or actual romantic partners. In the context of romance, the diversity in these portrayals of femininity collapses and even Buffy, the girl who routinely saves the day, is suddenly dependent on a man to save her. Both thin, white, and beautiful, these characters are similarly submissive, passive, overly emotional, and concerned with appearance in the presence of men,[2] thus illustrating that conventional femininity messages can exist in spite of a feminist subtext.

Differences Between Subsamples

Using *t* tests to compare the two groups of girls, we found no differences in either femininity ideology or reported sexual behaviors between the group identifying Buffy as their favorite television character and the group identifying Rachel as their favorite character. However, the two groups were statistically different in the tendency to watch television with a boyfriend as well as their scores on the masculinity ideology scale (AMIRS): Girls choosing Rachel as a favorite character expressed more conventional views about masculinity and less often watched with a boyfriend (Table 2.2). Further, these two groups differed from the full sample of girls in that certain sexual experiences were positively associated with more conventional masculinity ideology scores: reports of sexual intercourse for the Buffy group, $r(9) = .90$, $p < .001$, and touching under clothing for the Rachel group, $r(10) = .64$, $p < .05$.[3]

DISCUSSION

In this chapter, we have explored a number of factors that might be important in the process of influencing adolescent viewers as well as the complexity of the relationships between these factors. At this point, the con-

---

[2]Willow, another character on *Buffy the Vampire Slayer*, and the only character from either of these two shows endorsed by the National Organization for Women Feminist Primetime Report (2002), was not a favorite among these girls. Willow is extremely resistant to characteristics of femininity ideology and conventional dating scripts normally portrayed on television, including having serious and meaningful relationships with both men and women.

[3]Because of the small sample size, however, we interpret these results with caution and acknowledge the need for more systematic analyses with larger samples and a more extensive content analysis.

TABLE 2.2
Comparing Buffys With Rachels

Variable	Girls who report that their favorite character is Buffy ($n = 9$)	Girls who report that their favorite character is Rachel ($n = 10$)
Average hours of viewing per night	5.29	3.75
Watch soap operas (%)	78**	20
Watch talk shows (%)	100	70
Watch with boyfriend[a]	2.1*	0.9
Average age at first date (years)	9.1	11.3
Have held hands (%)	78	100
Have kissed on the mouth (%)	67	80
Have touched someone under that person's clothing (%)	33	30
Have been touched under their clothing (%)	33	50
Have had sexual intercourse (%)	11	10
"I can see myself responding and behaving to situations the same way the character does"[b]	6.1*	4.6
Masculinity ideology (AMIRS)	1.52	1.87*
Femininity ideology (ISR)	3.09	3.09
Femininity ideology (ORB)	3.38	3.07

Note. AMIRS = Adolescent Masculinity Ideology in Relationships Scale; ISR = Inauthentic Self in Relationship; ORB = Objectified Relationship to Body.
[a]On a scale from 0 (*never*) to 4 (*always*).
[b]On a scale from 1 (*strongly disagree*) to 7 (*strongly agree*).
*$p < .05$. **$p < .01$. Difference indicated by *t* tests ($df = 17$).

sistency of the relationships between sexual behaviors and both what adolescent girls are watching and with whom suggests that these factors deserve continued investigation. In particular, our finding that girls who watch television with a boyfriend tend to have more sexual experiences whereas those watching with parents tend to have fewer is striking, though not entirely surprising; it offers a new way to think about past studies of the ways parents influence perceptions of sexual content (Courtright & Baran, 1980; Gerbner et al., 1986; Morgan & Rothschild, 1983) and the influence of peers in terms of what and how much sexual content is being watched (Courtright & Baran, 1980; Greenberg, Lingsangan, et al., 1993). Though no less promising, the role that gender ideology may play in this system of relationships seems much less straightforward: Conventional femininity (ORB) is associated on one hand with the people with whom a girl watches television and on the other hand (ISR) with certain sexual behaviors. The complexity of these relationships was particularly clear in our exploratory analysis of the subsample of girls where we found relationships between masculinity ideology (AMIRS) and sexual behaviors that did not exist when we looked across the entire sample; this finding suggests that for particular groups of girls, beliefs about what makes a good girl or boy may play different roles in these relationships.

To unravel the role of gender ideology, we used sexual scripting theory (Simon & Gagnon, 1986), which is especially relevant to understanding the process by which adolescents might take in prime-time television messages about how to enter into and maintain sexual relationships. Scripting theory provides an alternative to earlier applications of social learning theory to the study of media effects (e.g., Brown & Steele, 1995), suggesting that television may act more immediately by providing adolescent viewers with certain informative "scripts" that dictate a variety of behaviors (in this case, sexual behaviors). The theory suggests that the scripts become so internalized and automatic that adolescents may become quite nonreflective about behaviors such as who makes the first move and, as suggested cryptically by the girl quoted at the beginning of this paper, who is likely to leave the relationship and why.

In addition to these scripts, the female characters on television seem to exhibit a continuum of conventionality regarding gender ideology, which has been associated with sexual outcomes among adolescent girls (Tolman, 1999). Past research (e.g., Ward, Gorvine, & Cytron, 2002) has suggested a circularity in the relationships between viewers, television portrayals, and personal beliefs: Viewers with certain personal attitudes identify more strongly with what they see on television, which then strengthens those attitudes and beliefs. Girls who identify strongly with the characters they see on television may thus be more likely to emulate behaviors and beliefs represented by those characters, though particular responses to television may also have to do with race and class (see, e.g., Press, 1989, 1991). Overall, however, as indicated by Ward and Harrison (see chap. 1, this volume), television's range of gender roles for girls tends to be constricted; given our findings, it seems as though even when television does offer girls choices about how to be in the world (i.e., whether they would like to be more like Buffy or more like Rachel), it tends to restrict them to a single script in terms of romantic relationships. This suggests that ever more complex and nuanced investigations may be necessary to understand how the sexual behaviors of girls may be associated with what, how much, and with whom they watch television.

CONCLUSION

Assumptions about how to account for television viewing in earlier research on media effects may have led to a simplification of the process of influencing viewers, particularly girls, who may be more strongly affected than boys in this realm (see chap. 1, this volume). Our research suggests that the ways we think about and measure television consumption could be instrumental in identifying patterns in associations between consumption and sexual behavior. Extending our concept of consumption beyond simply hours per day watched to include prime-time genres, identification with characters, and relational context of viewing has proven to be informative, as has the expansion of our exploration to the sexual behaviors beyond intercourse.

Considering the complex role of gender ideologies has also proven to be informative. The importance of evaluating both femininity and masculinity ideologies as a potential factor in the relationship between consumption and sexual behavior is particularly evident in our small exploratory analysis contrasting girls who chose different female characters as a favorite. This exploration highlights the fact that masculinity ideology might play a role for young women even when femininity ideology does not, and that the role played by masculinity might be of particular importance for certain groups of girls, such as those who, for example, might be worried about "being left for an alien." The importance of masculinity in this study of girls prompts us to remember that providing girls with more flexibility in expressing femininity needs to be coupled with equal attention toward alternatives for boys, both in and out of romantic relationships. Following the lead of Ward (1995), we continue to move forward in our efforts to understand the content of sexual interactions on television, the ways they reflect scripts about sexuality in our culture, and the impact these portrayals might have on adolescent sexuality.

REFERENCES

Austin, E. W., Roberts, D. F., & Nass, C. I. (1990). Influences of family communication on children's television-interpretation processes. *Communication Research*, 17(4), 545–564.

Bartky, S. L. (1990). *Femininity and domination: Studies on the phenomenology of oppression*. New York: Routledge.

Bronfenbrenner, U. (1970). *Two worlds of childhood: U.S. and U.S.S.R.* New York: Russell Sage Foundation.

Brown, J. D., & Newcomer, S. F. (1991). Television viewing and adolescent's sexual behavior. *Journal of Homosexuality*, 21(1/2), 77–91.

Brown, J. D., & Steele, J. R. (1995). *Sex and the mass media*. Chapel Hill: University of North Carolina at Chapel Hill.

Brown, J. D., Steele, J. R., & Walsh-Childers, K. (2002). *Sexual teens, sexual media: Investigating media's influence on adolescent sexuality*. Mahwah, NJ: Erlbaum.

Brown, J. D., Walsh-Childers, K., & Waszak, C. S. (1990). Television and adolescent sexuality. *Journal of Adolescent Health Care*, 11, 62–70.

Bryant, J., & Zillman, D. (Eds.). (1994). *Media effects: Advances in theory and research*. Mahwah, NJ: Erlbaum.

Chilman, C. S. (1983). The development of adolescent sexuality. *Journal of Research and Development in Education*, 16(2), 16–26.

Chu, J., Porche, M. V. & Tolman, D. L. (in press). The Adolescent Masculinity Ideology in Relationships Scale: Development and validation of a new measure for boys. *Men and Masculinities*.

Comstock, G., & Paik, H. (1991). *Television and the American child*. New York: Academic Press.

Cope-Farrar, K. M., & Kunkel, D. (2002). Sexual messages in teens' favorite prime-time television programs. In J. D. Brown, J. R. Steele, & K. Walsh-Childers (Eds.), *Sexual teens, sexual media: Investigating media's influence on adolescent sexuality* (pp. 59–78). Mahwah, NJ: Erlbaum.

Corder-Bolz, C. (1981). Television and adolescents' sexual behavior. *Sex Education Coalition News, 3*, 40.

Courtright, J. A., & Baran, S. J. (1980). The acquisition of sexual information by young people. *Journalism Quarterly, 57*, 107–114.

Gerbner, G., Gross, L., Morgan, M., & Signorelli, N. (1986). Living with television: The dynamics of the cultivation process. In J. Bryant & D. Zillman (Eds.), *Perspectives on media effects* (pp. 17–40). Hillsdale, NJ: Erlbaum.

Greenberg, B. S., Brown, J. D., & Buerkel-Rothfuss, N. L. (1993). *Media, sex and the adolescent*. Cresskill, NJ: Hampton Press.

Greenberg, B. S., Lingsangan, R., Soderman, A., Heeter, C., Lin, C., Stanley, C., & Siemicki, M. (1993). Adolescents' exposure to television and movie sex. In B. S. Greenberg, J. D. Brown, & N. L. Buerkel-Rothfuss (Eds.), *Media, sex and the adolescent* (pp. 61–98). Cresskill, NJ: Hampton Press.

Hayes, C. (Ed.). (1987). *Risking the future: Adolescent sexuality, pregnancy, and childbearing*. Washington, DC: National Academy Press.

Lerner, R. M., Petersen, A. C., & Brooks-Gunn, J. (1991). *The encyclopedia of adolescence*. New York: Garland.

McCaffree, K. (1989). Adolescent sexuality: Male and female adolescent developmental needs. *SIECUS Report, 18*(1), 3–4.

Moore, K. A., Miller, B. C., Glei, D., & Morrison, D. R. (1998). *Adolescent sex, contraception and childbearing: A review of recent research*. Washington, DC: Child Trends.

Morgan, M. (1987). Television, sex-role attitudes, and sex-role behavior. *Journal of Early Adolescence, 7*(3), 269–282.

Morgan, M., & Rothschild, N. (1983). Impact of the new television technology: Cable TV, peers, and sex-role cultivation in the electronic environment. *Youth and Society, 15*(1), 33–50.

National Organization for Women. (2002). *Watch out, listen up! 2002 Feminist Primetime report*. Washington, DC: National Organization for Women Foundation.

National Television Violence Study 1. (1996). Thousand Oaks: Sage Publications.

National Television Violence Study 2. (1997). Thousand Oaks: Sage Publications.

National Television Violence Study 3. (1998). Thousand Oaks: Sage Publications.

Nielsen Media Research. (1998). 1998 *Nielsen report on television*. Northbrook, IL: Nielsen.

Nielsen Media Research. (2000). *2000 Nielsen report on television*. Northbrook, IL: Nielsen.

Paul, E. L., & White, K. M. (1990). The development of intimate relationships in late adolescence. *Adolescence, 25*(98), 375–399.

Peterson, J. L., Moore, K. A., & Furstenberg, F. F. (1991). Television viewing and early initiation of sexual intercourse: Is there a link? *Journal of Homosexuality, 21*(1–2), 93–118.

Piaget, J. (1972). Intellectual evolution from adolescence to adulthood. *Human Development, 15,* 1–12.

Pleck, J. H., Sonenstein, F. L., & Ku, L. C. (1993). Masculinity ideology and its correlates. In S. Oskamp & M. Costanzo (Eds.), *Gender issues in contemporary society* (pp. 85–110). Thousand Oaks, CA: Sage.

Porche, M. V., Rosen-Reynoso, M., & Sorsoli, L. (2002, April). *Parental guidance suggested: An evaluation of measures of adolescent television consumption.* Paper presented at the biennial meeting of the Society for Research on Adolescence, New Orleans, LA.

Press, A. (1989). Class and gender in the hegemonic process: Class differences in women's perceptions of television realism and identification with television characters. *Media, Culture and Society, 11,* 229–251.

Press, A. (1991). *Women watching television: Gender, class, and generation in the American television experience.* Philadelphia: University of Pennsylvania Press.

Simon, W., & Gagnon, J. H. (1986). Sexual scripts: Permanence and change. *Archives of Sexual Behavior, 15*(2), 97–120.

Singh, S., & Darroch, J. E. (1999). Trends in sexual activity among adolescent American women: 1982-1995. *Family Planning Perspectives, 31*(5), 211–219.

Strasburger, V. C. (1995). Adolescent sexuality and the media. In A. Kazdin (Series Ed.) & V. C. Strasburger (Vol. Ed.), *Developmental Clinical Psychology and Psychiatry, Vol. 33. Adolescents and the media: Medical and psychological impact* (pp. 38–56). Thousand Oaks, CA: Sage.

Tolman, D. L. (1999). Femininity as a barrier to positive sexual health for adolescent girls. *Journal of the American Medical Women's Association, 54*(3), 133–138.

Tolman, D. L., & Porche, M. V. (2000). The adolescent femininity ideology scale: Development and validation of a new measure for girls. *Psychology of Women Quarterly, 24*(4), 365–376.

Ward, L. M. (1995). Talking about sex: Common themes about sexuality in the prime-time television programs children and adolescents view most. *Journal of Youth and Adolescence, 24*(5), 595–615.

Ward, L. M., Gorvine, B., Cytron, A. (2002). Would that really happen? Adolescents' perceptions of sexual relationships according to primetime television. In J. D. Brown, J. R. Steele, & K. Walsh-Childers (Eds.), *Sexual teens, sexual media: Investigating media's influence on adolescent sexuality* (pp. 95–123). Mahwah, NJ: Erlbaum.

Ward, L. M., & Rivadeneyra, R. (1999). Contributions of entertainment television to adolescents' sexual attitudes and expectations: The role of viewing amount versus viewer involvement. *The Journal of Sex Research, 36*(3), 237–249.

3

THE MEDIA'S ROLE IN BODY IMAGE AND EATING DISORDERS

STEFANIE C. GILBERT, HELENE KEERY, AND J. KEVIN THOMPSON

Eight years ago, girls who lived in Fiji had never seen a soap opera, a miniseries, or a commercial. Then, in 1995, the country introduced its first television channel. Within three short years, girls began reporting concern about their weight and body size. In a country that had traditionally prized a voluptuous female figure, girls began dieting and became determined to lose weight. Eating disorders, which had been virtually nonexistent prior to the introduction of television, suddenly became common. Anne Becker, the Harvard researcher who documented this change in eating habits (Becker, 1995), found that many of the girls wanted to lose weight to be more socially or professionally successful— goals that they now believed were associated with a thin body (Becker, Burwell, Gilman, Herzog, & Hamburg, 2002).

For more than 40 years, researchers and clinicians have focused on the role of various media influences as a contributor to body-image and eating problems (Cash & Pruzinsky, 2002; Thompson, Heinberg, Altabe, & Tantleff-Dunn, 1999). The media are believed to promote eating disorders by consistently portraying only thin, stereotypically attractive bodies, glorifying thinness as the essence of beauty and success, and denigrating fatness by linking it to such negative characteristics as laziness, ugliness, and failure (Rothblum, 1994). The feminine body ideal changed throughout history and became much more uniform with the growing influence of the mass media. As a result of this influence, the ideal female body shape has become increasingly thin, even as the size of the average woman has become progressively larger (see Thompson et al., 1999). In this chapter, we review some of the survey, experimental, and longitudinal data indicting media as a formative and pervasive factor in women's and girl's body-image disturbance and eating dysfunction (Thompson & Heinberg, 1999), outline recent theoretical approaches, and summarize promising new avenues in the prevention and early intervention arena.

BACKGROUND: STUDIES OF MEDIA EXPOSURE

Images of the ideal woman's figure became increasingly thin and tubular beginning in the 1950s and continuing well into the 1970s (Garner, Garfinkel, Schwartz, & Thompson, 1980). The number of diet articles in girls' and women's magazines also increased during this period and continued to do so through the 80s and 90s (Thompson et al., 1999; Wiseman, Gray, Mosimann, & Ahrens, 1992). At the same time, a marked gender difference in the incidence of eating disorders developed, favoring women by the same 2:1 ratio that characterized the number of diet articles found in women's magazines relative to that found in men's (Andersen & DiDomenico, 1992; Cusumano & Thompson, 1997). By the end of the 20th century, the image of the ideal woman was between 13% and 19% below normal weight for her age and height.

Given the remarkable pattern by which the incidence of eating disorders has paralleled the rise in media messages promoting the thin ideal, many theorists have suggested that exposure to media influences plays an important role in the development of eating disorders (Becker et al., 2002; Levine & Harrison, 2004; Stice & Shaw, 1994; Thompson et al., 1999). For instance, exposure to print media that emphasizes the cultural ideal has been associated with greater body dissatisfaction and eating disturbance in girls and young women (Harrison & Cantor, 1997; Levine & Harrison, 2004; Thompson & Heinberg, 1999).

Middle-school-age girls (between ages 10 and 14) read at least one fashion magazine each week and consider such publications an important source of beauty and fitness information (Levine, Smolak, & Hayden, 1994). Girls who read fashion magazines frequently are two to three times more likely than those who read magazines infrequently to diet or exercise to lose weight because of a magazine article and to feel that magazines influence their concept of the ideal female body shape (Field, Cheung, Wolf, Herzog, Gortmaker, & Colditz, 1999). Those who value magazine advertisements and articles that emphasize achieving a thin body are significantly more likely to express a desire to be thinner, diet, and have eating disorder symptoms (Gonzalez-Lavin & Smolak, 1995; Harrison, 2000a; Levine et al., 1994).

The impact of television exposure has received less evaluation than that of the print media, but also appears problematic and may be a function of the nature of the programs viewed. Middle school girls who watch more than 8 hours of television weekly are significantly less satisfied with their body shape than are girls who watch less television (Gonzalez-Lavin & Smolak, 1995). Those who spend their viewing time watching soap operas, movies, or music videos are at greater risk, as exposure to these types of programming has been positively associated with body dissatisfaction and restrictive dieting (Tiggemann & Pickering, 1996). Even elementary school children and boys are not immune to the impact of television. A recent survey of 303 first- to third-grade children (Harrison, 2000b) found that television viewing predicted increased eating disorder symptomatology among both boys and girls in this age group.

These correlational findings have been consistent with the results of experimental studies. For instance, in several studies, commercials preselected to represent the thin ideal produced increased levels of depressed mood, anxiety, anger, and body dissatisfaction when compared with control conditions (Cattarin, Thompson, Thomas, & Williams, 2000; Heinberg & Thompson, 1995; Levine & Harrison, 2004), but only in women with high levels of awareness and internalization of the thin ideal. These women were significantly less depressed after exposure to non-appearance-related commercials than they were following exposure to appearance-related commercials.

Other, cross-cultural studies have provided further support for the media exposure–eating disorder link, although some results have been contradictory. Several studies have examined whether exposure to Western media that depict very thin beauty ideals differentiates immigrant women who live in Western countries from their non-westernized counterparts on measures of body dissatisfaction and eating pathology. The results have been mixed, with some researchers reporting that women in cultures with minimal access to Western influences hold more positive views of their bodies and are less likely to exhibit eating pathology than are their female counterparts who have migrated to westernized countries (Akiba, 1998; Choudry & Mumford, 1992; Fichter, Weyer, Sourdi, & Sourdi, 1983; Nasser, 1986). Other researchers have found few or no differences between women exposed to Western media and those who have been shielded from such influences (Abdollahi & Mann, 2001; Stephens, Schumaker, & Sibiya, 1999; Tiggemann & Ruutel, 2001).

Becker (1995), whose dramatic study of the women of Fiji introduced this chapter, reported marked increases in levels of body satisfaction and eating behaviors within 3 years after the introduction of television in that country. Becker et al.'s (2002) results may offer the most convincing evidence of the media's power to elicit body dissatisfaction and eating pathology because the women in this study did not immigrate to an entirely different culture, as did individuals in other studies assessing this process. Rather, the one variable that changed in the Fiji sample's environment was the introduction of televised media. Lack of significant findings in other studies of women who immigrated to westernized countries may merely indicate that these women did not experience the dramatic increase in exposure to television (or possibly other mass media) that the women in Fiji experienced.

With numerous empirical studies indicating that both print and television media exert a powerful influence on the body ideals and eating behaviors of girls and women (for a more extensive review, see Levine & Harrison, 2004; Thompson et al., 1999), the following questions become paramount: What potential pathways might explain the media exposure effect? Are certain women more greatly affected by exposure? What variables seem to be protective?

POTENTIAL MECHANISMS OF A MEDIA EFFECT

Social Comparison

Two variables that may contribute to the media effect are the tendency to engage in social comparison with media images and psychologically internalizing the societal thin beauty ideal. Each of these variables has received substantial research attention.

Social comparison theory posits that human beings have an innate tendency to compare themselves with others in an effort to self-evaluate (Festinger, 1954). This tendency may be at work, either consciously or unconsciously, while people are viewing images of others in the mass media. According to Richins (1995), advertisers present idealized images of people to generate social comparison tendencies and, ultimately, demand for their products. The idealized images are presented as if they are real, even though they have been extensively edited, airbrushed, and cropped. As audience members self-evaluate and discover that they fall short of the idealized images, they are expected to increase their efforts to measure up.

As advertisers expect, social comparison with media images is associated with negative self-evaluation of one's appearance. This has been demonstrated in numerous experimental studies (Cash, Cash, & Butters, 1983; Cattarin et al., 2000; Irving, 1990; Martin & Gentry, 1997; Stice & Shaw, 1994). Social comparison tendencies have also been linked to eating disorders (Paxton, Schutz, Wertheim, & Muir, 1999; Rieves & Cash, 1996; Stice & Shaw, 1994; Thompson & Smolak, 2001; Veron-Guidry, Williamson, & Netemeyer, 1997). For example, Botta (1999) found that a tendency to compare one's body with those of female television characters predicted higher levels on numerous eating pathology indices, including body dissatisfaction, thin-ideal endorsement, drive for thinness, and bulimic symptomatology.

Social comparison theory may help to explain why girls and women of color have historically reported greater body and weight satisfaction (Akan & Grilo, 1995; S. M. Harris, 1994) and have been less likely than their White counterparts to develop an eating disorder (Altabe, 1996; Wildes & Emery, 2001), despite having a higher average body mass (Akan & Grilo, 1995; Pike, Dohm, Striegel-Moore, Wilfley, & Fairburn, 2001). Although Eurocentric societal standards of beauty hold the potential to elicit appearance dissatisfaction in girls and women of color (Gilbert, 2003; D. J. Harris & Kuba, 1997; Root, 1991), these individuals may engage less frequently in self-comparisons with media images because the majority of these images depict thin, White women (Parnell, Sargent, Thompson, Duhe, Valois, & Kemper, 1996). This may be protective and ultimately may contribute to the greater acceptance of larger female body types (Flynn & Fitzgibbon, 1996; Hebl & Heatherton, 1998; Kemper, Sargent, Drane, Wanzer, Valois, & Hussey, 1994) and higher levels of body satisfaction (Dounchis, Hayden, &

Wilfley, 2001) observed in girls and women of certain ethnic groups. However, research on this topic has been surprisingly sparse, offering scant empirical evidence that girls and women of color do, in fact, engage in fewer self-comparisons with images of women in the mass media. Existing research suggests that some girls of color do express a desire to be thinner (Joiner & Kashubeck, 1996; Striegel-Moore, Schreiber, Pike, Wilfley, & Rodin, 1995) and report levels of body dissatisfaction on par with their White counterparts (Snow & Harris, 1989). It is possible that girls and women of color who report levels of body anxiety and dissatisfaction comparable to White girls and women may have experienced greater exposure to media pressures for thinness, greater reinforcement of these messages from family members or peers, or internalization of these messages to a greater degree than is typical for others in their ethnic group. Inasmuch as thin images of women of color can be expected to become increasingly prevalent in the media, girls and women of color can subsequently be expected to engage in social comparisons with these images to the same extent that White girls and women engage in comparisons with White images, which increases the likelihood that they will also experience progressively greater levels of body dissatisfaction and eating disturbance (Botta, 2000).

Internalization

The second variable that has received extensive examination as a potential moderator or mediator between exposure and body-image or eating disturbances is internalization of the thin ideal (Thompson & Stice, 2001). Internalization refers to both buying into cultural ideals of attractiveness and engaging in behaviors aimed at achieving this ideal (Thompson et al., 1999). Thin-ideal internalization may result from social reinforcement of these ideals by family members, peers, and the mass media. When social reinforcement of the thin ideal occurs, the ideal is promoted and expectations of the benefits associated with being thin are enhanced (Hohlstein, Smith, & Atlas, 1998). These expectations play a powerful part in perpetuating the thin ideal for women (Thompson & Stice, 2001).

In theory, internalization of the thin ideal leads to body dissatisfaction because the thin ideal is virtually unattainable for the majority of girls and women (Thompson et al., 1999). Body dissatisfaction, in turn, may lead to restrictive dieting practices and, ultimately, to disordered eating behaviors. Stice, Shaw, and Nemeroff (1998) theorized a dual pathway model of bulimia nervosa in which sociocultural pressures to be thin lead to internalization, which in turn elicits body dissatisfaction. Body dissatisfaction then leads to dieting and negative affect, which subsequently lead to bulimic symptoms.

Several measures have been developed to assess the role of internalization in the development of body-image and eating disturbance. The Sociocultural Attitudes Towards Appearance Questionnaire (SATAQ; Heinberg, Thompson, & Stormer, 1995) evaluates the extent to which an individual is influenced by the media along two distinct dimensions: awareness of the thin ideal and internalization of the ideal. Awareness indicates that an individual recognizes society's influence, whereas internalization suggests that the person endorses or accepts society's message regarding the thin ideal. Research that has utilized the SATAQ, an updated version of the SATAQ called the Multidimensional Media Influence Scale (Thompson, van den Berg, Roehrig, Guarda, & Heinberg, 2004), or a scale designed specifically to assess internalization in adolescents—the Media Internalization Scale for Adolescents (Keery, Thompson, Shroff, Wertheim, & Smolak, 2004)—suggests that the internalization factor more strongly predicts body dissatisfaction and eating disturbance and accounts for significant variance beyond that explained by awareness (Cusumano & Thompson, 1997, 2001; Heinberg & Thompson, 1995).

Internalization may act in such a way as to moderate the impact of media influence. For example, in one study, college women with high levels of body-image disturbance and awareness or internalization of attractiveness ideals became significantly more depressed after watching 10 minutes of appearance-related commercials and significantly less depressed following 10 minutes of exposure to non-appearance-related commercials (Heinberg & Thompson, 1995). Exposure to the appearance-related commercials resulted in increased anger in women high on the awareness–internalization measure and increased body dissatisfaction in women with high levels of body-image disturbance. In a similar study, Cattarin et al. (2000) found that exposure to media images of the thin societal ideal led to increases in anger, anxiety, and depressed mood and that these findings were moderated by internalization of the societal ideal of thinness and attractiveness.

Prospective designs have examined the predictive effects of internalizing media pressures on subsequent body-image and eating symptoms. Stice et al. (1998) evaluated high school students over a 9-month period and found that internalization had a direct effect on body dissatisfaction, even when the effects of body mass and perceived pressure were controlled, and an indirect effect on subsequent bulimic symptoms (mediated via body dissatisfaction, restraint, and negative affect).

The research in this area thus suggests that internalization may be critical for the media to exert an impact on female viewers' mood, body satisfaction, drive for thinness, and eating behaviors. This theory may explain why, despite similar levels of exposure to the mass media, some women do not develop body dissatisfaction or engage in efforts to alter their body shape, whereas others react strongly to media images not only by experiencing negative appearance evaluation, but also by adopting deleterious coping strategies designed to dramatically alter their physical appearance.

PREVENTION STUDIES BASED ON
MODIFYING A MEDIA INFLUENCE

A variety of different types of early intervention and prevention programs have been developed for body-image and eating problems and many of these include a component that targets the media (Stice, 2001; Stice & Hoffman, 2004). For instance, media literacy programs educate participants about the techniques used by the media to alter images and make models look perfect, thus enabling participants to verbally and cognitively challenge the thin ideal promoted in the mass media (Levine, Piran, & Stoddard, 1999).

Irving, DuPen, and Berel (1998) designed a peer-led media literacy program for high school sophomores that combined media literacy with feminist psychotherapy, which aims to empower women by teaching them to challenge cultural norms and derive self-esteem from areas other than appearance. The experimental group watched a short video about techniques used to alter media images and participated in a discussion about media images, including how these images are reinforced by the way people think and behave, ways of challenging the images on a personal and political level, methods to evaluate and deconstruct media images, and the importance of basing self-esteem on factors other than appearance. The control group did not receive the intervention. At postintervention, the media literacy group reported significantly less internalization of the cultural ideal of thinness and lower perceived realism of media images than did the control group. However, the two groups did not differ significantly on measures of body dissatisfaction, anxiety about physical appearance, or affective state. Thus, the intervention seemed to impact participants' endorsement of the thin ideal but failed to lead to changes in body concerns.

Neumark-Sztainer, Sherwood, Coller, and Hannan (2000) evaluated a media literacy program that encouraged girls to be activists in helping peers and in changing mass media to establish healthier norms. Participants wrote letters to businesses to advocate for healthier images in advertisements and also posted notices on an eating disorder awareness website to encourage activism and advocacy by other girls. Following the intervention, thin-ideal internalization was reduced and participants' belief in their ability to be activists increased. However, the intervention had no effect on dieting behaviors and minimal maintenance of improvements in body-related knowledge and body-size acceptance. Perhaps the length or intensity of the intervention was insufficient to produce such effects.

Similar strategies were incorporated into a five-session prevention program implemented in Australia with adolescents (Wade, Davidson, & O'Dea, 2003) that was designed to enhance media literacy, increase activism to "protest or praise media products conveying unhealthy or healthy messages" (p. 375), and promote advocacy to enable communities to "express their own story in their own words" (p. 375). The authors compared their media-targeted program with a self-esteem program focused on self- and other acceptance and a control group that participated in a religious education class during the same period as both of the interventions. Following the interventions, the media literacy group reported lower levels of weight concern than did the religious education group. No other differences on measures of body dissatisfaction or eating pathology were observed between the groups, and even this difference was not maintained at 3-month follow-up. The self-esteem program group showed no improvements in weight concern or risk factors for eating disorders.

A recent longitudinal study designed to promote body-image satisfaction and prevent eating problems in middle school girls incorporated both media literacy about the dangers associated with the thin ideal and training in life skills, including self-esteem enhancement, stress management, and peer relations (McVey & Davis, 2002). The researchers found no differences in these variables between girls in schools where the intervention was implemented and those in the control schools, which did not receive the intervention. Instead, both groups experienced significant increases in body satisfaction and decreases in eating pathology over the course of the 1-year study. One potential explanation for this result is that the content of the regular health education curriculum at the control schools included information on healthy eating, active living, and body image.

Although some media literacy programs have led to reductions in weight-related anxiety and body-image concerns (Levine et al., 1999) and internalization of the thin ideal (Piran, Levine, & Irving, 2000), others have shown no effect on body dissatisfaction or eating disorder risk indices (Irving & Berel, 2001; Levine et al., 1999; McVey & Davis, 2002; Smolak, Levine, & Schermer, 1998).

Another type of program that has been the subject of investigations is the dissonance-based preventive intervention developed by Stice and colleagues (Stice, Trost, & Chase, 2003). In this program, women participate in verbal, written, and behavioral exercises in which they present self-generated arguments against the thin ideal. In theory, the strategy induces dissonance in women who have been preselected to have high levels of an endorsement of the thin ideal (i.e., high internalization). Stice, Mazotti, Weibal, and Agras (2000) found that women who received the dissonance intervention experienced decreases in internalization, body dissatisfaction, negative affect, and bulimic symptoms at termination that remained at a 1-month follow-up. Although Stice and colleagues have replicated these findings (Stice, Chase, Stormer, & Appel, 2001), a subsequent study found that the dissonance intervention modified internalization, negative affect, and bulimic symptoms but failed to impact dissatisfaction or dieting efforts (Stice, Trost, & Chase, 2003). The contradictory findings from these studies suggest the importance of identifying the most effective types of interventions. Some interventions are didactic in nature and target participants' knowledge, awareness, or adherence to the thin ideal as well as media techniques that promote it. Others engage the participants at a more personal or cognitive–emotional level by requiring them to verbally and actively combat the thin ideal and seem to produce reductions in body dissatisfaction and disordered eating behaviors as well as reductions in internalization of the thin ideal. These interactive interventions appear to result in more pronounced results than those interventions that are primarily didactic in nature (Stice & Hoffman, 2004).

Furthermore, studies that have assessed individuals who are at elevated risk for eating pathology have shown more positive effects postintervention than those intervention programs that have been directed at the more general population. The former targeted, or secondary intervention, programs may have greater impact than the latter universal, primary prevention programs simply because they are assessing individuals who have substantial problems in the eating and body-image areas being assessed. Those in the universal programs may have such low levels of eating pathology and risk factors for eating pathology that their problems are difficult to detect (Stice & Hoffman, 2004). Another issue to be considered is the developmental level of the participants in an intervention. For example, a universal intervention promoting a healthy lifestyle might be appropriate for elementary and middle-school-age girls, whereas a dissonance-based intervention may be more effective with high school and college females capable of engaging in a cognitive intervention.

Even when risk factors for eating pathology are reduced, these changes do not always result in changes in internalization about social comparison. For example, several studies that reported changes in body dissatisfaction did not report parallel changes in internalization (e.g., Stice & Hoffman, 2004). Possible explanations include the variability in sample sizes, therapists (graduate students vs. seasoned therapists) or teachers, and the exact nature of the intervention (i.e., media literacy, dissonance reduction). Finally, even when studies have reported changes in body-image or eating concerns, these effects are not always maintained at follow-up (Stewart, Carter, Drinkwater, Hainsworth, & Fairburn, 2001; Wade et al., 2003). Intensive, interactive, longer term designs may be needed to produce lasting changes in these variables.

CONCLUSIONS AND RECOMMENDATIONS

A substantial research database suggests a link between the high incidence of body dissatisfaction and eating disorders in Western societies and the Western media's promotion of a European American standard of female beauty that is characterized by extreme thinness. Girls and women who engage in greater consumption of popular media, including girls' and women's magazines and certain types of television shows, are more likely than others to compare themselves with these images, find a discrepancy between their bodies and the societal ideal, internalize the media-promoted ideal, and strive to attain the ideal being promoted. As a result, they tend to be less happy with their bodies and to believe that they need to lose weight, often using extreme strategies such as self-induced vomiting, laxative use, and excessive caloric restriction. As media images of women of color become more prevalent, girls and women of color may face an increasing risk for developing the high levels of body dissatisfaction, weight concern, and disordered eating behaviors that have become so common among White girls and women.

It is important to note that simply being exposed to media influences is insufficient to elicit the levels of body dissatisfaction and drive for thinness necessary for the development of eating disorders. What is clear from existing research is that girls and women must not only be exposed to media images perpetuating the beauty ideal but must also compare themselves negatively with these images or engage in a cognitive process of internalizing those messages. Girls who buy into these messages and try to emulate the images of women they see in movies, television, and magazines are more likely to engage in dieting behaviors and are at greater risk for developing an eating disorder.

Prevention efforts in this area are still in the formative stages, yet evidence to date suggests the potential benefit of programs focusing on increasing literacy and inducing dissonance regarding one's belief in the veracity of the media's messages. These interventions appear to be superior to earlier efforts that were primarily didactic in nature. However, there is still no clear consensus in this research area. Some findings suggest that even one-session intervention programs may have an immediate impact on young women's internalization of traditional messages about thinness and attractiveness, whereas other studies have failed to find any effect at all. Still others have reported an effect at termination of the study but no effect at follow-up.

Researchers might also consider even greater inclusion of feminist methods and strategies in various programs that are designed to challenge the thin ideal. Readings of feminist literature that address, evaluate, and challenge the thin ideal (e.g., excerpts from Naomi Wolf's *The Beauty Myth*, 1991) might be incorporated into future prevention efforts as could advocacy components requiring study participants to create publicity campaigns at their schools challenging the thin ideal. Appearance-related commercials could be part of classroom or school-wide debates designed to engage study participants in evaluating whether such images are harmful to women and men.

In the years to come, new media sources (i.e., the Internet) and accessibility can be expected to bombard girls and young women with media images at a staggering rate. If extant research is any indication, the pervasive body dissatisfaction common in girls and young women today will only continue to escalate unless effective prevention and intervention efforts are put in place. Before these efforts can be undertaken, it is imperative that a context for understanding the media's contribution be outlined, not only in relation to negative body image but also in its further relevance to the etiology of eating disturbance in girls and young women. With a framework of understanding in place, prevention efforts can prepare young people to cope with the media more effectively, leaving their self-esteem, their self-worth, and their physical and emotional health intact.

REFERENCES

Abdollahi, P., & Mann, T. (2001). Eating disorder symptoms and body image concerns in Iran: Comparisons between Iranian women in Iran and in America. *International Journal of Eating Disorders, 30,* 259–268.

Akan, G. E., & Grilo, C. M. (1995). Sociocultural influences on eating attitudes and behaviors, body image, and psychological functioning: A comparison of African-American, Asian-American, and Caucasian college women. *International Journal of Eating Disorders, 2,* 181–187.

Akiba, D. (1998). Cultural variations in body esteem: How young adults in Iran and the United States view their own appearance. *Journal of Social Psychology, 138,* 539–540.

Altabe, M. N. (1996). Issues in the assessment and treatment of body image disturbance inculturally diverse populations. In J. K. Thompson (ed.), *Body image, eating disorders, and obesity: An integrative guide for assessment and treatment* (pp. 129–147). Washington, DC: American Psychological Association.

Andersen, A. E., & DiDomenico, L. (1992). Diet vs. shape content of popular male and female magazines: A dose-response relationship to the incidence of eating disorders. *International Journal of Eating Disorders, 11,* 283–287.

Becker, A. E. (1995). *Body, self, and society: The view from Fiji.* Philadelphia: University of Pennsylvania.

Becker, A. E., Burwell, R., Gilman, S. E., Herzog, D., & Hamburg, P. (2002). Eating behaviours and attitudes following prolonged exposure to television among ethnic Fijian adolescent girls. *British Journal of Psychiatry, 180,* 509–514.

Botta, R. A. (1999). Television images and adolescent girls' body image disturbance. *Journal of Communication, 49,* 22–41.

Botta, R. A. (2000). The mirror of television. A comparison of Black and White adolescents' body image. *Journal of Communication, 50,* 144–159.

Cash, T. F., Cash, D. W., & Butters, J. W. (1983). "Mirror, mirror, on the wall. . .?": Contrast effects and self-evaluations of physical attractiveness. *Personality and Social Psychology Bulletin, 9*(3), 351–358.

Cash, T. F., & Pruzinsky, T. (2002). *Body image: A handbook of theory, research, and clinical practice.* New York: Guilford.

Cattarin, J., Thompson, J. K., Thomas, C. M., & Williams, R. (2000). The impact of televised images of thinness and attractiveness on body image: The role of social comparison. *Journal of Social and Clinical Psychology, 19*(2), 220–239.

Choudry, I. Y., & Mumford, D. B. (1992). A pilot study of eating disorders in Mirpur (Pakistan) using an Urdu version of the Eating Attitudes Test. *International Journal of Eating Disorders, 11*, 243–251.

Cusumano, D. L., & Thompson, J. K. (1997). Body image and body shape ideals in magazines: Exposure, awareness, and internalization. *Sex Roles, 37*(9/10), 701–721.

Cusumano, D. L., & Thompson, J. K. (2001). Media influence and body image in 8-11-year-old boys and girls: A preliminary report on the Multidimensional Media Influence Scale. *International Journal of Eating Disorders, 29*(1), 37–44.

Dounchis, J. Z., Hayden, H. A., & Wilfley, D. E. (2001). Obesity, body image, and eating disorders in ethnically diverse children and adolescents. In J. K. Thompson & L. Smolak (Eds.), *Body image, eating disorders, and obesity in youth* (pp. 67–99). Washington, DC: American Psychological Association.

Festinger, L. (1954). A theory of social comparison processes. *Human Relations, 7*, 117–140.

Fichter, M. M., Weyer, S., Sourdi, L., & Sourdi, Z. (1983). The epidemiology of anorexia nervosa: A comparison of Greek adolescents living in Germany and Greek adolescents living in Greece. In P. L. Darby, P. E. Garfinkel, D. M. Garner, & D. V. Coscina (Eds.), *Anorexia nervosa: Recent developments in research* (pp. 95–105). New York: Liss.

Field, A. E., Cheung, L., Wolf, A. M., Herzog, D. B., Gortmaker, S. L., & Colditz, G. A. (1999). Exposure to the mass media and weight concerns among girls. *Pediatrics, 103*, 660.

Flynn, K., & Fitzgibbon, M. (1996). Body images and obesity risk among Black females: A review of the literature. *Annals of Behavioral Medicine, 20*, 13–24.

Garner, D. M., Garfinkel, P. E., Schwartz, D., & Thompson, M. (1980). Cultural expectations of thinness in women. *Psychological Reports, 47*, 483–491.

Gilbert, S. (2003). Eating disorders in women of color. *Clinical Psychology: Science and Practice, 10*, 444–455.

Gilbert, S., & Thompson, J. K. (1996). Feminist explanations of the development of eating disorders: Common themes, research findings, and methodological issues. *Clinical Psychology: Science and Practice, 3*, 183–202.

Gonzalez-Lavin, A., & Smolak, L. (1995, March). *Relationships between television and eating problems in middle school girls.* Poster session presented at the Convention of the Society for Research in Child Development, Indianapolis, IN.

Harris, S. M. (1994). Racial differences in predictors of college women's body image attitudes. *Women & Health, 21*, 89–104.

Harris, D. J., & Kuba, S. A. (1997). Ethnocultural identity and eating disorders in women of color. *Professional Psychology: Research and Practice, 28*, 341–347.

Harrison, K. (2000a). The body electric: Thin-ideal media and eating disorders in adolescents. *Journal of Communication, 50*, 119–143.

Harrison, K. (2000b). Television viewing, fat stereotyping, body shape standards, and eating disorder symptomatology in grade school children. *Communication Research, 27,* 617–640.

Harrison, K., & Cantor, J. (1997). The relationship between media exposure and eating disorders. *Journal of Communication, 47,* 40–67.

Hebl, M. R., & Heatherton, T. F. (1998). The stigma of obesity in women. The difference is black and white. *Personality and Social Psychology Bulletin, 24,* 417–426.

Heinberg, L. J., & Thompson, J. K. (1995). Body image and televised images of thinness and attractiveness: A controlled laboratory investigation. *Journal of Social and Clinical Psychology, 14*(4), 325–338.

Heinberg, L. J., Thompson, J. K., & Stormer, S. (1995). Development and validation of the sociocultural attitudes towards appearance questionnaire. *International Journal of Eating Disorders, 17*(1), 81–89.

Hohlstein, L. A., Smith, G. T., & Atlas, J. G. (1998). An application of expectancy theory to eating disorders: Development and validation of measures of eating and dieting expectancies. *Psychological Assessment, 10,* 49–58.

Irving, L. M. (1990). Mirror images. Effects of the standard of beauty on the self- and body-esteem of women exhibiting varying levels of bulimic symptoms. *Journal of Social and Clinical Psychology, 9,* 230–242.

Irving, L. M., & Berel, S. (2001). Comparison of media-literacy programs to strengthen college women's resistance to media images. *Psychology of Women Quarterly, 25,* 103–111.

Irving, L. M., DuPen, J., & Berel, S. (1998). A media literacy program for high school females. *Eating Disorders: The Journal of Treatment and Prevention, 6,* 119–131.

Joiner, G. W., & Kashubeck, S. (1996). Acculturation, body image, self-esteem, and eating disorder symptomatology in adolescent Mexican American women. *Psychology of Women Quarterly, 20,* 419–435.

Keery, H., Thompson, J. K., Shroff, H., Wertheim, E., & Smolak, L. (2004). The Sociocultural Internalization of Appearance Questionnaire–Adolescents (SIAQ-A): Psychometric and normative data for three countries. *Eating and weight disorders: Studies on anorexia, bulimia, and obesity, 9,* 56–61.

Kemper, K. A., Sargent, R. G., Drane, J. W., Wanzer, J., Valois, R. F., & Hussey, J. R. (1994). Black and white females' perceptions of ideal body size and social norms. *Obesity Research, 2,* 117–126.

Levine, M. P., & Harrison, K. (2004). Media's role in the perpetuation and prevention of negative body image and disordered eating. In J. K. Thompson (Ed.), *Handbook of eating disorders and obesity* (pp. 695–717). New York: Wiley.

Levine, M. P., Piran, N., & Stoddard, C. (1999). Mission more probable: Media literacy, activism, and advocacy as primary prevention. In N. Piran, M. P. Levine, & C. Steiner-Adair (Eds.), *Preventing eating disorders: A handbook of interventions and special challenges* (pp. 1–25). Philadelphia: Brunner/Mazel.

Levine, M. P., Smolak, L., & Hayden, H. (1994). The relation of sociocultural factors to eating attitudes and behaviors among middle school girls. *Journal of Early Adolescence, 14,* 471–490.

Martin, M. C., & Gentry, J. W. (1997). Stuck in the model trap: The effects of beautiful women in ads on female pre-adolescents and adolescents. *Journal of Advertising, 26*(2), 19–33.

McVey, G. L., & Davis, R. (2002). A program to promote positive body image: A 1-year follow-up assessment. *Journal of Early Adolescence, 22*, 96–108.

Nasser, M. (1986). Comparative study of the prevalence of abnormal eating attitudes among Arab female students of both London and Cairo universities. *Psychological Medicine, 16*, 621–625.

Neumark-Sztainer, D., Sherwood, N., Coller, T., & Hannan, P. J. (2000). Primary prevention of disordered eating among pre-adolescent girls: Feasibility and short-term impact of a community-based intervention. *Journal of the American Dietetic Association, 100*, 1466–1473.

Parnell, K., Sargent, R., Thompson, S., Duhe, S., Valois, R., & Kemper, R. (1996). Black and white adolescent females' perceptions of ideal body size. *Journal of School Health, 66*, 112–118.

Paxton, S. J., Schutz, H. K., Wertheim, E. J., & Muir, S. L. (1999). Friendship clique and peer influences on body image concerns, dietary restraint, extreme weight-loss behaviors and binge eating in preadolescent girls. *Journal of Abnormal Psychology, 108*, 255–266.

Pike, K. M., Dohm, F., Striegel-Moore, R. H., Wilfley, D. E., & Fairburn, C. (2001). A comparison of Black and White women with binge eating disorder. *The American Journal of Psychiatry, 158*, 1455–1460.

Piran, N., Levine, M. P., & Irving, L. M. (2000). GO GIRLS! Media literacy, activism, and advocacy project. *Healthy Weight Journal, 14*, 89–90.

Richins, M. L. (1995). Social comparison, advertising, and consumer discontent. *American Behavioral Scientist, 38*(4), 593–607.

Rieves, L., & Cash, T. F. (1996). Social developmental factors and women's body-image attitudes. *Journal of Social Behavior & Personality, 11*, 63–78.

Root, M. (1991). Disordered eating in women of color. *Sex Roles, 22*, 525–536.

Rothblum, E. D. (1994). I'll die for the revolution but don't ask me not to diet: Feminism and the continuing stigmatization of obesity. In P. Fallon, M. A. Katzman, & S. C. Wooley (Eds.), *Feminist perspectives on eating disorders* (pp. 17–52). New York: Guilford Press.

Smolak, L., Levine, M., & Schermer, F. (1998). A controlled evaluation of an elementary school primary prevention program for eating problems. *Journal of Psychosomatic Research, 44*, 339–353.

Snow, J. T., & Harris, M. B. (1989). Disordered eating in South-western Pueblo Indians and Hispanics. *Journal of Adolescence, 12*, 329–336.

Stephens, N. M., Schumaker, J. F., & Sibiya, T. E. (1999). Eating disorders and dieting behavior among Australian and Swazi university students. *Journal of Social Psychology, 139*, 153–158.

Stewart, D. A., Carter, J. C., Drinkwater, J., Hainsworth, J., & Fairburn, C. G. (2001). Modification of eating attitudes and behaviour in adolescent girls: A controlled study. *International Journal of Eating Disorders, 29*, 107–118.

Stice, E. (2001). Risk factors for eating pathology: Recent advances and future directions. In R. Striegel-Moore & L. Smolak (Eds.), *Eating disorders: Innovative directions in research and practice* (pp. 51–74). Washington, DC: American Psychological Association.

Stice, E., Chase, A., Stormer, S., & Appel, A. (2001). A randomized trial of a dissonance-based eating disorder prevention program. *International Journal of Eating Disorders, 29,* 247–262.

Stice, E., & Hoffman, E. (2004). Eating disorder prevention programs. In J. K. Thompson (Ed.), *Handbook of eating disorders and obesity* (pp. 33–57). New York: Wiley.

Stice, E., Mazotti, L., Weibal, D., & Agras, W. S. (2000). Dissonance prevention program decreases thin-ideal internalization, body dissatisfaction, dieting, negative affect, and bulimic symptoms: A preliminary experiment. *International Journal of Eating Disorders, 27,* 206–217.

Stice, E., & Shaw, H. E. (1994). Adverse effects of the media portrayed thin-ideal on women and linkages to bulimic symptomology. *Journal of Social and Clinical Psychology, 13,* 288–308.

Stice, E., Shaw, H., & Nemeroff, C. (1998). Dual pathway model of bulimia nervosa: Longitudinal support for dietary restraint and affect-regulation mechanisms. *Journal of Social and Clinical Psychology, 17,* 129–149.

Stice, E., Trost, A., & Chase, A. (2003). Health weight control and dissonance-based eating disorder prevention programs: Results from a controlled trial. *International Journal of Eating Disorders, 33,* 10–21.

Striegel-Moore, R., Schreiber, G. B., Pike, K. M., Wilfley, D. E., & Rodin, J. (1995). Drive for thinness in black and white preadolescent girls. *International Journal of Eating Disorders, 18,* 59–69.

Thompson, J. K., & Heinberg, L. J. (1999). The media's influence on body image disturbance and eating disorders: We've reviled them, now can we rehabilitate them? *Journal of Social Issues, 55,* 339–353.

Thompson, J. K., Heinberg, L. J., Altabe, M., & Tantleff-Dunn, S. (1999). *Exacting beauty: Theory, assessment, and treatment of body image disturbance.* Washington, DC: American Psychological Association.

Thompson, J. K., & Smolak, L. (2001). *Body image, eating disorders and obesity in youth: Assessment, prevention and treatment.* Washington, DC: American Psychological Association.

Thompson, J. K., & Stice, E. (2001). Thin-ideal internalization: Mounting evidence for a new risk factor for body image disturbance and eating pathology. *Current Directions in Psychological Science, 10,* 181–183.

Thompson, J. K., van den Berg, P., Roehrig, M., Guarda, A., & Heinberg, L. J. (2004). The Sociocultural Attitudes Towards Appearance Scale–3 (SATAQ-3): Development and validation. *International Journal of Eating Disorders, 35,* 293–304.

Tiggemann, M., & Pickering, A. S. (1996). Role of television in adolescent women's body dissatisfaction and drive for thinness. *International Journal of Eating Disorders, 20*(2), 199–203.

Tiggemann, M., & Ruutel, E. (2001). A cross-cultural comparison of body dissatisfaction in Estonian and Australian young adults and its relationship with media exposure. *Journal of Cross-Cultural Psychology, 32,* 736–742.

Veron-Guidry, S., Williamson, D. A., & Netemeyer, R. G. (1997). Structural modeling analysis of body dysphoria and eating disorder symptoms in preadolescent girls. *Eating Disorders: The Journal of Treatment and Prevention, 5,* 15–27.

Wade, T. D., Davidson, S., & O'Dea, J. A. (2003). A preliminary controlled evaluation of a school-based media literacy program and self-esteem program for reducing eating disorder risk factors. *International Journal of Eating Disorders, 33,* 371–383.

Wildes, J. E., & Emery, R. E. (2001). The roles of ethnicity and culture in the development of eating disturbance and body dissatisfaction: A meta-analytic review. *Clinical Psychology Review, 21,* 521–551.

Wiseman, C. V., Gray, J. J., Mosimann, J. E., & Ahrens, A. H. (1992). Cultural expectations of thinness in women: An update. *International Journal of Eating Disorders, 11*(1), 85–89.

Wolf, N. (1991). *The beauty myth.* New York: Doubleday.

II

DEFINING REALITY

4

CLASH OF CULTURES: WOMEN AND GIRLS ON TV AND IN REAL LIFE

DIANA ZUCKERMAN AND NICOLE DUBOWITZ

We've come a long way baby, but to where? Are there any positive role models on TV for girls? Ask their mothers, who will say no. Ask the daughters, and they will say yes.

In the 1950s and early 1960s, TV families tended to portray an ideal: attractive parents and children, homes where nothing was out of place and families ate all their meals together, and kids playing outside in safe neighborhoods on manicured lawns. The closest approximation to reality TV was Ozzie and Harriet Nelson and their two sons starring as a suburban family with the same names on *Ozzie and Harriet*. In those days, watching TV was a family activity, because many families had only one television.

Those days are over. Today, most families in the United States have at least two or three TVs and dozens of channels, so families rarely watch programs together. And when they try to watch programs with their children, many parents are embarrassed or disgusted. A 2002 poll found that two thirds of American parents believe that TV programs on between 8:00 and 10:00 p.m. are usually "inappropriate for children" and 7 out of 10 parents said they had been "shocked or offended" by something on TV in the past year (Parental Guilt, 2002).

These statistics raise an interesting question about the other 30% of parents: What could it possibly take to shock or offend them?

Despite parental despair, parents exercise surprisingly little control over their children's TV viewing. The same polls showed that half of the parents had put a TV in a child's bedroom; an amazing 40% of all 5- to 9-year-olds and half of all 10- to 12-year-olds had TVs in their bedrooms (Public Agenda, 2002).

TV and other media influence what people say, think, and believe for a wide range of topics, including appropriate roles for women and girls. Sometimes the influence is very superficial, such as hairstyles (e.g., Farrah Fawcett's mane of hair in the 1970s and Jennifer Aniston's hairstyle today) and fashion trends (e.g., Mary Tyler Moore's conservative outfits in the 1970s and Britney Spears' belly-button exposure starting today's low-rise jeans). However, TV also influences people in more substantial ways; for example, without realizing it, adolescents repeat the expressions and ideas they hear on TV, ask for the products they see advertised on TV, and imitate the celebrities and characters that they see on TV.

In addition to these imitations, research shows a rather consistent but modest correlation between TV viewing and gender stereotypes (Herrett-Skjellum & Allen, 1996; Morgan & Shanahan, 1997). In chapter 1 (this volume), L. Monique Ward and Kristen Harrison quote research indicating that TV viewing influences viewers' attitudes about jobs held by women, appropriate roles and behaviors for women, and their own personal preferences regarding the kinds of activities that interest them. Children who were exposed to nontraditional women on TV expressed more nontraditional attitudes and opinions, and those exposed to more traditional women on TV gave more traditional responses. Most of these studies were conducted in the 1970s and 1980s, which raises questions about whether those studies are still relevant to life in the 21st century. After all, in the past decade, most girls have seen or heard of women in occupations that were once considered nontraditional for women: doctors, politicians, police officers, and lawyers. Wouldn't seeing such characters on TV be much less important as children are exposed to them in their daily lives?

In this chapter, we summarize how the roles of women on TV programs have changed through the years, briefly describe what we know about the impact of these role models for girls and women, and provide some examples from popular TV programs that girls and women are likely to watch. These examples are not based on a representative sample of programs or attitudes, but we focus on describing women and girls depicted on the most popular network prime-time programs, syndicated series, and cable programs from 2002 and early 2003. One anecdotal example of the conflicting views of one mother and daughter is also included.

WOMEN ON TV PROGRAMS: A HISTORICAL PERSPECTIVE

Understanding women on TV today requires a historical context. Early television portrayed women in limited roles on programs and in commercials. Analyses in the 1960s and 70s documented a lack of female characters compared with male characters, an abundance of stay-at-home moms (called homemakers in those days), and few women in other jobs (Signorielli, 1991). The TV world was inhabited almost entirely by White women and a disproportionate number of young women; women of color and older women were rare (Huston et al, 1992). In commercials, men were the voice of authority: Regardless of the product being sold, the voice-overs were male and women usually sold cleaning products rather than cars or appliances. Of course, sex was sometimes used to sell products, and in those commercials beautiful, sexy women enticed men to buy products, not as the voice of authority, but as the voice of seduction.

When women started breaking out of the homemaker role in the 1960s, they did so in the supernatural realm: *I Dream of Jeannie* portrayed a genie living with an astronaut and *Bewitched* portrayed a witch with magical powers pretending to be a suburban wife-next-door. The cultural breakthroughs were much heralded: *Julia* was the first series starring an African American woman with a professional job (Diahann Carroll as a widow working as a nurse) in 1968, and Mary Tyler Moore's Mary Richards debuted in 1970 as the first attractive, unmarried, and unattached career woman (working in a TV newsroom). From 1970 to 1977, Mary Richards was a role model to millions of women—a beautiful, smart career woman who did not obsess about her lack of a husband or boyfriend. Even so, the program was careful not to be too radical; Mary was surrounded by more traditional women characters.

The late 1970s saw new breakthroughs, such as *Charlie's Angels*. Now beautiful young women were single and had exciting careers as some special kind of private investigators. The trend continued in the 1980s with Cybil Shepherd in *Moonlighting* and Stephanie Zimbalist as the owner of her own private investigation business. Both were beautiful, smart, and competent women who competed with their male partners (Bruce Willis and Pierce Brosnan). And so the role models of TV women changed from one narrow and unrealistic ideal (the beautiful, contented housewife) to another (the beautiful, smart, and athletic private detective). TV's world was suddenly inhabited by many single women and single mothers, but not many traditional families. The families with traditional mothers and daughters tended to be set in the past, such as in *The Waltons* (starting in 1972, with TV movies through the 1990s) and *Little House on the Prairie* (1974–1983).

By the 1980s, there were a much wider range of women characters on TV: married moms and single moms—most of them employed—and single career women, divorced or widowed. From the early 1980s on, more and more of the women were lawyers, policewomen, doctors, and other highly educated and well-paid professionals.

Describing women and girls on TV in the 1990s and 21st century is much more difficult because there are so many more TV channels and a greater range of programs than ever before. At almost any hour of the day or night, millions of American families with cable or satellite TV can watch new reality programs, new movies, old movies, and dramas and situation comedies produced sometime between the 1950s and last week.

When there were just a few TV channels, each tried to appeal to a mainstream audience, but cable TV stations can survive with a smaller audience and can afford to offend many viewers as long as their audience is sufficient to attract advertisers. This situation has resulted in a much wider range of images on TV, some of which are extremely negative portrayals of women. Howard Stern's show and MTV music videos that portray women in degrading situations are especially egregious examples, but even prime-time network television has been influenced by cable programs and the new pressure to succeed against so many more competitors by being edgier and sexier. *The Osbournes* and *Sex in the City* are obvious examples of programs with language and themes that were not acceptable a decade or more ago, but even programs that were popular with elementary- and middle-school children in the 1990s, such as *The Simpsons* (consistently in the top-50 prime-time programs) and *Boy Meets World*, included ideas and language that differed greatly from those of previous prime-time TV.

Even in programs that depict positive values such as the importance of friendship and family or the wisdom of teachers, mothers might wonder why teenage girls on TV dress like street walkers. In contrast, their daughters would probably be shocked by that perception and may be oblivious to how teen and even preteen fashions are shaped by what they see on TV. In the real world, meanwhile, principals of middle schools and high schools are struggling to write and enforce dress codes that prohibit very low rise jeans, cleavage, miniskirts, micro-mini shorts, and other distractions (Anderson, 2002), having to make explicit rules that used to be taken for granted, such as "no underwear should be visible" (Massey, 2003).

Sex sells, and some of the most highly acclaimed TV programs aimed at adult audiences have been baring bodies for years. Nudity on *NYPD Blue* (which ranked in the top 20–30 prime-time programs from 1999 to 2002) and sex and nudity in *Sex in the City* (a top-rated HBO program that is now widely available in a slightly toned-down version) are the most obvious examples. There are many other examples of TV's use of women's bodies to increase market share: *ER* (a top-ten program since its inception) and the *CSI* series (consistently rated in the top ten) feature doctors, police, and other professional women with tight, low-cut tops under their white coats or jackets. In fact, the main woman character on top-rated *CSI* was an exotic dancer prior to becoming a medical technician. Is this really how women who are doctors and investigators dress on the job? Most professionals would say no, but TV is influential and as has happened in schools, office attire is changing as more and more viewers buy the revealing types of clothes they see on TV and want to wear them to work (Kalita, 2003).

WOMEN ON COMMERCIALS

Commercials in the 1960s and 1970s were criticized by researchers for portraying women who were apparently ecstatic about cleaning their homes. Women were rarely portrayed in car commercials as potential buyers, although they were used as decorative accessories.

One thing hasn't changed: the use of sex to sell products. What has changed is the explicitness of the ads. Early ads were suggestive; for example, a sexy voice sold shaving cream by urging "Take it off—take it all off." Today, ads for Victoria's Secret are not just suggestive, they are revealing: Close-ups of beautiful women in skimpy underwear are selling an image rather than the actual items of clothing. These ads are shown throughout prime time, when adolescent girls (many of whom are already feeling inadequate about their bodies) will see them, whether they choose to or not. The bodies in these ads are enhanced by breast implants, liposuction, and computer enhancement, resulting in images of a perfect body that rarely occurs in nature.

BODY IMAGE

As the prevalence of traditional and nontraditional characters on TV has become less important in a culture where fewer careers are considered men's or women's, more research has focused on what women look like on TV. Current complaints about TV women are different from those in the past. For example, in recent years, the National Organization for Women has issued an annual *Feminist Primetime Report*, which examines all the prime-time programs on the six broadcast networks (ABC, CBS, Fox, NBC, UPN, and WB). Although their concerns about lack of women characters and lack of real women on news programs are similar to the complaints dating back to the 1970s, they are much more concerned about the appearance of women on TV and the lack of older women, minority women, and women with realistic bodies.

One doesn't need to be a researcher to notice that the vast majority of actresses on TV are thinner, younger, and more beautiful than women in real life. It is not just their Barbie doll bodies; most also have extremely white teeth and perfect noses and other features. Even the teenagers have no pimples (unless it is part of the story line) and the "fat friends" are often attractive and many are not even very overweight.

It is therefore not surprising that recent research studies have emphasized how TV viewing increases dissatisfaction with one's looks and body image (e.g., Grogan, Williams, & Conner, 1996), lowers self-esteem (Thornton & Maurice, 1997), and increases anger and depression (Pinhas, Toner, Ali, Garfinkel, & Stuckless, 1999). Teenage viewers may feel especially lacking as they see these ads, but research indicates that grown women also tend to feel inadequate in comparison.

For example, Ogden and Mundray (1996) found that medical students were more dissatisfied with their bodies after viewing media images of thin models than they were after viewing images of overweight individuals. A study of ninth-grade California girls found no link between total TV viewing and perceived importance of weight and appearance, but girls who watched more music videos were slightly but significantly more concerned about weight and appearance (Borzekowksi, Robinson, & Killen, 2000). This was especially true of African American and White girls. However, a careful review of these studies indicates that the correlations between TV viewing and attitudes about one's body are modest. Is TV's influence on body image cause for concern?

Very little is known about how TV influences an individual, but research on TV violence suggests that the impact on some children and adults can be substantial and on others it can be nonexistent. The image of girls and women on TV probably influences some girls and women more than others, but with those images even harder to avoid than TV violence, their influence is probably more pervasive and therefore nearly impossible to measure.

CLASH OF CULTURES

For individual women and girls watching TV, the impact will vary according to which of the hundreds of programs they watch. Thanks to cable TV and VCRs, today's viewers can spend all their time watching programs and movies with the best available role models, or they can watch the most exploitative or misogynist programs imaginable, or anything in between. Unlike 30 or more years ago, there are strong women and admirable women on today's popular TV series who provide role models for adult women. And yet, despite the dizzying array of programs, there are surprisingly few programs that mothers are likely to identify as ones they would want their adolescent daughters to watch that adolescent girls would find interesting. Instead, many mothers struggle with a clash of cultures as they try to teach their daughters to grow up to try to be the best they can be—and find love and a great career—when so few TV programs portray women with attractive and appealing personal traits, personal lives, and careers.

There are many TV characters that would be perceived as role models for women but would not be especially appealing to girls. For example, three award-winning series—The West Wing, Law and Order, and The Practice—portray smart, accomplished, often admirable women in important but real jobs. Most of the women are very attractive and very thin, but there are even some role models with less-than-perfect physical attributes. The most unusual character was Eleanor Frutt, the plus-size lawyer on The Practice; unfortunately, she left TV when *The Practice* became *Boston Legal*, and was replaced with a bevy of almost unbelievably beautiful young lawyers and one beautiful, over-50 law partner played by Candace Bergen. *The West Wing's* CJ is often cited as a role model by young professional women, because although attractive, she looks less glamorous and perfect than do most TV characters. *The West Wing's* First Lady often seems too flashy and opinionated for a political wife, but on the positive side she is portrayed as a very intelligent woman who is an accomplished physician and who cares about improving public policies for women. *Law and Order*, which is the only one of these three programs that has remained in the top ten, has always included beautiful, smart, young lawyers, but they seem believable compared to lawyers on many other TV programs. These three programs provide an array of role models for adult women, but they are not programs aimed at children or teenagers and it is unlikely that the characters would be seen as role models by most adolescent girls.

What do teen girls watch? The Nielsen ratings do not make demographic data available to the public, but programs such as *Friends* and *Sex in the City* certainly attracted a teenage audience during their many years in prime time and their continued presence as reruns. *Friends* was one of the top-five-ranked programs on TV for several years, and in 2002–2003, the situation comedy's story line revolved around having a baby outside of marriage after a fling with a friend. Although the women on *Friends* are attractive and generally supportive of each other, their sometimes casual attitudes toward sex and careers make it unlikely that most mothers would point to any of them as desirable role models for their daughters. *Sex in the City* focuses on women on their own in the big city, one of whom has the kind of casual attitude toward sex that makes public health workers panic about the spread of sexually transmitted diseases. *Sex in the City* is very popular among teens and young women and portrays friendships that are very strong and sometimes inspiring, but this is not a program that mothers are likely to encourage their school-age daughters to watch.

Although the ratings of *Gilmore Girls* (below the top 100) do not compare with those of the other programs described in this chapter, the show is worth noting because it is supported by corporations wanting to sponsor family-friendly programming and is clearly aimed at a mother and daughter audience. It features a mother and daughter as best friends, with the fun-loving mother overcoming her past as a teen mom and often seeming more like a sister than a mom. Daughter Rory is the serious one (she was a high school student when the series premiered and entered Yale in the fall 2003 television season). Its heart seems to be in the right place, but credibility is strained as the mother and daughter do things such as dance with each other in a marathon. The daughter frequently sounds like she's reading a script rather than saying things that teen girls say in real life. Mothers all over America would like their daughters to be as close to them and be as hard-working, but for most mothers, this daughter is not a role model but rather a fantasy.

The programs named above feature women and girls who are potential role models, but they are not necessarily currently top-ten-ranked programs. In the last few years, "reality" programs such as *Survivor* and various dating and makeover programs have frequently made the top-ten. *Survivor* often shows women to be as sexually uninhibited and as tough as men. *The Bachelor*, *The Bachelorette*, and similar programs are all throwbacks to the Cinderella story in which women vie to find or attract Mr. Right, and preferably Mr. Rich (even when, as in *The Bachelorette*, the woman is doing the choosing, rather than hoping to be chosen). The makeover programs are like endless infomercials for plastic surgery, conveying that changing as much of your appearance as possible is the way to improve your life.

Even more appalling are MTV's *Real World*, a very raunchy reality program about men and women sharing a house, and programs such as *Extreme Dating* and *Victoria's Secret Fashion Show*. The latter is a prime-time infomercial for sexy underwear and plastic surgery, whereas *Extreme Dating* follows real people on sometimes sexually explicit blind dates. Howard Stern's program, featuring women stripping and men critiquing their bodies, is so demeaning to women that it is distressing that parents have not banded together to try to get it off the air.

These are the kinds of programs that are likely to cause the most anguish for mothers, because it is so difficult to ensure that their children do not watch them. Not so long ago, such programs could be avoided by not subscribing to cable TV, but now some of them are on major networks, many of them during prime time. And with so many children and teens with TVs in their rooms, it is likely that many parents who assume that their children are not watching these programs would be in for a rude surprise if they checked up on their children's TV viewing more often.

In addition to prime-time network programs, syndicated series also attract large audiences. Several of the top-rated syndicated programs are older versions of the top-rated shows on prime time, such as *Everyone Loves Raymond* and *Will & Grace*. Other popular programs are game shows such as *Wheel of Fortune* and *Jeopardy*, court TV shows such as *Judge Judy*, and talk shows such as *Oprah* and *Dr. Phil*. Of these, Oprah is the most positive role model for many women because of her personal accomplishments, but girls probably see her as representing an unattainable status.

The Generational Divide: A Mother and Daughter Compare Views

15-year-old daughter: It's hard to think of a good role model from programs today. I think my favorite is Topanga Lawrence from *Boy Meets World*. Topanga is a very positive role model because she stands up for what she believes in, like abstinence until marriage, and she is very focused on school and doing well. When her parents broke up she had to deal with whether she could be in a marital relationship with Cory, and eventually decided to follow her heart and marry Cory.

Mother responds: *Boy Meets World* is still on reruns. At the time it was on ABC on prime time, it seemed too sexy for its 8:00 p.m. time slot, and I didn't like my preteen children watching it. Now that my daughter is older, I can appreciate the program more.

Daughter: Other good role models are the three main women on the show *Friends:* Monica, Phoebe, and Rachel. While all of them are very different, each has good qualities that could be looked up to. Monica is very ambitious and responsible. Phoebe is fun-loving and carefree. Rachel is confident and caring. These characters are very realistic because while each have strong points in their values and attributes, they make mistakes and have flaws just like any regular person. When they come to realize their mistakes, though, they always try to rectify them and they want the best for all their friends and look out for one another.

Mother responds: Unfortunately, Rachel is a single mother who can't seem to figure out that the friend who is the father of her baby loves her and wants to marry her. Phoebe seems like the stereotypic ditsy blond. The thought of these women as role models is depressing.

Daughter: Rory Gilmore (from *Gilmore Girls*) doesn't have much time for boys because she is very studious and has an extremely close relationship with her mother. While this is a little unrealistic, a lot of teenage girls would probably be better off with morals like Rory. I'm not sure if girls could relate to her because not many girls are super close with their moms. Her mom is very outgoing and fun, and more like a friend than a mom, which I think is pretty unusual. Unfortunately, a real-life girl who acted like Rory wouldn't probably have friends her own age.

Mother responds: I'm in full agreement on this one!

Daughter: One of the worst role models is Trishelle on MTV's *Real World*. Trishelle comes off very sweet and innocent, but on the inside she is a partying skank dying to get out. She agrees with Stephen to not sleep with any other people, yet she still flirts with practically every guy around. Then, Stephen gets angry at her because Trishelle is totally hypocritical and gets mad when Stephen does so much as talk to another girl. What the hell! I think she is sleazy and dishonest.

Mother responds: Sounds about right to me, but what is my daughter doing watching this awful program?

Daughter: One of my best friends likes Hillary, the quirky host on *TRL*, a music video show on MTV. Another close friend likes Bridget, the attractive popular daughter on 8 *Simple Rules for Dating My Teenage Daughter*.

Mother responds: I've never watched *TRL* so I have no opinion on that one. Of course, I prefer the more studious daughter on 8 *Simple Rules for Dating My Teenage Daughter*.

Despite the many programs available, the TV role models mothers would chose for girls are scarce. Mothers are in an untenable position, trying to teach values that are antithetical to many of the explicit and implicit values that are conveyed on TV programs every hour of the day and every day of the week. Regardless of their ideology, it is unlikely that most mothers feel good about what TV is teaching their daughters (and sons!). Where are the women characters who enjoy their jobs, friends, and family, while behaving admirably in their personal and professional lives?

The public may want to blame network executives and producers, but unfortunately that blame needs to be shared. Programs are on TV because they attract viewers. If parents did not let their children watch programs that the parents do not approve of, and did not watch them either, many of these programs would be off the air. If parents took televisions out of their children's rooms and limited TV viewing, these programs would lose much of their audience. If parents formed groups that threatened to boycott companies that advertise on these programs, the programs would be off the air. Most parents have not done any of those things, and everyone must live with the results.

REFERENCES

Anderson, W. (2002, Fall). *School dress codes and uniform policies* (Policy Report No. 4). Eugene, OR: ERIC Clearinghouse on Educational Management. Retrieved March 9, 2005, from http://eric2.uoregon.edu/pdf/policy_reports/policy%20report%20dress%20code.pdf

Borzekowski, D. L., Robinson, T. N., & Killen, J. D. (2000). Does the camera add 10 pounds? Media use, perceived importance of appearance, and weight concerns among teenage girls. *Journal of Adolescent Health, 26,* 36–41.

Grogan, S., Williams, Z., & Conner, M. (1996). The effects of viewing same gender photographic models on body-esteem. *Psychology of Women Quarterly, 20,* 569–575.

Herrett-Skjellum, J., & Allen, M. (1996). Television programming and sex stereo-typing: A meta-analysis. *Communication Yearbook 19*, 157–185.

Huston, A. C., Donnerstein, E., Fairchild, H., Feshbach, N. D., Katz, P. A., Murray, J. P., et al. (1992). *Big world, small screen.* Lincoln: University of Nebraska Press.

Kalita, S. M. (2003, July 8). Toeing the line on appropriate attire: Suits or shorts? *The Washington Post*, p. B1.

Massey, J. (2003, August 21). Skimpy styles spur dress code scrutiny. *Boston Globe*, Globe South, p. 1.

Morgan, M., & Shanahan, J. (1997). Two decades of cultivation research: An appraisal and meta-analysis. *Communication Yearbook 20*, 1–46.

Ogden, J., & Mundray, K. (1996). The effect of the media on body satisfaction: The role of gender and size. *European Eating Disorders Review, 4*, 171–182.

Parental guilt. (2002, November 17). *The Washington Post*, p. B5.

Pinhas, L., Toner, B., Ali, A., Garfinkel, P., & Stuckless, P. (1999). The effects of the ideal of female beauty on mood and body satisfaction. *International Journal of Eating Disorders, 25*, 223–226.

Signorielli, N. (1991). *A sourcebook on children and television.* New York: Greenwood Press.

Thornton, B., & Maurice, J. (1997). Physique contrast effect: Adverse impact of idealized body images for women. *Sex Roles, 37*, 433–439.

5

OUTWIT, OUTLAST, OUT-FLIRT? THE WOMEN OF REALITY TV

LAURA S. BROWN

On the TV screen, a group of emaciated, scantily dressed women and men can be seen huddling around a campfire. From time to time, one of them appears by him- or herself on the screen, chatting to the unseen interviewer about how he or she is going to eliminate another member of the group from the game. The viewers watch and wonder, who will be voted off tonight?

In the fall of 2000, I spent 2 months as the resident psychologist for a popular reality TV show while it was in production. Another psychologist and I screened the finalists for the show. As a result, I knew a great deal about each person's dynamics and much about their personal histories, foibles, and values. I then lived among and debriefed the show's participants about their feelings as filming progressed. I was able to spend a number of hours talking to and observing the work of field producers, camera and sound crews, and other staff involved in the 24-hour-a-day, 7-day-a-week work required for the creation of the 40 or so minutes that made it on the TV screens of America each week the show aired.

Because of the in-residence nature of my job, I came to know, in very personal and intimate ways, people who were portrayed in brief, edited segments on-screen. These people were not precisely clients (because the network was my client, and thus, along with the reality show, remains anonymous here), but certainly not my friends, given the extreme artificiality of the circumstances in which we encountered one another. I nonetheless had a view of the show's participants that was full and rich and founded in daily interactions rather than only in psychological evaluation. Many of the participants were people whom I came to like and admire, even though our lives and values were frequently at extreme variance.

After filming ended, I returned to my usual life, fascinated by the phenomenon of reality television. I watched the show with which I had been involved like any other consumer of network TV and was frequently surprised to see how these people whom I had come to know so well had been portrayed. I recognized some of the characters on the screen, but they lacked the depth and color of the people with whom I had spent time.

When I went online to read the chat-room discussions about the perceptions of the show's participants by the general viewing public, as part of my ongoing job of assisting show participants in dealing with their new-found fame (or infamy), I found perceptions among chat-room writers that often were wildly at variance with what I knew of some of these individual's actual psychological makeup or ways of being. Persons who were portrayed on-air, and perceived by the public, as evil or scheming often were loving, decent, and compassionate individuals. The public saw as funny and charming people who were occasionally shallow and manipulative. Yet because this show and others like it are defined as "reality," that is, television that arises from the unscripted interactions of nonacting cast members, the general audience experienced their perceptions of the show's characters as real. Jane Doe must be this sort of person because it was how she appeared to behave on the show.

Things were not as they seemed. Reality television was definitely not reality as I had experienced it interactively with the show's participants, and frequently not the reality lived by those participants themselves. My experience of dissonance did not surprise me. As a long-time social critic and feminist who has always looked at popular media with a jaundiced eye, I had assumed before beginning this job that even a show that purported to show its viewers real unscripted interactions between people who were not actors was nonetheless a product of the mainstream media industry, and consequently a reflection of that industry's vision of reality. I knew, from three decades of feminist analysis, that media images of White women, women and men of color, poor people, old people, fat people, lesbians, and anyone else who departed from the dominant norm were distorted pictures, if and when members of those groups were included in media-constructed reality at all.

When I watched the first season of the show for which I subsequently worked, I had been struck by how embedded in the show's narrative were the common stereotypes of gender, social class, and race (Wright, 2001). It seemed impossible to me that the show's producers had picked people who fell so neatly into these preconceived boxes; and, in fact, the producers had, as I learned when observing them make decisions about who would get on the show, gone to some pains to cast people who did not fall into easily identifiable niches in the popular discourse. The producers consciously wanted people who appeared to play against stereotype, so as to keep viewers engaged and uncertain as to what a particular person might do. Despite these conscious intentions to cast against stereotype, in the editing room those stereotypes provided the most interesting story lines for the producers who were creating the final footage of each episode. The stereotypes felt real, embedded as they were in the social narrative. The nonconscious motives of the editors and producers overcame their conscious desires to portray people as they really were. Thirty years later, the nonconscious ideology of sexism (Bem & Bem, 1970) continued to rule.

This was especially striking given the people who were enacting this nonconscious ideology. The stereotypes created by reality TV stand in sharp contrast to the realities of those who make the shows. The women and men who create reality TV shows are themselves people who defy the stereotypes, according to my direct observations. This is especially true of those shows in which crew members must follow a cast into situations of physical danger, difficulty, and deprivation (e.g., *Survivor* or *The Amazing Race*). The 200-plus-person crew of the show on which I worked was full of women who were mechanically capable, avid players of extreme sports, and technologically savvy. Women were in positions of power and authority at every level and in every aspect of production, and there was little room for stereotypical femininity in the show's crew. As the on-site psychologist with few demands on my stamina and physical (non) prowess, I was probably the least fit woman in the entire crew. Many of these women were simultaneously very engaged with certain aspects of conventional femininity. For instance, the sight of my unshaven armpits gave rise to extensive discourse by several crew members on the waxing of body parts hitherto unthought-of by me as candidates for depilation.

Although many of the men on the crew fell well within masculine gender stereotypes, more than a few, including one of the most visible members of the crew, were more androgynous than macho in their interests, interpersonal styles, and self-presentations. It was not unusual to see powerful men in the production team being in the role of nurturing parent with their children who were visiting the production site.

A fairly large percentage of the crew with whom I interacted described having worked on a number of reality shows; although my sample is neither representative nor scientific in nature, I think that my assessment of the absence of rigid gender stereotypy in the lives of those creating reality TV is likely to apply more of the time than not. The crewmembers I met worked in reality television because they enjoyed the special challenges created by the genre as well as the somewhat edgy personalities of those involved with these shows.

Subsequent to my experience in what I have come to think of as the interesting foreign culture of the television industry I have become a regular observer of a wide range of reality television shows. I have become fully engaged with the phenomenon; although I rationalize my interest as offering opportunities to observe the mores of popular culture, the truth is that the human drama of reality TV is not dissimilar from the more painful private dramas that drew me to the work of psychotherapy, only far more entertaining.

These shows vary greatly on several dimensions; production values range from magnificent to tacky; story lines may go on for weeks, or resolve within the 30 minutes in which the show airs. Some shows put strangers together for the purpose of social manipulation. The grandparent of these shows is MTV's *The Real World*, which, beginning in 1990, placed seven strangers in a house and allowed them to pursue their lives and relationships under the eye of the camera. More recent iterations of this genre include the shows *Survivor*, on which 16 people are divided into two competing teams in semi-wilderness tropical environments; *Big Brother*, on which 13 people are placed together into a house, under observation and viewable online, 24 hours a day, 7 days a week, and unable to leave or interact with anyone outside the house until voted out; and the dating shows, such as *Blind Date* or *Elimidate*, in which the show's producers play matchmaker and young women and men decide with whom, or whether, to continue dating relationships. The alleged upscale version of the dating shows is *The Bachelor*, a hybrid of the other two genres, in which one man interacts for a period of several weeks with a large group of women, eliminating one each week until he picks one for his fiancée. A more recent version is Fox TV's *Joe Millionaire*, which combines deception (poor construction worker–underwear model being portrayed to a group of women as recent heir to 50 million dollars) with the who-will-he-pick theme. This group of shows also includes a genre that I call relationship-challenge shows, such as *Temptation Island*, in which members of committed heterosexual pairs are given the opportunity to cheat with nubile members of their preferred sex.

Other shows work entirely with preexisting social or interpersonal groups. *The Amazing Race* pits teams of two people in extant relationships against one another as they travel around the world and solve problems, with one team being eliminated in each leg of the race. Race teams have included sibling, mother–daughter, and father–son pairs; many heterosexual couples, both married and otherwise; and long-time female friends. *While You Were Out* and *Trading Spaces* are reality decorator shows; in the former, one member of a couple redecorates a room in the couple's home for his or her partner, whereas in the latter, two couples trade homes for a weekend redecorating project. *The Last Resort* offers on-air marital therapy, with heterosexual couples in trouble seen working through their problems and allegedly receiving couples counseling from self-identified relationship therapists.

Yet another genre of reality shows are those purporting to show the actual daily lives of real people. This subgroup has its roots in the classic 1973 PBS special, *An American Family*, which documented the lives of the Loud family of Marin County (Rowen, 2002). More recent reality shows have included video vérité of the lives of minor celebrities, such as Anna Nicole Smith, who has her own show on a cable network, and the Osbourne family, who are entering their second season on MTV. These last two shows are pseudodocumentary in nature, most closely resembling *An American Family*; their subjects are indeed leading their own lives, in their own homes, but the hand of the videotape editor is ever-present, albeit invisible. Finally, there are true-life-story shows, such as *COPS*, which follows police officers through their duty shifts, or *Maternity Ward*, which follows women from the late stages of pregnancy through labor and delivery.

Because of the huge variability in genre, it can be difficult to make sweeping generalizations about women in reality TV. The minor celebrities of the Anna Nicole Smith and Osbourne family shows obviously have more control over how they are portrayed, as they are more involved in the production and editing process, than do any of the contestants on *Survivor, Big Brother,* or *The Amazing Race,* who have absolutely no say in what component of their behaviors will appear on the small screen in America's living rooms. The vignettes of *Maternity Ward* are different in that they are briefer than the ongoing story lines of *The Real World*. In addition, because the different genres are attempting to attract different audiences, the ways in which women are positioned in a show's narrative reflect attempts to grab and keep audience attention. With all of these caveats in mind, it is still possible to observe some apparently common themes emerging from the reality shows.

THEMES OF WOMEN IN REALITY TV

Reality shows do a remarkable job of reflecting the social construction of gender within dominant culture. In that regard, no matter how contrived the story lines, the stereotypes of women on reality shows appear highly consistent with those seen in other aspects of popular media. These images arise from the decision of producers and editors about who will appear and how they will appear. I have sampled this genre extensively, watching multiple episodes of most of the shows that I discuss in this paper (for research purposes only!) as well as reading show-related chat rooms, both official and unofficial, and websites. My sampling has not been systematic, nor do my speculations in this analysis represent formal research; rather, they are the views of an observer informed by 30 years of feminist psychology, seasoned with the real-life experience of work on one such show. There is minimal scholarly literature on this particular topic; a thorough search of online databases yielded a small number of articles by media critics (Bennett, 2002; Kumbier, 2001; Putnam, 2001; Renshaw, 2001; Rowen, 2002; Wright, 2001), all of whom have used the same methodology as I have in arriving at their conclusions.

There Are No Lesbians Here

Gay men are plentiful in reality TV shows. The first season of *Survivor* was won by a gay man who outed himself early in the show and made the issue of his gayness a prominent feature in his manipulation of other players. Several episodes of that show, *Big Brother,* and *The Amazing Race* have featured openly gay men, several of whom have done quite well in competition. Gay men are portrayed by reality TV in the range of their complexity; viewers have seen older gay men, fat gay men, gay men of color, gay men in happy relationships with their families of origin, and gay men in happy long-term committed relationships.

Lesbians, or at least clearly identified lesbians, are, in contrast, virtually nowhere to be found in the universe of reality TV. Lesbians do try out for reality shows and frequently do well enough to almost get on the show; several lesbians, including a lesbian of color, were among the finalists that I screened for the show on which I worked. Some participants on reality shows could very well be lesbians; these women are strong and capable women who work in nontraditional fields and thereby fall into one stereotype of lesbians. For example, on *Survivor: Marquesas,* one contestant was the Xena: Warrior-Princess look-alike Zoë, who captains a fishing boat in Maine and never spoke of attachments to a boyfriend, although the show's publicity did list her as having a son. She became a topic of discussion in some lesbian circles: Was she or wasn't she? A hostile fellow-player on that episode lesbian-baited her, referring to her as a dyke. If Zoë was a lesbian, she wasn't saying; none of these possibly lesbian women have self-identified as lesbian on-air. Because many producers of reality TV shows give their casts the right to decide what to share or not about themselves with their peers, it is possible that viewers have seen plenty of lesbians on reality TV. Not all of the gay men who've been on these shows have chosen to come out on-air. But lesbian invisibility is almost as consistent in reality TV as in any other aspect of mainstream U.S. media.

There are three exceptions to this exclusion, all of them interesting in regard to how they portray lesbians. One exception occurred during a November 2002 episode of *While You Were Out* on the TLC cable channel. This episode featured a Caucasian lesbian couple who were treated in a manner similar to that afforded the heterosexual couples who made up the remainder of the show's participants. The couple's circumstances of meeting (at a *Xena: Warrior Princess* convention) and their shared hobbies (rodeo riding) were integrated into the fabric of the show. The show treated the pair's lesbian relationship in a matter-of-fact manner; the word *lesbian* was never mentioned, but it was clear that this was a committed couple, not simply roommates.

The Bravo Network also pierced through this barrier with its show *Gay Weddings*. This quasi-documentary show that aired in the fall of 2002 featured a gay male couple and a lesbian couple as they prepared for and went through their wedding ceremonies. With the focus of this show on gay weddings, it would have been difficult to exclude lesbians; but note that the title of the show was not *Gay and Lesbian Weddings*.

Finally, *The Real World* has had three lesbian cast members (out of a total of 84 cast members) over its 12 seasons. All of these shows aired on cable networks. Cable has always been more willing to portray marginalized groups than network television has been. Yet even with cable's greater openness to diversity, I have managed to unearth only nine open lesbians among the scores of women appearing on reality shows on cable. Most of the lesbians were also members of other marginalized groups (people of color or Jews), and all of them were portrayed as adhering to conventions of femininity (e.g., long hair, wearing makeup). Although reality TV has shown us "nelly" gay men, no butch lesbians have been on reality TV; the only butch women in the reality universe have been aggressively defined as heterosexual through continuous references to husbands, boyfriends, or offspring.

In the time since this chapter was written, lesbian invisibility has diminished significantly with the appearances of Ami Cusack and Scout Cloud Lee, both open lesbians, on the Fall 2004 episode of *Survivor*. Ami and Scout were visible to the audience as lesbians; their partners both appeared in one episode, and each woman referred to her partner during the course of the show. Lee (personal communication, January 2005) noted that when she first auditioned for the show she was not open about her lesbianism, but that when she reauditioned she made a decision to be out. She speculates that this one changed piece of personal data may have made the difference for her getting on the show.

Strong Women Are Bitches

There is no absence of strong women in reality TV, particularly in the subset of the genre that involves competition in physically challenging, strenuous tasks. Many of the women who compete in reality TV are veterans of nontraditional work environments; participants in *Survivor*, for example, have included fire fighters, police officers, a prison guard, one Navy Seal swimming instructor, the aforementioned fishing boat captain, a truck driver, and factory workers. Participants in this show and *The Amazing Race* have demonstrated feats of skill, strength, and stamina that require unusually high levels of fitness and fearlessness.

But many of these women, picked for precisely the same qualities as the men on the show, end up depicted as mean or bitchy, consistent with stereotypes of women who are competent in other nontraditional work settings (Putnam, 2001; Renshaw, 2001). On first two seasons of *The Amazing Race*, several of the teams consisted of heterosexual couples in which the woman was clearly the more powerful member of the pair. Inevitably, footage would be shown in which the woman appeared to be not simply more powerful, but domineering, insensitive, and pushy. On *Survivor*, similar themes emerged repeatedly; women might be powerful and competent, but if they failed to smile or be socially smooth under all circumstances, they found themselves cast on-screen as problematic, whereas their socially less skillful male counterparts got off easy in the editing process and the chat rooms alike, being viewed as being clumsy rather than evil. Women who attempted to visibly outwit and outplay were seen as "two-faced," "manipulative," or "mean" (Putnam, 2001), whereas similarly Machiavellian behaviors by a man were portrayed as part of his strategy for winning (Putnam, 2001; Renshaw, 2001).

Apparent sexual scheming by women plays especially badly on reality TV. Men's interest in and sexual manipulation of women is coded as "sexy bad boy" or simply as normative male behavior. Women's sexual interest in and manipulation of men was, on the other hand, frequently portrayed as evidence of that woman's badness and failure to deserve a good outcome on the show. One Australian commentator observed that "Survivor, CBS's best-known reality show, has brought a whole new dimension to assertive women being labeled 'bitches'" (Putnam, 2001, p. 1).

Exemplifying this trend, two of the three times that a woman has won *Survivor*, she has been a woman whose persona, as supplied by the editors of the show, was that of the nice girl. These women were portrayed as good Christians and good caretakers of their fellow participants (e.g., willing to cook and facilitate smooth social relationships). As Putnam (2001) notes, "It's pretty clear: if a woman survives the last vote, she sure can't be a bitch" (p. 3). Although the winner of *Survivor: Amazon* was neither married nor aggressively Christian in her identification, she was edited as sweet and feminine; the fact that she won the game in part because she exhibited strength and skill in many of the final immunity challenges, thus keeping herself in the game until the end, was downplayed on-screen.

An exception to this trend of strong-women-finish-last emerges in the one show where the strong woman in question, Sharon Osbourne, apparently has important creative and editorial input into the show's content. Osbourne, whose entire family has been filmed for MTV, emerges as the powerful, capable glue that holds her family together. Her husband (rock star Ozzy Osbourne) makes a point of his valuing of her skills, emotional strength, and competency in managing his career and containing his emotional lability.

Maternity Ward is devoted almost entirely to nice women. All of the women shown laboring and birthing on this show do so under the tutelage of physicians, who clearly know best. There are no feisty consumers of obstetric services, no midwives, no lesbian moms—only meekly grateful married women. One episode exemplifying this trend showed a woman giving birth to her fifth child in 10 years; because no baby-sitter was available, the other four children came along for the delivery, even though this was not what this woman had apparently wished for or planned. This stunning example of Madonna-like motherhood powerfully communicates the good-woman message to viewers.

Old Age and Treachery Triumph Over Youth and Skill

Older women do astonishingly well in some aspects of the reality genre. The NOW Foundation's *Feminist Primetime Report* noted that "even on TV, a number of older, 'everyday' women on reality shows like 'Survivor' and 'Amazing Race' make our case" about the more general stereotyping of women in nonreality shows (Bennett, 2002). Older, nonstereotypically attractive women have gone into the final rounds of five of the six seasons of *Survivor*. A 40-year-old woman won the Australia season of that show, and a woman with grey hair, wrinkles, and grandchildren was the second-place contestant on the Africa season. A wrinkled 50-something woman was the third-place contestant on the Thailand show.

The visibility and success of older women in reality TV stand in contrast to what Renshaw (2001) describes as the "hyper-masculine ethos" of many of the reality TV shows. Almost all of these shows reward individualistic striving for success and appear to devalue an ethic of caring. Is it possible that old women succeed in reality TV because the implicit ageism of both their fellow participants and the viewers makes their strategizing and manipulation less visible? My sense as a critical viewer is that this may be so. The interaction of ageism and sexism operates to the benefit of these women, who are erroneously perceived by other participants as less strong, less of a threat, and nicer (e.g., motherly or grandmotherly). Older women on these shows rarely win the competitions of skill and strength but frequently remain in the running because of their high levels of interpersonal abilities and their capacities to create the appearance of caring relationships, even while they are actively scheming to eliminate the competition or manipulating a younger, stronger fellow player to bring them along into the finals of the game.

Older women are not, however, portrayed as sexy. Exclusively young, nubile women populate the dating shows. On *The Bachelor*, a woman in her 30s was constructed as old. Old women may win money, but they are not seen as winning the hearts of men (or women) with their beauty.

Dragon Ladies, Sapphire, and Sexy Latinas

Women of color are somewhat underrepresented among the denizens of reality TV, although better represented than in nonreality shows. But the representation of women of color on reality TV is a near-mirror of racially gendered stereotypes. Women of Asian descent, as rare in this genre as elsewhere in the media, are edited to look smart, geeky, and dangerous. African American women, the most frequently seen women of color in reality TV, are shown as strong and emotionally expressive and, when seen in relationship to male partners, are constructed as dominating the relationship. For example, on the first season of *The Amazing Race*, Karen, an African American woman who is competing in a team with her fiancé, is seen as constantly verbally denigrating him and attempting to control his actions. On the second season of *Survivor*, Alicia, who was clearly among the physically strongest people on her tribe, was set up as the bitch who had to be eliminated early in the game because her strength made her a danger to others. Viewers had no idea from the show's editing how well liked she was by her peers. On *Survivor: Amazon*, Joanne, a strong African American woman, was depicted as annoyingly concerned with her faith; her early departure from the show was made to seem evidence of interpersonal difficulties, not, as the contestants revealed after the show's finale, because her strength threatened other members of her all-female tribe. On the dating shows, these themes in images of women of color are even more persistent.

The issue of race and culture is more strongly expressed on reality TV through the roles of men, however. The theme of the lazy African American man has resounded through all five seasons of *Survivor*, for instance. Women of color appear to fare somewhat better than men of color where reality TV is concerned, being given a slightly greater range of roles by those editing the footage for broadcast airing.

Women Will Be Girls

Season six of *Survivor* was set up as an erstwhile battle of the sexes, with the teams initially divided into all-women and all-men crews. The women's tribe was depicted in the editing process as klutzy, disorganized, and full of spite and backbiting, whereas the men's tribe was shown efficiently building their hut and engaging in hearty male-bonding. Women's relationships with one another are often similarly portrayed on reality TV; even when women on a show make deep, functional connections with one another, their relationships are portrayed as full of catfights, with the dating shows offering especially egregious examples of this theme.

SO WHY SHOULD WE CARE?

Why should these distortions of women in reality TV matter to feminist psychologists? After all, doesn't the average postmodern viewer realize that, in the words of one media critic, "the 'reality' we're viewing is quite artificial" (Kumbier, 2001, p. 3)? I suggest that there are several cogent reasons for feminists in general, and feminist psychologists in particular, to attend to gendered trends and themes in reality TV.

Although the postmodern viewer may be aware that he or she is watching a contrived, edited fiction that is no more real than an episode of *Friends* or *Law and Order*, the level of engagement between the viewers of reality TV and the participants in shows goes beyond such ironic detachment. Because the players on reality TV shows are real people, acting only as themselves, the viewing public believes that it knows them and frequently fails to perceive that the actors or the story lines are contrived and constructed.

Thus can be seen the greater power of the narratives of reality TV to influence and shape the nonconscious ideologies of sexism, racism, and heterosexism. These people are real; therefore, their apparent concurrence with social constructions of gender must demonstrate the truth of those gendered social constructions. At times, the participants in these shows seem to demonstrate their awareness of the power of these narratives, and sometimes these women resist the dominant paradigm. For example, on the fifth season of *Survivor*, the young woman cast in the role of "woman with large breasts" (of whom there is predictably one on almost every reality TV show) spoke of the importance, to her, of being strong and competent because she knew that she had been cast in that role and wanted to play against the parameters of that image (e.g., large breasts equals stupid and incompetent, a theme that has resounded loudly in reality TV, most notably in the Anna Nicole Smith show). It's one thing for a social commentator to critique media images of women for their artificiality; it's quite another to come up against media images of women that appear to spring, unimpeded by script writers, directly from women themselves.

When I told colleagues that I had taken a job with a reality TV show, their reactions ranged, with very few exceptions, from shocked to critical. Most of my feminist psychology colleagues had strong opinions about reality TV, almost all negative and almost entirely informed by a complete failure to have seen even one episode of a reality show. At current count, a total of seven psychologists of my acquaintance (out of probably 100 with whom I have discussed my experience on the show during the past three years) have admitted to actually watching reality TV shows (and two of those watched only the show I worked for, only because I had worked for it). None of my colleagues at the doctoral program where I teach has ever seen a reality show (one watches no television at all, another not uncommon choice made by psychologists of my acquaintance). Several colleagues suggested that, in working for this show, I had somehow sold out or abandoned my radical feminist stance.

Reality TV represents a media phenomenon that has enormous potential impact on cultural constructions of gender, culture, and sexuality, yet it remains virtually unknown and unobserved by feminist psychologists, who appear to have disdained it as representing the worst of commercial television. However, serious questions emerge from the landscape of reality TV that would benefit from feminist questions and rigorous psychological study. Following are questions for further research.

What are the effects of this powerful social construction of gender on those viewing reality TV, as contrasted with the impacts of watching clearly fictional portrayals of women in other commercial media? Is it, for instance, more undermining of women's power and competence to see three real women with obvious physical prowess (Zoë, Joanne, and Alicia) voted off of *Survivor* for being strong women than to see the fictional main character of *Judging Amy* portrayed as blown about by her emotions? I suggest that the answer to this and similar questions may be yes, but for a definitive answer the question, feminist-informed study of the effects of the reality TV genre is needed. Further, what is the impact of being a woman on reality TV? The participants in reality TV shows are not exploited victims, as I had feared before meeting them. They are highly agentic, having volunteered for their commodification. Frequently they avidly pursue postshow opportunities for further exposure, often in the pages of *Playboy*. There are no introverts among the denizens of reality TV. Yet is their willingness to be exposed in these ways an informed willingness? What does it do to a woman to see herself distorted by the editing process and vilified in chat rooms? One of my participants struggled mightily with this phenomenon. Although she was media-savvy enough to know intellectually that her portrayal as an evil schemer was simply the result of editing, she frequently felt hurt by people's attacks on her and had difficulty separating out her actual self from her on-air persona.

Is gender even a factor in these issues? The men who participate in reality TV experience just as much distortion of their images as do the women, and are subject to as much stereotypy related to gender, sexual orientation, social class, and ethnicity. Do the women of reality TV have the same kinds of strong needs for affiliation and approval that are seen in many general populations of women? If so, how does their celebrity, and the means by which that celebrity was attained, affect their well-being?

Reality TV is the wave of the commercial media future. It is immensely successful; reality shows have done exceptionally well and are less expensive to produce than are dramas or situation comedies, as there are no expensive star salaries to pay every year. Reality TV dovetails with other forms of voyeuristic entertainment that are becoming increasingly popular, such as webcams. And because it purports to be real, it is powerful in ways that fictional television cannot be.

Thus, feminist psychologists cannot afford to disdain reality TV. Feminist psychologists need to consider how to engage with this medium: how to study it, how to become involved as the screening and debriefing psychologists for shows, how to become willing observers of this aspect of popular culture. It is notable that, in my attempt to find scholarly research on this topic, I was unable to retrieve any work done by psychologists. Psychologists need to become actively involved in the world of media psychology and thus become part of the networks that generate psychologists who work for and with such shows. Feminist psychologists who have worked in the fields of assessment, personnel selection, and coaching are particularly well-suited for this work, as it draws on all of those skills; psychotherapists, however, will find themselves in truly foreign territory, as the average reality TV show participant is a superfunctioning person with few areas of distress (I have never seen so many normal MMPI–2 profiles in my career as I did among the 50 would-be contestants whom I had the pleasure to screen). Feminist psychologists need to bring their critical eyes and open minds to perusal of this medium; where are the special issues of feminist psychology journals on women in reality TV? By legitimizing interest in reality TV, feminist psychologists will discover an entirely new, and highly valuable, direction for an analysis of women in the media, and a powerful standpoint from which to observe emerging roles for women in dominant culture.

REFERENCES

Bem, S. L., & Bem, D. (1970). Training the woman to know their place: The power of a non-conscious ideology. In S. Fox (Ed.), *Female psychology: The emerging self* (pp. 180–191). Chicago: SRA Books.

Bennett, L. (2002, Fall). NOW Foundation criticizes TV's distorted image of women. *National NOW Times*. Available at http://www.how.org/nnt/fall-2002/wolu.html

Kumbier, A. (2001). *Why we watch*. Retrieved December 18, 2002, from http://www.poppolitics.com/articles/2001-09-18-tv.shtml

Putnam, A (2001). *Surviv*-ing women: 'Bitches' voted off first. *M/C Reviews, 4*. Retrieved December 18, 2002, from http://reviews.media-culture.org.au/sections.php?op=viewarticle&artid=111

Renshaw, S. (2001). The "reality" of television's latest gendered genre. *M/C Reviews, 4*. Retrieved December 18, 2002, from http://reviews.media-culture.org.au/sections.php?op=viewarticle&artid=112

Rowen, B. (2002). *History of reality TV*. Retrieved December 18, 2002, from http://www.infoplease.com/spot/realitytv1.html

Wright, C. (2001). *Borans don't cry*. Retrieved December 18, 2002, from http://www.poppolitics.com/articles/2001-10-22-borans.shtml

6

NARRATIVES OF GENDER IN COMPUTER ADVERTISEMENTS

LAURA J. BURLINGAME-LEE AND SILVIA SARA CANETTO

Katie's family is at the bookstore, looking at computer magazines. Her family will be buying a new computer soon. Together, they are gathering information about computer options. The family decides on two slick, colorful magazines with reviews of the latest in computer technology. Katie is excited she will soon have a chance to play the computer games her cousins Joe and Mark are talking about. Later that night, Katie leafs through the magazines, reading reviews of the newly released games. The advertisements show bright, action-packed screens. At first, Katie is entranced by the screen shots of the newest fantasy game. After looking at the pictures a little longer, Katie notices that only boys are shown playing the game.

Advertisements have been studied for decades. Social scientists have examined them for clues to social ideologies, including ideologies of gender. A major focus of attention has been the images of women and men in fashion and beauty advertisements. As a result, a great deal has been learned about the gender narratives of beauty, attraction, sex, and love conveyed by these images (Bartel, 1988; Courtenay & Whipple, 1983; Kilbourne, 1999; Lanis & Covell, 1995; Mackay & Covell, 1997; Merskin, 1999; Williamson, 1978, 1980).

So far, however, very little is known about computer advertisements and the stories they tell about gender. Why is it important to study gender narratives in computer advertisements? First, computers are technology, and technology, like science in general, has long been assumed to be a male domain, and facility with technology, a male talent (American Association of University Women [AAUW], 2000b; Barbercheck, 2001). Thus, computer advertisements can inform researchers about the current discourse on gender and science as well as the discourse about gender and technology. Second, jobs in computer science are well paid and do not require physical strength. In 1999 the gender salary differential was smaller in computer sciences compared with the differential in the life sciences (National Science Foundation, 2002). Expertise with computers may provide women with one avenue to overcoming the gender wage gap.

So far, only two studies have examined images of gender in computer advertisements (Demetrulias & Rosenthal, 1985; Ware & Stuck, 1985). Both were published in the mid-1980's and used content-analyses. One finding across the two studies is that women and girls were underrepresented in computer advertisements, as compared with boys and men. A second finding is that women and men were portrayed in stereotypical ways. For example, Demetrulias and Rosenthal found that images of women featured conventional feminine accessories (e.g., ribbons, cosmetics) and settings (e.g., kitchens). Similarly, Ware and Stuck noted that when women were present, they were typically cast in subordinate roles (e.g., as clerical workers) or in sexualized poses. Men, on the other hand, were typically featured in dominant or expert roles (e.g., as managers or technicians). The latter study also found that women were often portrayed in passive or decorative roles whereas men were often depicted as working with the computers.

An important contribution of these past studies (Demetrulias & Rosenthal, 1985; Ware & Stuck, 1985) is that they have documented the imbalance in the number of female and male characters in computer advertisements. They have also provided information about the gender messages typically communicated through these advertisements. One limitation is that they are dated. Another limitation is that they both rely on a content-analysis approach. As noted by Leiss, Kline, and Jhally (1986), content analyses are great for detecting patterns in large volumes of qualitative data, but they are "inadequate for the measurement of meaning." According to them, "meaning is dependent upon the place of any particular item within an entire system of language and image. Isolating any element alters the meaning of that element itself, as well as the meaning of the whole structure" (p. 174).

In this chapter, we report on a study of gender narratives in computer advertisements found in computer magazines and in general readership magazines. One goal was to replicate, update, and extend the findings reported in earlier quantitative content analyses of computer advertisements (Demetrulias & Rosenthal, 1985; Ware & Stuck, 1985). We were specifically interested in the demographic profile of the individuals typically featured in recent computer advertisements. We also assessed whether the type of diversity in age and ethnic look of people appearing in the advertisements. Finally, we wanted to know whether women's and men's magazines were equally likely to feature computer advertisements. A second goal of the study was to examine the gender stories told within individual computer advertisements with a discourse analysis method (Coyle, 1995). We were specifically interested in how the images and text of the advertisements worked together to convey these stories. We also wanted to understand to whom these advertisements might be directed and what narrative strategies were used in the advertisements to engage this potential computer consumer.

METHOD

The data for this study were computer and computer-related advertisements found in magazines published in 1999.

Sample

The advertisements comprising the sample were drawn from both computer and noncomputer magazines (see Table 6.1). The magazines were selected on the basis of circulation as well as readership. The computer magazines were *PC Magazine*, *MacWorld*, *Wired*, and *Family PC*. The noncomputer magazines encompassed a balance of primarily female-readership magazines (*Family Circle*, *Cosmopolitan*, *Shape*, *Entertainment*, *People*, and *Working Woman*) and primarily male-readership magazines (*Field & Stream*, *Playboy*, *Sports Illustrated*, *Time*, *Newsweek*, and *Money*), matched by content. Advertisements were included in the sample if they marketed computer hardware, software, peripheral devices, or computer-related services. An item was considered computer-related if it was a component or peripheral of a computer system (e.g., a modem) or if it was a device that could be used in conjunction with a computer (e.g., a digital camera). Advertisements for service or leisure Web sites (e.g., a financial Web site) or for computer companies advertising employment were excluded. Finally, to be included, advertisements had to be one half page or larger and had to feature human beings. Two individuals independently reviewed the advertisements for possible inclusion in the analyses. A third individual also selected advertisements through a random 10% of the sample. The three-way agreement was 96%. After reasons for disagreements were clarified across the three individuals, agreement reached 100%. The final study sample included 436 advertisements containing 1,151 people.

Sample Coding

Two coders recorded the sex, ethnicity, and age appearance of persons featured in the advertisements. Interrater reliability was calculated on an independently coded, common 20% of the sample. Agreement ranged from a high of 93% (sex appearance) to a low of 73% (ethnic appearance). Agreement on age appearance was 79%.

RESULTS

This study examined both quantitative and qualitative representations of gender in computer advertisements. The strength of this approach is that

TABLE 6.1
Magazine Category, Content, Names, and Readership

Magazine category	Content	Name of publication	Readership Female (%)	Male (%)
Computer	Window users	PC Magazine	13	87
	Apple OS users	MacWorld	Not available	
	Individual users	Wired	16	84
	Family user	Family PC	50	50
Predominantly female	Lifestyle/leisure	Family Circle	100	
	Lifestyle/fashion	Cosmopolitan	100[a]	
	Sports/fashion	Shape	100	
	News	Entertainment	57	43
	News	People	66	34
	Business/finance	Working Woman	98	2
Predominantly male	Lifestyle/leisure	Field & Stream	7	93
	Lifestyle/fashion	Playboy	14	86
	Sports/fitness	Sports Illustrated	21	79
	News	Time	46	54
	News	Newsweek	45	56
	Business/finance	Money	40	60

Note. In some cases, readership values were not available from either the publishers or media kits. Whenever possible, Standard Rate and Data Service (2000) information was used instead.
[a]Standard Rate and Data Service (2000).

it provides context that gives meaning to the qualitative analysis, through which a more accurate picture of gender messages may be understood.

Content Analyses: Profiles of Persons Typically Featured in Computer Advertisements

Frequency data for the sex, ethnicity, and age appearance of the people featured in the advertisements were analyzed with chi-square tests. Expected values for age, ethnicity, and sex in the U.S. population were obtained from the 1990 United States Census (United States Department of Commerce, 1995). Analyses indicated that males ($\chi^2 = 63.34, p < .001, w = .24$), Whites ($\chi^2 = 120.17, p < .001, w = .35$), and young adults ($\chi^2 = 299.65, p < .001, w = .56$) were overrepresented in computer advertisements, relative to their numbers in the population. The same trends were evident when only primary characters were included in the analyses. Again, males ($\chi^2 = 20.39, p < .001, w = .23$), Whites ($\chi^2 = 49.40, p < .001, w = .36$), and young-looking persons ($\chi^2 = 65.67, p < .001, w = .42$) were overrepresented in the sample. Males represented 60% of all characters and 60% of the primary characters depicted in the advertisements. Sex-by-ethnicity interaction analyses for primary characters revealed that White males were predominant in computer advertisements (χ^2 = 76.19, p < .001, V = .45). Asian American–looking males were also overrepresented, relative to their numbers in the U.S. population, whereas other sex-by-ethnicity groups (i.e., African Americans, Hispanics, Native Americans, and "Others") were underrepresented. Sex-by-age interaction analyses for primary characters showed that young adult males were overrepresented in computer advertisements, relative to population parameters (χ^2 = 91.47, p < .001, V = .49). On the other hand, older adults, regardless of sex, were underrepresented. Finally, ethnicity-by-age interaction analyses were conducted after ethnic groups other than Blacks and Whites were collapsed into one group because of small expected values. It was found that White young adults were the most overrepresented (χ^2 = 119.50, p < .001, V = .32). Black children and young adults were featured close to the level that would be expected on the basis of population numbers. However, Black teens and older adults were entirely absent as primary characters.

Additional Content Analyses: Distribution of Computer Advertisements Across Magazines

An analysis of variance was conducted to determine whether men's magazines had more computer advertisements than did women's magazines. There were in fact more computer advertisements in male-readership magazines (M = 19.33, SD = 17.06, Mdn = 17.5) than in female-readership magazines (M = 6.17, SD = 9.07, Mdn = 3). This difference, although large, was not statistically significant, $F(1,11)$ = 3.84, p = .079, because of large within-group differences, as indicated by the standard deviation values.

An analysis of the distribution of advertisements within high female-readership and high male-readership magazines showed that four (i.e., *Sports Illustrated*, *Time*, *Newsweek*, and *Money*) out of the six predominantly male magazines had 10 or more computer advertisements across the year; and only two (i.e., *Field & Stream* and *Playboy*) had fewer than five computer advertisements. However, of the six high female-readership magazines, only one (i.e., *Working Woman*) had 10 or more (to be precise, 24) advertisements across the year. All the other female-readership magazines (i.e., *Shape*, *Cosmopolitan*, *Family Circle*, *People*, and *Entertainment*) had fewer than 10 computer advertisements. In fact, three female-readership magazines (i.e., *Family Circle*, *Cosmopolitan*, and *Shape*) had one or no computer advertisements.

Discourse Analyses

Discourse analyses were conducted on three advertisements that had been randomly selected from the total pool of 436. Two were from computer magazines (*MacWorld* and *PC Magazine*) and one was from a female-readership magazine (*Working Woman*). A fourth advertisement was included in the discourse analyses because it had been published in a series with one of the randomly selected advertisements, and thus it included elements that were crucial in the interpretation of that randomly selected advertisement.

Consistent with past discourse analyses of advertisements (e.g., Kilbourne, 1999; Lester, 1996), we examined both structural (e.g., settings) as well as narrative (e.g., text) elements. As in past discourse analyses, we gave special attention to human characters. We noted presences and absences: who was foreground and dominant, who was background and ancillary, and who was absent. Our goal was to record and evaluate the multiple messages conveyed in concert by the individual elements of the advertisements (Brummett, 1991, 1994). We were interested in the stories that the computer advertisements told about women, men, and computers.

"You have got to see . . . [them] in . . . color"

Our first randomly chosen advertisement was drawn from *MacWorld* magazine. The product being marketed is a color printer. The advertisement features several agile female dancers in form-fitting body costumes designed to make them blend, like chameleons, against a tree. The point of the advertisement is that to see the dancers, the reader must print the image with the advertised printer. As the title of the advertisement notes, "You have got to see it in Epson color."

What does this advertisement say about gender and computers, and how does it do so? A first observation is that there are no men present in this advertisement. The only human beings portrayed are women. If one were to simply count female and male characters to make inferences about messages of gender in computer advertisements, this advertisement would add to the record of female presences in computer advertisements and thus could contribute to the conclusion that females are protagonists in the computer advertising discourse. If, however, one also examines the structural and narrative elements of this advertisement, a different story emerges.

In this advertisement, women are de-individuated and sexualized. Their faces are indiscernible, they are wearing skin-tight body suits, and they are posed in ways that emphasize their body curves. Whom might this erotic spectacle target and whom might the advertisement tease with an invitation to find all four "amazing dancers"? Although the text does not explicitly refer to a male interlocutor, the heterosexually eroticized female figures suggest a male audience and a male gaze. Again, this male character is not mentioned, but his presence feels in some way larger and more powerful because of his silence and invisibility. Taken together, the elements of the advertisement are consistent with the theme of "woman as image, man as bearer of the look" identified by Mulvey (1999) in her analyses of cinema conventions and artifices. According to her, in many films, women are not featured as active characters in the story. Rather they are brought in and "displayed . . .

for . . . visual and erotic impact. . . . as (passive) raw material for the (active) [and voyeuristic] gaze of man" (pp. 272, 274).

Another feature of this advertisement is that women are turned into part of an object, part of a tree, part of nature. This imagery builds on a tradition of associating women with nature and men with culture, women with immanence and men with transcendence, women with concrete thinking and men with abstract thinking (Ortner, 1996). The blending of woman with object heightens the de-individuation and objectification of the dancers, encouraging the viewer to see them as less human.

In conclusion, women are the sole human protagonists of this advertisement. However, they are featured in passive, animalized, and sexualized poses. The text invites the reader to search for the camouflaged and animalized female bodies—a message that suggests a male audience and a heterosexual male gaze. Thus, the message of this female-dominated advertisement is anything but empowering women as active, participatory agents in the world of technology.

"Give your kids an 'Advantage'"

The second randomly chosen advertisement appeared in *PC Magazine*. It markets computer systems by Future Power. At first impression, only one person appears to be featured in this advertisement. It is a White girl, seemingly between ages 5 and 7, who is sitting in front of a computer. However, on closer examination, one also notices an adult, male, White hand over the girl's hand. This male hand seems to be guiding the girl in the use of the computer's mouse. The image on the computer screen is that of a cartoon of a cat in a conventionally masculine outfit, reading a book. This image is TV-like and suggests passive viewing. At the top of the advertisement, one reads: "Give your kids an 'Advantage,'" which apparently refers to Advantage computer systems.

The protagonist of this advertisement appears to be a girl. Past studies (Demetrulias & Rosenthal, 1985; Ware & Stuck, 1985) have noted that girls are particularly rare in computer advertisements so in this sense, this advertisement seems to break new narrative ground. At the same time, as noted above, the girl in the advertisement is not actually the person using the computer. The hidden male character whose hand controls the mouse is in charge of the computer and its use.

The message about gender conveyed by this advertisement is convoluted and perplexing. On the one hand, the advertisement commands the reader to give kids the "Advantage" of Future Power computer systems. As the advertisement features a girl, one might conclude that the advertisement tells readers that girls should be given access to computers. However, the male hand overlaying the girl's hand communicates a different story. One could interpret the controlling presence of the male hand as suggesting that girls cannot or should not use computers independently. It could be also taken to imply that girls' computer access requires male supervision and guidance.

Messages about ethnicity and class are also embedded in this advertisement. First, both the child and the adult hand are light-skinned. Also, the girl's clothes resemble the uniforms used by private or parochial schools, suggesting affluence, conventionality, and, perhaps, a call to modesty. These elements could be read to imply that White children, and specifically well-to-do and well-behaved White children, have a special entitlement to "the advantage" of computer technology.

"The Best Way to Focus on Your Customer"

The third advertisement that was randomly selected for this analysis appeared in *Working Woman*, a magazine with 98% female readership. *Working Woman* targets top executives.

This advertisement features a young White male standing behind a large white piece of board that looks like an ophthalmologist's eye examination chart. The letters on the chart spell out, in capital letters, "THE BEST WAY TO FOCUS ON YOUR CUSTOMER." Above this picture, is a small black banner that reads, "Symantec Small Business Software." Underneath the main picture are thumbnail-size pictures of the software boxes produced by Symantec. In between is a small-print paragraph advertising the software made by this company. The text of this paragraph is as follows:

> As a small business owner, you know that keeping your customer in focus is critical to your success. That's why you need Symantec Small Business Software. You see, we've developed an entire line of products to help you be more productive and stay well protected. And that means more time to build a customer centered business with the least amount of PC downtime. Which is exactly the way it should be.

This advertisement is directed to small-business owners, not simply business owners. This is surprising because, according to Standard Rate and Data Service (2000), *Working Woman* targets women in top management positions, not small-business owners. One wonders if the reference to small-business owners implies that only owners of small businesses need the advertised software, or if it assumes that women own only small businesses.

Because this advertisement appeared in *Working Woman*, it presumably is aimed at female readers. Yet, the computer software expert in the advertisement is a young White man. The experts on the software boxes are also White men. Some may argue that having male-only experts in an advertisement of a female magazine is insignificant, or trivial. Others might see the choice of male-only experts as an oversight. However, given the time and money that go into crafting advertisements (Kilbourne, 1999), neither explanation is plausible. So what is left is a very peculiar gender message for a female executive magazine—the message that technical expertise is male.

There are more odd gender messages embedded in the text and images of this advertisement. One such message implied by the emphasis on customer service is that women should not get involved with technology. This message fits with the gender stereotype that it is a man's job to take care of machines and a woman's job to take care of people, expressed in this advertisement as the recommendation for women to focus on customer satisfaction. Also, the male character offers small-business owners "help" to be more "productive" as well as to "stay well protected." The assumption that women need male protection is an important theme in traditional gender ideologies. Given the patronizing content and tone of this advertisement, it is amazing it appeared in a magazine aimed at female executives.

"Customer: Fragile, Handle with Care"

This last advertisement was not randomly chosen. It was included for analysis because it represents the narrative premise to the one entitled "The best way to focus on your customer." "Customer: Fragile, Handle with Care" appeared in *Working Woman* one month earlier than did "The best way to focus on your customer." Together, these advertisements are like episodes one and two of the same story.

"Customer: Fragile, Handle with Care" features a middle-aged White woman with facial wrinkles and glasses. She wears a dark business-like suit and has a sticker pasted on her forehead that reads, in capital letters, "CUS-TOMER [framed in red] FRAGILE HANDLE WITH CARE [framed in white]." The text underneath the image reads, "Call me. Fax me. Help me. Please. It's called customer service." The bottom of this advertisement, as with "The best way to focus on your customer," has thumbnail-size pictures of the product boxes. At the top of the advertisement, in the yellow border surrounding the entire presentation, the text reads, "Symantec Small Business Software: We help you build a customer-centered business." As in the previous Symantec advertisement, this advertisement markets software to help small-business owners manage customer-service tasks.

In this advertisement the fragile customer is identified as a woman. She is presented as emotionally labile and technologically inept. She is the customer whom the young man of "The best way to focus on your customer" advertisement was offering to help. She is probably the computer customer that, according to the same Symantec advertisement, needs "to stay well protected." Taken together, these advertisements communicate a message of male dominance and female incompetence in regard to computer knowledge.

DISCUSSION

We live in a world packed with advertisements. It has been estimated that in the United States, each of us is exposed to 3,000 advertisements every day (Kilbourne, 1999).

Many people feel that advertisements are fun, playful, perhaps outrageous, but certainly not to be taken seriously. They may feel personally exempt from the influence of ads: "What I hear more than anything else, as I lecture throughout the country, is 'I don't pay attention to ads. . . . I just tune them out. . . . they have no effect on me,'" wrote Kilbourne (1999). "Of course, I hear this most often from young men wearing Budweiser caps," she added wryly (p. 27).

In fact, everyone is influenced by advertisements. "There is no way to tune out this information, especially when it is carefully designed to break through the 'tuning out' process," argued Kilbourne. The fact that everyone thinks he or she is immune to advertisements adds to, rather than detracts from, the power of advertising. "The most effective kind of propaganda is that which is not recognized as propaganda," Kilbourne (1999, p. 27) stated. Advertisements sell not only products; they sell lifestyles and ideals as well (Barbercheck, 2001).

What do computer advertisements communicate about gender and technology? We conclude that they demonstrate and reinforce the stereotype that computer technology is a White, young male domain. One line of evidence supporting our conclusion is content analyses of the demographic profile of human characters appearing in computer advertisements. Our study, consistent with those of others (Demetrulias & Rosenthal, 1985; Ware & Stuck, 1985), found that young- and White-looking males are the people typically featured in computer advertisements. Most other groups of people, particularly ethnic minority older adults, are essentially absent from computer advertisements.

A second line of evidence supporting our conclusions is the finding on the prevalence of computer advertisements in female- and male-readership magazines. In our study, we found three times as many computer advertisements in male-readership magazines as in female-readership magazines—though these differences were not statistically significant because of large variations in the number of advertisements across magazines. Our analysis of the distribution of advertisements within high female- and high male-readership magazines showed that four out of the six predominantly male magazines had 10 or more computer advertisements within the year, and only two had fewer than five. However, out of the six high female-readership magazines, only *Working Woman* had 10 or more advertisements across the year. These findings may suggest that, from the point of view of computer advertisers, women in executive positions are the only women engaged or worth engaging in computer technology.

A third line of evidence consistent with our conclusions is provided by studies of the themes of computer advertisements—whether through discourse analysis, as in the present study, or through content analysis, as in past studies (Demetrulias & Rosenthal, 1985; Ware & Stuck, 1985). These kinds of studies provide particularly compelling data in support of the conclusion that the primary message of computer advertisements is that computers are a masculine domain. Across studies, one finds a theme of female incompetence in using technology. There is a theme of women's fragility as well as a theme of women needing guidance, reassurance, and protection. Finally, across studies, there is evidence of women being displayed and objectified for erotic impact and for heterosexual male entertainment.

In sum, across studies, the basic message of computer advertisements seems to be that the world of technology and, by extension, the world of business and work, is a male space. There is an invitation for women to "stay protected" and let men deal with the "complexities" and "dangers" of computer technology. These studies also implied that women are better suited for expressive, human-relationship tasks as opposed to impersonal, technical tasks.

Why should one be concerned about these messages? Because there are signs of persistently low and even diminishing interest and involvement of girls and women in computer science. Recent surveys indicate that girls are underrepresented in computer clubs. They are less likely than boys to enroll in high school computer science classes, and this gap increases with more advanced classes. Girls are also five times less likely than boys to take the advanced-placement computer science exam (AAUW, 2000a, 2000b). According to data from the National Science Foundation (2002), the percentage of computer science bachelor's degrees awarded to women has never gone beyond 37%—a peak reached in 1984 and in 1998. At the same time, the percentage of women in computer science and mathematics postbaccalaureate programs is decreasing. In 1998, women received only approximately 25% of master's degrees and 22% of doctoral degrees in computer science and mathematics. Furthermore, the percentage of women in computer science and mathematics occupations has been declining by about 4% since 1993. Finally, as of 1996, women comprised only 19% of assistant professors, 10% of associate professors, and 6% of full professors in computer science (Cassell & Jenkins, 1998).

This gender gap in computer science participation appears to go hand in hand with a host of other attitudinal, motivational, and behavioral factors. For example, both females and males think of computers and computer science as a male domain (AAUW, 2000b; Hess & Miura, 1985; Margolis & Fisher, 2001). Girls in high school report less confidence than do boys in using technology. Girls also exhibit less computer efficacy and less positive affect about computers than do boys (Whitley, 1997). As the AAUW report frames it, girls seem to have serious reservations about the computer culture.

Does the gender discourse of computer advertisements reflect or influence female alienation from computers? Probably a bit of both. Advertising themes reflect what advertisers perceive as the important issues of their likely market. One reason computer advertisements assume a male audience and speak in a male voice likely has to do, at least in part, with the fact that, as noted above, men demonstrate more interest in computer products, activities, training, and careers.

At the same time, the gender discourse of computer advertisements also influences and, in many ways, probably reinforces different female and male attitudes and behaviors about using computers. Studies of advertisements as well as studies of stereotypes have demonstrated how cultural ideologies, including gender ideologies, can shape interests, motivation, self-efficacy, and ultimately behavior. Steele's (1997) stereotype-threat research has shown that individuals do not need to accept a prevailing intellectual inferiority stereotype to be affected by it. It is enough that they have to contend with it at a time when their mental abilities are tested, such as during an exam, for the negative prophecy to be fulfilled. For example, according to Steele's research, the cultural message that women are incompetent in math can depress their performance in math tests. According to him, a stereotype-threat message can also lead to "disidentification" and disengagement with a particular field. It is likely that similar messages about male facility with technology may affect the confidence with which girls approach computers and technology in general.

What can be done to counteract the potentially negative effects on girls and women of the dominant masculine discourse on computers? According to Steele's (1997) research, increasing a sense of one's presence, belonging, and entitlement in a field may help counteract negative stereotypes. Girls and boys tend to think of computers as a male domain and expertise. Changing the public image of computing may be a strategy to improve women's sense of belonging in computer fields. The media may be engaged in promoting active and positive images of women using computer technology across a variety of work and leisure domains (AAUW, 2000b). One goal of this media campaign would be to counteract the stereotype that the computer user is male, socially isolated, and working in impersonal technical fields. Increasing the visibility of women who are leaders in information technology design, programming, and entrepreneurship may also be helpful. According to the AAUW report (2000b), girls express an interest in knowing more about female computer pioneers and experts. Encouraging diverse points of entry will also be important. Some individuals will be drawn to computers through the arts, others through biology, and yet others through engineering. Some individuals may be interested in computers from childhood and because of the appeal of the Web, whereas others may come to computers later as adults, through vocational or personal needs. It will be crucial to reach out to women from a range of educational, economic, and occupational levels. A focus on non-college-bound women is critical because information technology training offers some of the better paying career options for persons with high-school-level education (AAUW, 2000b). Changing the way that girls and women are socialized in technology may also help. Women who have succeeded in technological fields may provide guidance, advice, and support for those beginning to explore the field. Developing mentoring programs for young adolescent women in junior high school and in high school, similar to the support groups for women in engineering, may provide yet another route to increasing women's sense of belonging in computer sciences. Last but not least, it will be important to increase the presence of positive female characters in computer and video games. It has been shown that the sexist and violent nature of many computer and video games alienates girls (see Cassel & Jenkins, 1998, for a review), which diminishes the number of female players. At the same time, "computer and video games provide an easy lead to computer literacy. . . . those children who aren't playing them at young ages may end up disadvantaged in later years," noted Cassel and Jenkins (p. 11).

Computers are the technology of the present. They have inserted themselves as key tools in all aspects of people's lives. Computers are also the way of the future. Clearly, it is important for girls and women not to be left out of a major technical and scientific field. And what is good for one group can be good for other groups. Getting more girls and women involved in computer science can transform the computer culture in ways that may benefit other computer-reticent or computer-disengaged groups, including older adults and some ethnic minorities. Girls complain about the passivity of much conventional computer use; they report disliking the narrow and technical focus of programming classes; they reject a computer culture primarily focused on playing with machines; and they reject both the tedium and the violence of computer games. What girls and women seem to be asking of computer designers and programmers may be meaningful to other consumers who, like girls and women, have been turned off by aspects of the computer culture (AAUW, 2002b). What girls and women bring to the computer field can benefit everybody. The key to innovation in computer sciences and future technology may be in the mind of a woman. Society cannot afford to waste the computer talents of half of humanity because of gender stereotypes.

REFERENCES

American Association of University Women. (2000a). *Tech report: Tech-savvy.* Washington, DC: Author. Retrieved May 16, 2000, from http://www.aauw.org/2000/techsavvy.html

American Association of University Women. (2000b). *Tech-savvy: Educating girls in the new computer age.* Washington, DC: Author.

Barbercheck, M. (2001). Mixed messages: Men and women in advertisements in *Science*. In W. Wyer, M. Barbercheck, P. Giesman, H. O. Öztürk, & M. Wayne (Eds.), *A reader in feminist science studies: Women, science and technology* (pp. 117–131). New York: Routledge.

Bartel, D. (1988). *Putting on appearances: Gender and advertising*. Philadelphia, PA: Temple University Press.

Brummett, B. (1991). *Rhetorical dimensions of popular culture*. Tuscaloosa, AL: The University of Alabama Press.

Brummett, B. (1994). *Rhetoric in popular culture*. New York: St. Martin's Press.

Cassell, J., & Jenkins, H. (1998). Chess for girls: Feminism and computer games. In J. Cassel & H. Jenkins (Eds.), *From Barbie to Mortal Kombat: Gender and computer games* (pp. 2–37). Cambridge, MA: The MIT Press.

Courtenay, A. E., & Whipple, T. W. (1983). *Sex stereotyping in advertising*. Lexington, MA: Lexington Books.

Coyle, A. (1995). Discourse analysis. In G. M. Breakwell, S. Hammond, & C. Fife-Schaw (Eds.), *Research methods in psychology* (pp. 243–258). London: Sage.

Demetrulias, D. M., & Rosenthal, N. R. (1985). Discrimination against females and minorities in microcomputer advertising. *Computers and the Social Sciences, 1,* 91–95.

Hess, R. D., & Miura, I. T. (1985). Gender differences in enrollment in computer camps and classes. *Sex Roles, 13,* 193–203.

Kilbourne, J. (1999). *Can't buy my love: How advertising changes the way we think and feel*. New York: Simon & Schuster.

Lanis, K., & Covell, K. (1995). Images of women in advertisements: Effects on attitudes related to sexual aggression. *Sex Roles, 32,* 639–649.

Leiss, W., Kline, S., & Jhally, S. (1986). *Social communication in advertising*. Toronto: Methuen.

Lester, P. M. (1996). *Images that injure: Pictorial stereotypes in the media*. Westport, CT: Praeger Publishers.

Mackay, N. J., & Covell, K. (1997). The impact of women in advertisements on attitudes toward women. *Sex Roles, 36,* 573–583.

Margolis, J., & Fisher, A. (2001). *Unlocking the clubhouse: Women in computing*. Cambridge, MA: The MIT Press.

Merskin, D. (1999). What every girl should know: An analysis of feminine hygiene advertising. In S. R. Mazzarella & N. O. Pecora (Eds.), *Growing up girls: Popular culture and the construction of identity* (pp. 113–132). New York: Peter Lang Publishing.

Mulvey, L. (1999). Visual pleasure and narrative cinema. In L. Braudy & M. Cohen (Eds.), *Film theory and criticism: Introductory readings* (pp. 833–844). New York: Oxford University Press.

National Science Foundation. (2002). Higher education in science and engineering. In *Science and engineering indicators 2002* (chap. 2). Retrieved September 15, 2003, from http://www.nsf.gov/sbe/srs/seind02/start.htm

Ortner, S. (1996). *Making gender: The politics and erotics of culture*. Boston: Beacon Press.

Standard Rate and Data Service. (2000, January). *Consumer magazine advertising source*. Des Plaines, IL: Author.

Steele, C. M. (1997). A threat in the air: How stereotypes shape intellectual identity and performance. *American Psychologist, 52*, 613–629.

United States Department of Commerce, Bureau of the Census. (1995, July). *1990 U.S. census data: Population summary*. Washington, DC: Author. Retrieved June 25, 2000, from http://venus.census.gov/cdrom/lookup/961975227

Ware, M. C., & Stuck, M. F. (1985). Sex-role messages vis-à-vis microcomputer use: A look at the pictures. *Sex Roles, 13*, 205–214.

Whitley, B. E. (1997). Gender differences in computer related attitudes and behavior: A meta-analysis. *Computers in Human Relations, 13*(1), 1–22.

Williamson, J. (1978). *Decoding advertisements: Ideology and meaning in advertising*. London: Marion Boyars.

Williamson, J. (1980). *Consuming passions: The dynamics of popular culture*. London: Marion Boyars.

7

HOLLYWOOD'S PORTRAYAL OF PSYCHOLOGISTS AND PSYCHIATRISTS: GENDER AND PROFESSIONAL TRAINING DIFFERENCES

HARRIET T. SCHULTZ

Woman meets man. They play, help each other with their problems, flirt, fall in love, start a torrid affair—nothing unusual, a common movie scenario. She is his therapist.

My interest in Hollywood's portrayal of psychotherapists was piqued a few years ago after viewing several movies that featured members of my profession as unethical boundary violators (*Prince of Tides*, 1992; *Tin Cup*, 1996; *First Wives Club*, 1996). The films, though enjoyable, were most memorable for their depiction of therapists having romances with their patients, and I questioned what cumulative impact these depictions might have on audiences.

I discovered a small body of literature on psychiatry and film, which I reviewed in this chapter, and realized that these movies were simply the latest additions to Hollywood's longstanding tradition of presenting mental

Dr. Schultz wishes to thank the following colleagues for their careful review and helpful critique of this chapter or earlier versions: Lisa Balick, Robin Burks, Susan Dickson, Shirley Glass, Linda Jackson, Robert McLaughlin, and Constance Wood.

health professionals as stereotypes. The authors use the term *psychiatry* in a general sense with no distinction among different kinds of mental health practitioners. It is not always clear what the professional's training is, and many viewers do not understand the differences anyway.

Although lawyers, dentists, and others may grumble when portrayed as stereotypes, the close historical link between psychiatry and film makes this a field worthy of continued study. Psychiatry and film both developed during the same period (at the turn of the past century); both deal with human emotions and motivations; and each displays a fascination with the other. Film psychiatrists often serve as a vehicle through which characters express thoughts and feelings, and psychological themes are a frequent and rich source of high drama (Farber & Green, 1993; Gabbard & Gabbard, 1999; Schneider, 1977).

THE STEREOTYPES

Schneider (1987) identified three common stereotypes of movie psychiatrists which continue to the present time: Dr. Dippy, Dr. Evil, and Dr. Wonderful. Dr. Dippy, crazier and zanier than the patients, is exemplified by Mel Brooks in *High Anxiety* (1977), Richard Dreyfuss in *What About Bob* (1991), and Billy Crystal in *Analyze This* (1999).

Dr. Evil is sometimes portrayed as a corrupt mind-controller, like Patrick Stewart in *Conspiracy Theory* (1997), who programs people to be assassins, and sometimes as a homicidal maniac such as Alan Alda in *Whispers in the Dark* (1992). One of the most famous Dr. Evils is Dr. Lecter, or Hannibal the Cannibal, played by Anthony Hopkins in *Silence of the Lambs* (1991).

Dr. Wonderful is the warm, caring, competent therapist who has endless time to devote to patients and often cures with the uncovering of a single traumatic event—a kind of supertherapist. The psychiatrists in *Three Faces of Eve* (1957) and *Ordinary People* (1980) are Dr. Wonderfuls.

I identified two additional stereotypes: Dr. Rigid and Dr. Line-Crosser (Schultz, 1998). Dr. Rigid stifles joy, fun, and creativity like the spoil-sport psychologist in *Miracle on 34th Street* (1947) who tries to have Santa Claus committed as a dangerous lunatic. The most common movie stereotype, however, may be Dr. Line-Crosser. He or she crosses boundaries of different types, typically becoming romantically involved with patients. This is a recurring theme, portrayed with the strong implication that such love affairs are curative for both patient and therapist.

Even some Dr. Wonderfuls are tarnished. Barbra Streisand in *Prince of Tides* (1992) devotes a great deal of time to patient Nick Nolte, does not charge him for sessions, and cures him by uncovering a traumatic event, all typical of Dr. Wonderful. She also has a passionate affair with him. In *Good Will Hunting* (1997), Robin Williams plays a highly effective therapist who connects well with his difficult patient, but he crosses, or at least pushes at, the boundaries by grabbing Will roughly by the throat, revealing his own issues, and breaking confidentiality by discussing him with his math professor.

Hollywood has its own special way of portraying female therapists. Gabbard and Gabbard (1989, 1999) conducted analyses, reviewing films dating back to 1935. They identified a pattern in which the female psychotherapist starts out as a cold intellectual professional woman with no romantic attachments. In movie after movie she is eventually cured of this problem by falling in love with her male patient, who diagnoses her, sweeps her off her feet, and shows her how to become a true woman, loving and submissive. The classic film of this genre is Hitchcock's *Spellbound* (1945) with Gregory Peck as an accused murderer and Ingrid Bergman as the psychoanalyst who cures his amnesia, proves he is not the murderer, and falls in love with him.

Gabbard and Gabbard (1989, 1999) found far more movie female therapists violating boundaries than males, even though in real life, statistics consistently show the reverse. The majority of sexual offenses are perpetrated by male therapists with female patients. Possible reasons for this reversal are explored below.

Why does Hollywood persist in these neverending caricatures? First, there is more than a grain of truth in many of the portrayals. Probably all psychologists know therapists they consider Dippy, and everyone knows there are therapists who violate boundaries. My concern has been with the degree of Hollywood's distortion, portraying most therapists as outrageous or unethical.

Second is the nature of Hollywood—Hollywood does what Hollywood does. Their business is to produce stories that will bring in big bucks. There is a lot of appeal in stories about therapists who are crazy, are homicidal, or carry on affairs with patients. Filmmakers sexualize most relationships, so why not this one? Given the intimate nature of the therapist–patient relationship, this situation is a natural setup for the screen.

Third, it turns out that many Hollywood psychotherapists are as starstruck and entranced with the glamour of their celebrity patients as the rest of us. A book entitled *Hollywood on the Couch: A Candid Look at the Overheated Love Affair Between Psychiatrists and Moviemakers* (1993) reveals that in real life it has been common among Hollywood therapists to overstep their bounds. Some regularly socialize with and date their patients or brag openly about who they are treating. According to this book, Marilyn Monroe's psychoanalyst was so concerned about her fragility that he essentially adopted her into his family to provide her with some stability. From the perspective of some moviemakers, then, what they are showing is reality.

Finally, what is seen on screen may be a literal acting out of love fantasies, fears, and rage that moviemakers and their audiences have toward therapists (Schultz, 1998). Patients sometimes do place therapists on a pedestal as

Dr. Marvelous; at the same time there is concern about their power. In social situations when a psychologist reveals his or her profession, it is not uncommon for people to make rather nervous remarks about their minds being read. The fear is that therapists can control patients or force treatment against their will. Hence, the malevolent Dr. Evils are ready to hospitalize (*High Anxiety*, 1977), lobotomize (*One Flew Over the Cuckoo's Nest*, 1975), or cannibalize their patients (*Silence of the Lambs*, 1991). Komrad (2000) summed this up by suggesting that the three archetypes of Drs. Wonderful, Dippy, and Evil correspond to three kinds of feelings that people have when they go for treatment: the wish for healing and rescue, the fear of incompetence, and the fear of pain, madness, and death.

What impact do these stereotypes have on the public? Is help-seeking behavior affected in any way by these portrayals? The answer is not known because of lack of research in the area. However, the American Psychological Association (1996), in its Public Education Campaign, revealed that 76% of the public cite "lack of confidence in the outcome" as a barrier to seeking help from therapists. It seems reasonable to assume that for those who are ambivalent about seeking help or who already hold negative opinions about psychotherapy, these stereotypes could reinforce and resonate with their fears, especially if movies are their only source of information about the profession. Why would billions of dollars be spent on advertising if the image had no power?

GENDER AND PROFESSIONAL TRAINING DIFFERENCES

As noted, few researchers who study film therapists make distinctions among different mental health practitioners. This issue is important because Hollywood may be reflecting the impressions—or misimpressions—of the public. It would be useful to know what perceptions patients have when they enter therapists' offices after having watched them satirized, devalued, or idealized on screen for years.

As a psychologist, I wondered how Hollywood portrays this field in comparison to psychiatrists. Are there any differences in the depictions?

Two studies that touched on these differences show that movie mental health professionals are more likely to be identified as psychiatrists than psychologists. Bischoff and Reiter (1999) identified 99 therapists in films that opened from 1988 through 1997. They found 29% were psychiatrists, 6% were psychologists, and the rest had unspecified training. Lipsitz, Rand, Cornett, Sassler, and White (2000) identified movie therapists in 45 movies from 1990 to 1997. Nearly half were psychiatrists, 22% were psychologists, and the rest were unspecified. Even among researchers there are discrepancies about the professional's identity because of ambiguity or inconsistencies in the depiction.

The trend continues. Updating an earlier study (Schultz, 2000), I could find only two movies released from 2000 to 2002 that featured psychologists (in videos available at the local branches of a chain video store): *Saving Silverman* (2001) and *Vanilla Sky* (2001). During the same period at least five films had psychiatrists as a main character: *Don't Talk to Anyone* (2001), *Lantana* (2001), *K-Pax* (2001), *Analyze That* (2002), and *Antwone Fisher* (2002).

Why this underrepresentation for movie psychologists when in real life there are so many more psychologists than psychiatrists? (The American Psychiatric Association reported approximately 39,000 members in 2002. The Research Office of the American Psychological Association reported 85,000 doctoral-level members the same year. As membership in both organizations is voluntary, neither figure represents the full total of licensed practitioners in these fields.) Psychiatrists may be perceived as having more power, or the term *psychiatrist* may be more familiar to both filmmakers and the audience, so it is used almost generically. It is common knowledge that many Hollywood figures are in therapy, with most likely seeing psychiatrists. Featuring psychiatrists in their movies may be a way for filmmakers to both honor and devalue them.

SURVEY OF MOVIE PSYCHOLOGISTS

Because there was no research examining how film psychologists as a group are depicted, I did an informal survey.

Method

I identified movies that included a psychologist, examined the types of professional roles taken by the psychologist, and compared these with roles played by movie psychiatrists during the same period. There were no specific hypotheses about how psychologists might be portrayed differently from psychiatrists, but on the basis of previous literature the expectation was that there would be gender differences among movie psychologists, with more females than males acting out sexually with patients.

Names of movies that included a psychologist came from previous research, colleagues, my own knowledge of film, and the Internet Movie Data Base. To be counted as a psychologist, the professional had to self-identify or be identified as such elsewhere, as on an office nameplate or in a newspaper. I found and viewed 23 movies released from 1990 to 2002 that met this criterion (see Exhibit 7.1; Schultz, 2000, 2002). I might add that in the process, I watched a lot of really bad movies!

EXHIBIT 7.1
Movies Featuring Psychologists

Male (n = 11)	Female (n = 12)
Raising Cain (1992)	*Basic Instinct* (1992)
There Goes the Neighborhood (1992)	*Knight Moves* (1992)
Color of Night (1994)	*Sleepless in Seattle* (1993)
IQ (1994)	*Body Chemistry 3* (1994)
Kiss the Girls (1997)	*Copycat* (1995)
Good Will Hunting (1997)	*Jade* (1995)
Sphere (1998)	*Never Talk to Strangers* (1995)
Sixth Sense (1999)	*Primal Fear* (1996)
Mumford (1999)	*Flirting With Disaster* (1996)
The Haunting (1999)	*Tin Cup* (1996)
Vanilla Sky (2001)	*Night Caller* (1998)
	Saving Silverman (2001)

Results

There were 11 male and 12 female psychologists. All had major roles, except in *Sleepless in Seattle*, although the invisible radio psychologist in that movie plays a major part in bringing the two leads together.

Looking at the psychologists' professional roles, one can see male–female differences. Among the males, 5 of the 11 are therapists (in *Sixth Sense, Good Will Hunting, Mumford, Color of Night*, and *There Goes the Neighborhood*) but only 3 of the 12 women are (in *Tin Cup, Basic Instinct*, and *Saving Silverman*). Three women are media psychologists (in *Sleepless in Seattle, Night Caller*, and *Body Chemistry 3*); none of the men are.

There were about equal numbers of researchers—four males (in *IQ, The Haunting, Raising Cain, Sphere*) and five females (in *Copycat, Jade, Body Chemistry 3, Knight Moves, Flirting With Disaster*)—and about equal numbers doing forensics—three males (in *Color of Night, Kiss the Girls*, and *Vanilla Sky*) and four females (in *Copycat, Primal Fear, Never Talk to Strangers*, and *Knight Moves*). Forensics refers here to the evaluation of criminals (e.g., Frances McDormand in *Primal Fear*) or to using expertise to help the police catch serial murderers (Sigourney Weaver in *Copycat*). Some of the psychologists are shown taking more than one role, such as researcher and forensics expert.

In contrast to the varied roles played by movie psychologists, movie psychiatrists are almost always shown doing talk therapy, contrary to real life where psychiatrists perform a range of functions. Psychiatrists as therapists appear in *Prince of Tides* (1992), *Final Analysis* (1992), *Mr. Jones* (1993), *Silent Fall* (1994), *Don Juan de Marco* (1995), *Gross Pointe Blank* (1997), *Lantana* (2001), *Don't Talk to Anyone* (2001), *K-Pax* (2001), *Analyze That* (2002), and many more. Only occasionally are psychiatrists seen prescribing medications as in *What About Bob?* (1991), *Mr. Jones* (1993), and *Don Juan de Marco*

(1995). There is one radio movie psychiatrist, played by Mark Harmon in *Magic in the Water* (1995).

Other striking differences were found in portrayals of male and female psychologists. Male psychologists can be divided into two groups at the extremes: One set is skilled, the other is inept or extremely evil.

Morgan Freeman in *Kiss the Girls* is the hero who solves serial kidnappings and murders. In *Color of Night*, *Good Will Hunting*, and *Sixth Sense*, male therapists are depicted as warm and caring, but they are also emotionally wounded healers who cure their patients and in turn are cured by them. Robin Williams in *Good Will Hunting* is grieving his wife's death. Bruce Willis in *Sixth Sense* and *Color of Night* plays a psychologist (a different one in each movie) who has misdiagnosed patients, with disastrous results, but redeems himself by helping future patients.

These male Dr. Wonderfuls contrast with their fake, imaginary, inept, or evil male counterparts. Loren Dean in *Mumford* is portrayed as the best psychologist in town, but he turns out to be a fake, in a not-so-subtle devaluation of professional training. Forensic psychologist Kurt Russell is dismissed as imaginary at the end of *Vanilla Sky*. Jeff Daniels in *There Goes the Neighborhood* is ineffectual and ridiculed by his prisoner patients. Even they sense it is not appropriate to use Rorschach cards as a way to stimulate discussion during group therapy!

Of the male psychologists who are researchers, three of the four are rigid, unfeeling, extremely evil scientists who commit egregious human subject violations. Stephen Fry, in *IQ*, has locked up a screaming man to conduct a time deprivation experiment. Liam Neeson in *The Haunting* deceives his subjects, telling them that they are participating in an insomnia study when in reality he is studying fear. The situation goes out of control when fear turns to terror and death in a haunted house. To say these psychologists show complete disdain and disregard for informed consent and institutional review boards would be a gross understatement.

John Lithgow in *Raising Cain* is perhaps the most evil psychologist of all. He murders young mothers and steals their crying babies so he can take them to his even more evil researcher father for child development study. Dustin Hoffman in *Sphere* has falsified a government report and slept with a patient, actions almost benign in comparison.

Many of the female psychologists are sexualized Line-Crossers. Jeanne Tripplehorn in *Basic Instinct* and Rene Russo in *Tin Cup* are therapists having affairs with patients. Diane Lane, as a forensic expert in *Knight Moves*, has sex with the man she is evaluating, and Tea Leoni, the adoption researcher in *Flirting With Disaster*, more than flirts with her married subject. These are standard depictions of female therapists, whether psychologists or psychiatrists. Hollywood sexualizes women in general, and when filmmakers see a close male–female relationship, they cannot pass up the opportunity to portray a romance.

However, there was a new and unexpected finding: the extent to which the female psychologists act out or study sexual or aggressive impulses. Many of the women are portrayed as brainy, proper, and controlled in their professional lives. They are the experts who deliver lectures or publish books. (None of the male psychologists are depicted in this manner.) But in their personal lives, the women are seething with aggressive sexuality, as exemplified by Shari Shattuck in *Body Chemistry 3*, Linda Fiorentino in *Jade*, and Rebecca De Mornay in *Never Talk to Strangers*. Their research focuses on aggression: violence in the workplace (*Jade*), sex and violence (*Body Chemistry 3*), and serial murderers (*Knight Moves* and *Copycat*).

Further, there is a strong connection between these women and murder. Two are murderers, in *Never Talk to Strangers* and *Body Chemistry 3*. Two others are very strong murder suspects, in *Jade* and *Basic Instinct*. The psychologist in the latter movie was not the serial killer, but there is a strong suggestion that she murdered her former husband, and she herself is murdered. Two female psychologists are the victims of obsessions of serial murderers who attempt to kill them (*Copycat* and *Night Caller*) and, as already mentioned, two specialize in studying serial murderers.

In *Saving Silverman* the psychologist is not only a controlling, sexy, and tough martial arts expert, amply illustrated in the film, but she defends herself at one point by trying to drown her attacker in the toilet. Later she becomes a target for murder.

It is noteworthy that when female psychologists are portrayed as evil, they are killing or accused of killing men with whom they have a relationship—as in *Jade*, *Basic Instinct*, *Never Talk to Strangers*, and *Body Chemistry 3*. When male psychologists are evil, they are manipulating or abusing research subjects, as in *IQ* and *The Haunting*. An exception is the one male killer psychologist in this sample, in *Raising Cain*, who murders his wife and some of his female friends. Only in the film *Color of Night* is a male psychologist shown as the target of murder. This is also the only film in which a male psychologist exhibits strong sexuality.

By contrast, female movie psychiatrists are not as deadly or as victimized as female psychologists, even in an earlier period. Among female psychiatrists in *Spellbound* (1945), *Zelig* (1983), *Agnes of God* (1985), *House of Games* (1987), *Whispers in the Dark* (1992), *Prince of Tides* (1992), *Mr. Jones* (1993), *12 Monkeys* (1995), and *Lantana* (2001), there is only one who kills: Lindsay Crouse in *House of Games*. One is the target of murder (Annabella Sciorra in *Whispers in the Dark*), and one has written a book and lectures about her daughter who was murdered (Barbara Hershey in *Lantana*). Most female movie psychiatrists are too busy falling in love with their male patients and curing themselves to have time for murder or mayhem (*Prince of Tides*; *Mr. Jones*, *12 Monkeys*). As mentioned, some male psychiatrists in film are murderous Dr. Evils, but many are depicted as ineffectual or warm and caring.

Results of this survey indicate that among movie psychologists and psychiatrists it is the female psychologists as a group who are most strongly associated with violent interests and impulses. They are murderers, possible murderers, targeted victims of murderers, or experts on murderers.

Discussion

It is not news that Hollywood thrives on sex and violence, but why are female psychologists the black widow spiders of the group? Answers lie in the realm of socially acceptable gender roles and power differentials. The Gabbards (1989, 1999) have theorized that a woman in the role of a powerful authority figure stirs up primitive fears in men. The mostly male moviemakers, catering to the males in the audience, revel in showing the sexual conquest of a female therapist by her male patient. This allows male viewers to master their anxiety.

Samuels (1985) made an observation along the same line, as did Bischoff and Reiter (1999), who found that female mental health professionals in the movies were more likely than males to be portrayed as sexualized. The later authors see the authoritative female therapist as gender-incongruent, given that the stereotypical female in our society is viewed as less powerful than males.

To expand on this: A male patient being treated by a female therapist may feel vulnerable and emasculated. He may fear that talking to her about his inner life will prove deadly to him. He sees a professional woman in front of him, but he may be fantasizing about what's underneath. These movies become a vehicle to de-fang the woman and reduce her to sex object (Schultz, 2000). Women in film cannot have it all; being a career woman excludes being wife and mother (Walker, 1993).

These observations may explain why moviemakers show more female than male therapists romancing patients. Man seducing woman is nothing new. But when a professional woman crosses the boundary, the drama is heightened. The good female authority figure topples and becomes a sex object; the Madonna turns into a whore.

As for male movie mental health professionals, Bischoff and Reiter (1999) found that they were more likely than females to be shown as incompetent. This was interpreted also on the basis of gender-incongruity because society tends to view men as poorly equipped to handle emotional and relationship issues. Male therapists, as presumed experts in these areas, are put down by being made to look silly and inept. They can be warm and caring, but only if emotionally wounded.

Why are female film psychologists as a group so strongly associated with murder? This likely relates to the roles they play in the movies described here. These women are not warm, fuzzy therapists but intelligent, sexy powerhouses, experts in their fields, lecturing from the podium or giving advice over the airwaves. They are tough cookies, ready to kick or shoot when threatened. As public "experts," these women may be viewed by men as even more threatening than therapists in a private office.

As mentioned, the female psychologists kill, or are accused of killing, someone with whom they have a relationship. The two female killers literally get away with murder. They are shown planting the murder weapon on a man they have just shot, the police buy their story, and the women happily carry on with successful careers. As with the issue of sexuality, these portrayals may be interpreted as a way for the male moviemakers to deal with the threat they experience from strong women. The filmmakers may be projecting their fears, anger, and aggressiveness onto the female psychologists in their films (Lisa Balick, personal communication, May 19, 2003). Career women in these portrayals are dangerous. They kill and get away with it, they are suspected to have killed, or someone wants to kill them. They are shot down—too powerful for their own good.

From a societal point of view, Carll (1999) pointed out that there is a public fascination with women and violence, especially when women are the perpetrators. When women kill or maim husbands or kill their children, it becomes instant news worldwide because the behavior is contrary to the stereotype of woman as loving wife and mother. The stalking homicidal female in the movie *Fatal Attraction* (1987) generated tremendous press coverage despite the fact that the overwhelming majority of rejected stalkers and perpetrators of domestic violence are males (Carll, 1999). Portraying the female movie psychologist as aggressive or having potential for violence fits this general pattern of routine media sensationalism.

In summary, there is good and bad news here. The good news is that psychologists are being shown taking a variety of professional roles and in equal numbers of males and females. But the stereotypes and distortions continue. The perceived power of mental health providers is still devalued, with the men dippy, wounded, or manipulative, the women sexualized or aggressive.

Yet in a way there has been progress. Samuels (1985) reported making a slip of the tongue, telling an audience that she was writing a paper on how female movie psychotherapists were *betrayed* when she meant to say *portrayed*. She was referring to early movies showing female therapists as unassertive buffoons. At least this label does not apply to the latest crop of female psychologists!

WHAT CAN BE DONE ABOUT THESE PORTRAYALS: MEDIA WATCH COMMITTEE, APA DIVISION 46

In response to these problematic portrayals, Dr. Shirley Glass founded the Media Watch Committee for the American Psychological Association's Media Psychology Division (Division 46) in 1998. A major concern was that audiences may not recognize that certain commonly depicted movie psychologists' behaviors are violations of the ethical code and, in real life, could lead to loss of the license to practice. Murdering patients is likely to stand out as illegal, but actions allowable in other professions may not be viewed as inappropriate, especially in the arena of dual relationships, such as dating a client's sister in *Final Analysis* (1992) or terminating the professional relationship to pursue a romance in *Tin Cup* (1996). Many nonpsychologist friends tell me that they do not see anything wrong with these behaviors.

The committee (which I chair) monitors portrayals of fictional mental health professionals in the movies, television, and books, looking for creative ways to heighten awareness among our colleagues and the public about the possibly negative impact of these portrayals. The group devised a system to rate the fictional psychologists' professional and ethical behaviors as these were the areas that we wanted to target for public education. We did not want to come across as defensive or humorless, complaining about satires and spoofs, which can be very funny.

We rate the professionals' behavior for professional competence, respect for boundaries, maintaining confidentiality, and overall professional conduct. We also rate the show's producers or the author of a book for responsible portrayal of professional standards: either the practitioner has portrayed appropriate behavior or, if the behavior is inappropriate, it is clearly labeled as such. All too often the professional's unethical conduct is presented either as curative or as comical. In *Analyze This* (1999) the psychiatrist's son eavesdrops on sessions and spreads the gossip at cocktail parties.

The committee has also created the Golden Psi Media Award, which is given to a producer or author who has shown excellence in the responsible portrayal of ethical standards. To date, awards have been given to specific episodes of five television programs: *The Sopranos, Chicago Hope, Once and Again, Law & Order,* and *Law & Order Special Victims Unit.* In 2002 the recipient was Stephen White, PhD, a clinical psychologist who writes mysteries in which the main character is a clinical psychologist who grapples with complex ethical dilemmas.

There has been national media coverage of these awards and of the symposia presented by the committee at APA's annual convention. We plan to expand coverage of our ratings so that they reach a wider audience of psychologists and the public. Over time we hope to see more portrayals of ethical, nonlethal male and female mental health professionals and more depictions of unethical practitioners called to account before a licensing board. New stereotypes may develop: Dr. Healthy Competent and Dr. Line-Crosser who loses his license!

REFERENCES

American Psychological Association, Practice Directorate. (1996). *Public education campaign kit.* Washington, DC: Author.

Bischoff, R. J., & Reiter, A. D. (1999). The role of gender in the presentation of mental health clinicians in the movies: Implications for clinical practice. *Psychotherapy, 36,* 180–189.

Carll, E. K. (1999). *Violence in our lives: Impact on workplace, home, and community.* Boston: Allyn & Bacon.

Farber, S., & Green, M. (1993). *Hollywood on the couch: A candid look at the overheated love affair between psychiatrists and movie makers.* New York: William Morrow and Company.

Gabbard, G. O., & Gabbard, K. (1989). The female psychoanalyst in the movies. *Journal of the American Psychoanalytic Association, 37,* 1031–1049.

Gabbard, G. O., & Gabbard, K. (1999). *Psychiatry and the cinema* (2nd ed.). Washington, DC: American Psychiatric Press.

Komrad, M. (2000, August). *How Hollywood portrays psychiatrists.* Paper presented at the annual convention of the American Psychological Association, Washington, DC.

Lipsitz, A., Rand, K., Cornett, J., Sassler, M., & White, A. (2000, June). *Out of focus: The image of psychology in current cinema.* Poster session presented at the annual convention of the American Psychological Society, Miami Beach, FL.

Samuels, L. (1985). Female psychotherapists as portrayed in film, fiction, and nonfiction. *Journal of the American Academy of Psychoanalysis, 13,* 367–378.

Schneider, I. (1977). Images of the mind: Psychiatry in the commercial film. *American Journal of Psychiatry, 134,* 613–620.

Schneider, I. (1987). The theory and practice of movie psychiatry. *American Journal of Psychiatry, 144,* 996–1002.

Schultz, H. T. (1998, August). *Hollywood therapists and psychology's public image.* Paper presented at the annual convention of the American Psychological Association, San Francisco, CA.

Schultz, H. T. (2000, August). *Hollywood psychologists: Gender and professional training differences.* Paper presented at the annual convention of the American Psychological Association, Washington, DC.

Schultz, H. T. (2002, August). *Movie psychologists: How Hollywood portrays gender differences.* Paper presented at the annual convention of the American Psychological Association, Chicago, IL.

Walker, J. (1993). *Couching resistance: Women, film, and psychoanalytic psychiatry.* Minneapolis: University of Minnesota Press.

III

AGGRESSION AND VIOLENCE: VICTIMS AND PERPETRATORS

8

VIOLENCE, SEX, RACE, AND AGE IN POPULAR VIDEO GAMES: A CONTENT ANALYSIS

KAREN E. DILL, DOUGLAS A. GENTILE, WILLIAM A. RICHTER, AND JODY C. DILL

After dinner in a suburban American home, a 13-year-old boy plays a video game alone in his bedroom. On the screen, the boy's hero, Duke Nukem, approaches a strip club where, before entering, he guns down the local authorities. Duke is a young, White man—blond and tan, with huge, rippling muscles. On entering the club, he sees several virtually naked young women dancing on poles, moaning and gyrating. He shoots and kills one of the young women. As her screams fade, Duke fires his witty retort, "Too bad, she was cute."

INTRODUCTION

This scene is all too typical of what is happening nightly in homes across America. The Duke Nukem 3D video game is the 11th most popular selling PC video game of all time (*PC Data Top Games of 1999*, 2000). Forty-nine percent of children have a video game player or computer in their bedrooms (Song & Anderson, 2001). Griffiths and Hunt (1998) reported that 98.7% of the adolescents they studied were video game players. Ninety-four percent of eighth and ninth graders reported playing video games, with 59% reporting playing at least once a week (Gentile, Lynch, Linder, & Walsh., 2004). Finally, Paik (2001) reported that 87% of younger children and 70% of adolescents play computer games, and that more boys (87%) than girls (79%) play. Among eighth- and ninth-grade students, boys reported playing an average of 13 hours per week, with girls playing an average of 5 hours per week (Gentile et al., 2004). Males also reported preferring games in the sports or violence categories, whereas females prefer intellectual–creative or action–

115

fantasy games. Finally, worldwide annual video game sales reached $20 billion by the year 2000 (Cohen, 2000; Video game sales, 2001). Furthermore, the U.S. video game industry has become "the fourth pillar of the entertainment business, alongside movies, music and television. Games sales regularly rival box-office receipts, and the top game publishers routinely exceed $1 billion in annual revenue" (Reuters, 2005a, p. 14).

Video Games as a Source of Information

Mass media act as an agent of socialization. Individuals learn cultural rules from the stories told in that culture (Ryan & Wentworth, 1999). Whereas stories used to be told person-to-person within communities, the media are now telling the stories (Walsh, 1997); thus, individuals learn rules from the media (Ryan & Wentworth, 1999). The past two decades have seen an explosion of information sources including the Internet, video games, and an expanding array of television channels. The stories told by the media include messages about social roles as they relate to race, sex, and age. Many of these stories are violent and describe, in terms of race, sex, and age, who is the powerful aggressor and who are the victims. A person's community loses moral authority as messages come from outside that community. The self becomes isolated and the definitions of acceptable and deviant behavior change (Ryan & Wentworth, 1999). Therefore, it is important to analyze the content of media and its role in socialization, especially with regard to character portrayals.

Portrayal of Gender in Video Games

There has been little examination of the role of female characters in video games. One notable exception is a study by Tracy Dietz (1998), who analyzed aggressive content and the portrayal of women in the top-selling Sega and Nintendo video games. She found that 79% of the games included aggression, with 21% depicting violence toward women. Twenty-eight percent of the games portrayed women as sex objects. Only 15% of the games portrayed women as heroic characters, and even those heroic roles were mostly sexualized or trivialized. In games with female characters, the females were most likely to be depicted as victims or as damsels in distress. Other common depictions included females portrayed as visions of beauty, as evil or obstacles to the game, and in devalued or insignificant roles.

It is interesting that Dietz (1998) found that the most common depiction of female characters was no depiction at all: Most games simply did not have female characters. Similarly, Braun and Giroux (1989) found that in arcade video games, female screen displays and synthetic voice emissions were practically nonexistent.

The Media Education Foundation (Huntemann, 2000) noted that video games tend to send blatant messages about gender in Western culture. A female character is often the damsel in distress or someone who simply fulfills male desires. Female characters are portrayed with distorted body images. These images are hypersexual, with disproportionately large breasts and small waists and hips, and are often physically impossible, especially given the athletic prowess of the characters (Huntemann, 2000). For men, the gender portrayal is equally stereotypical and blatant, showing men as symbols of power and dominance. Male physical appearance is hypermasculine, often featuring chest and arm muscles in massive and unrealistic proportions. This is the male hero fantasy: the muscular giant who wins battles and women alike (Huntemann, 2000).

In some recent video games, female aggressive heroines are emerging. *Tomb Raider*'s heroine, Lara Croft, is perhaps the most notable, but is accompanied by others such as *Perfect Dark*'s Joanna Dark. Are these characters positive or negative role models? Although the idea of female heroines is positive, the highly sexualized way they are portrayed robs them of dignity. On the surface, they may appear empowered, but they are actually created to appeal to the young, male game player (Huntemann, 2000).

Race and Age in Violent Video Games

The Media Education Foundation (Huntemann, 2000) reported that 8 of the 10 top-selling games feature White characters. Racial minorities are depicted primarily in stereotypical ways. For example, in the game *Kingpin*, in which Blacks are portrayed as street thugs and prostitutes, a White, male character tries to overpower the Black criminal element.

Vasil and Wass (1993) analyzed research on the treatment of age in several different media sources including television and print media. They concluded that, across these studies, the elderly, especially women, were underrepresented. When elderly characters were portrayed, they were depicted negatively, cast in minor roles, and underdeveloped as characters. The apparent ages of video game characters have never, to our knowledge, been studied empirically. If characters are similar in age to the player, this may help the player identify with the character. Identification with an aggressor has been shown to increase aggressive behavior in those exposed to aggressive media (see Berkowitz, 1993, for a discussion).

Content Analyses: Violence

A handful of studies have examined the percentage of popular games that are violent. A content analysis of Canadian arcade games revealed that 71% were violent (Braun and Giroux, 1989). Provenzo (1991) found that about 85% of the most popular games were violent. Funk (1993) asked adolescents to report their favorite video games and found that 50% included a violent game on their list. Buchman and Funk (1996) reported the same numbers in their study of fourth through eighth graders.

Similarly, Dietz (1998) found that 79% of the popular Sega and Nintendo titles she studied were aggressive in nature. Twenty-one percent included violence specifically directed toward women. Nearly half the games included violence directed specifically at other characters, with the majority of these characters being human or human-like and including graphic violence.

Video Game Violence Linked to Aggression

Anderson and Bushman (2001) conducted a meta-analysis on 35 different studies of violent video games to see if these would reveal similar patterns in their findings. They identified the following consistent pattern: Exposure to violent video games increases physiological arousal, aggressive thoughts, aggressive emotions, and aggressive actions and decreases positive, prosocial actions. Thus, there is reason to be concerned about the prevalence of violence in video games (for reviews of the literature, see Dill & Dill, 1998; Gentile & Anderson, 2003).

Rationale for the Present Investigation

For this study we measured the prevalence of violence in top-selling video games with emphasis on a detailed description of the nature of the violence. Special attention was given to the interaction of video game violence with the demographics of the video game characters. Of primary interest was how the race, sex, and age of the characters related to roles of power, dominance, and aggression. Also reported are the demographics and portrayals of characters in general, notwithstanding the violent content of the game. This study is unique in its analysis of the content of video games and provides important information about this growing medium. Because the content of video games changes rapidly over time, follow-up investigations are necessary.

METHOD

The Games

The games chosen for this analysis came from a published list of the 20 top-selling PC video games of 1999 (*PC data top games of all time*, 1999; *PC data top games*, 2000). PC games were chosen because they are available to a wide audience and because past content analyses of video games have studied other game formats such as dedicated game systems and arcade games. Following is the list of the games and their publishers: *RollerCoaster Tycoon* (Hasbro Interactive), *SimCity 3000* (Electronic Arts), *Who Wants To Be a Millionaire?* (Disney), *Age of Empires II: The Age of Kings* (Microsoft), *StarCraft* (Havas Interactive), *Half-Life* (Havas Interactive), *Command & Conquer: Tiberian Sun* (Westwood), *Microsoft Flight Simulator* (Microsoft), *Frogger* (Hasbro Interactive), *Baldur's Gate* (Interplay), *Cabela's Big Game Hunter 2* (Activision), *Wheel of Fortune* (Hasbro Interactive), *Tom Clancy's Rainbow Six Gold Edition* (Red Storm), *StarCraft Expansion: Brood War* (Havas Interactive), *Need for Speed 3: Hot Pursuit* (Electronic Arts), *Monopoly* (Hasbro Interactive), *Deer Hunter III* (GT Interactive), *Star Wars Episode I: Phantom Menace* (LucasArts), *Microsoft Combat Flight Simulator* (Microsoft), and *Tom Clancy's Rainbow Six: Rogue Spear* (Red Storm).

Each game was played by a professional male gamer in his early 20s. His game play was recorded on videocassettes, which were subsequently viewed by the coders. Game play was standardized in the following ways: Wherever applicable, the same game settings were used. For example, if there was a choice of difficulty level, the highest level was chosen. For each game, the opening segments and control screen were recorded so the coders could view the story line and the general game controls. The time each game was recorded was set at a minimum of 10 minutes and a maximum of 30 minutes. The minimum time was used on games with straightforward and relatively unvarying story lines; the maximum time was used for games with different levels or story lines, with an attempt made to demonstrate all the major play modes. Because these are samples of game play, not all characters and settings were necessarily recorded, although an attempt was made to sample each of the main actions of the game in question.

Three trained coders (a male and a female psychologist and a male communications professor) rated each of the 20 video games. After watching the complete video recording of each game, each coder independently rated the game according to the categories described below. Next, the coders compared ratings. Any discrepancies were resolved by viewing disputed footage (e.g., to determine the race of a character whose race was disputed). After discrepancies were resolved, a single list of characteristics resulted. Interrater reliability was acceptably high. The average reliability coefficient for the scaled items was $r = 0.81$. The average reliability coefficient for the categorical items was kappa = 0.98.

Demographics of Video Game Characters

Sex, Race, and Age

Coders judged each character's gender, race (Black, White, Latino, Asian, Indian, or other), and age (child, adolescent, adult, or senior).

Role

Coders categorized the character's role in the game as being a main character (hero or primary player), target (object of violence in aggressive games), or secondary character (other).

Life-Form Type

Raters coded the life-form type of the video game characters according to the following categories: human, humanoid/alien, animal, cartoon, and robot/mechanical. Life-form type is an important variable, because where modeling behavior is concerned, media viewers tend not only to imitate the aggressive behavior they witnessed but to take into account the personal characteristics of the perpetrator and victim. Phillips (1986) found increases in homicide rates after highly publicized prizefights. It is interesting that the races of the murderer and victim matched those of the winner and loser in the prizefight. Violence that is perceived as more realistic is more likely to incite violence in the viewer (see Geen, 2001, for a review). Humans, animals, and robots are all concrete characters, whereas cartoons and aliens are less concrete.

Characterization

For each video game character, raters selected whether the character fit any of the following important roles: sexualized, comrade, obstacle, needs rescue, positive role, and negative role. The six categories were considered independent. Characters were rated as sexualized if they were depicted as scantily clad, as sex objects, or with sexualized features such as large breasts, or if the dialogue surrounding that character was sexual in nature. Comrades were secondary characters who aided or otherwise befriended the main character. The obstacle category followed from Dietz's (1998) description. Dietz (1998) also found that female video game characters were often depicted as damsels in distress. This study expanded the term *damsel in distress* to include characters of both sexes with the term *needs rescue*.

Finally, a rating of whether characters were depicted particularly positively or negatively during game play was included. These terms were confined to anything outside the main action of the game (a soldier in a war game would not be coded as a negative role, but characters who demonstrated vices aside from the main action of the game were rated as negative).

Aggressive Content of the Video Games

Realism

Several items tapping into this realism were constructed. All items described below were rated on five-point Likert scales with 0 (*not at all*) and 4 (*extremely*) being the endpoints. The first set of questions was as follows:

"How aggressive is this video game?" "When violence happens, how violent are the visual graphics?" and "When violence happens, how violent are the auditory elements?"

Highly concrete aggressive stimuli elicit more aggression than do less concrete stimuli (Turner & Goldsmith, 1976). The next set of questions distinguished between the terms *realistic* and *reality-based* for several dimensions of the games. *Realistic* referred to the quality of the computer graphics. Something was *reality-based* if "it exists or could exist in the real world." Both the realistic and reality-based nature of the settings, main characters, targets, and weapons were assessed.

The next questions expanded the idea of realism for the weapons. Included was the question "How accessible are the weapons?" Weapon accessibility was defined as the perceived likelihood that a person could attain the weapons in real life. With a checklist, weapons were placed into the following categories: real, science fiction, fantasy, and hands. More than one category could be chosen for a given game. *Real* weapons were weapons that are currently available in the real world. *Hands* denoted aggression through hand-to-hand combat. The science fiction and fantasy categories were used for categorizing nonreal weaponry. The difference between the two is that fantasy weapons do not exist and cannot theoretically be created (e.g., magic wands) whereas science fiction weapons do not exist, but could theoretically be created in the future on the basis of scientific theory (e.g., spaceships that fire lasers).

Next, the main view of the game was coded by checking one of four categories: from person's eyes (e.g., seeing hands shoot), shows main character's entire body (or vehicle) from behind, shows characters (vehicle) as seen from directly above, or shows characters (vehicles) interacting from a distance. The first category is the most realistic, and the categories decline in realism from there. These categories are also theoretically related to the degree that the player would be likely to identify with the aggressor. It was theorized that identification should be greatest when seeing the action through the character's eyes and least when seeing the game characters interact from a distance. Finally, whether any of the targets of aggression were objects or implicit targets was rated. *Objects* were defined as nonliving entities, and *implicit targets* were defined as targets that were supposed to be life forms but could not be directly viewed by the player (e.g., ships that would presumably be piloted by a living being).

Categories

According to a modified version of Buchman and Funk's (1996) video game categories, all games were classified as life-form violence, general entertainment, sports violence, or nonviolent sports.

RESULTS

Game Characteristics

Of the top-20 selling games from 1999, 12 (60%) have violence as a major theme. The games were classified as life-form violence (50%), general entertainment (35%), sports violence (10%), and nonviolent sports (5%). The amount of aggression was rated on a 0–4 scale, with 4 representing *extremely aggressive*. Sixty-five percent of games have nonzero aggression scores, and 12 (60%) have scores greater than the midpoint of the scale, hereafter referred to as high scores. Among the 12 games with violence as a major theme, the mean aggression score is 3.6 ($SD = 0.47$).

Half of the top 20 games are presented from the player's eyes (first-person viewpoint), 45% are presented showing the characters interacting from a distance, and 5% show characters as seen from directly above. Within violent games, half are presented from a first-person viewpoint, and half show the characters interacting from a distance. Three of the 20 games (15%) include profanity (all three are violent games and constitute 25% of the violent games).

Games are very realistic, both in terms of the portrayals of characters and settings and in terms of how realistic the graphics are. When considering how reality-based the settings are, raters gave scores at or above the scale midpoint for 100% of the games ($M = 3.6$ on the 0–4 scale, $SD = 0.67$). When considering how reality-based the main characters are, raters again gave high scores to 100% of the games ($M = 3.6$, $SD = 0.54$). Raters gave high scores to 85% of games when considering how realistic the graphics depicting the game setting are, and to 57% of games when considering the realism of the graphics depicting the game characters. The results are similar for violent video games.

Violent Game Characteristics

A number of game characteristics of the 12 violent games were rated (again on a 0 to 4 scale). Two thirds of violent games received scores at or above the scale midpoint for how violent the graphics are ($M = 2.2$, $SD = 0.77$), and 58% received high scores for how violent the auditory elements are ($M = 1.9$, $SD = 0.63$). Although most games (83%) received high scores for how reality-based the weapons are, only 50% received high scores for how realistic the weapons graphics are. Two thirds of games similarly received high scores for how reality-based the targets of violence are, although only 50% received high scores for how realistic the target graphics are. Half of violent games include objects as targets, and 42% include implicit targets (e.g., airplanes piloted by unseen living beings). Among violent games, 92%

include real weapons, 33% include science fiction weapons, and 8% include fantasy weapons.

Eighty-three percent of violent games received high scores for how instrumental the aggression was. Although only 45% of violent games received high scores regarding their extent of having a theme of retributional aggression, 82% had nonzero scores, indicating at least some amount of aggression as justified retribution. All of the violent games received high scores for rewarding aggressive behaviors. Twenty-five percent of violent games combine aggression and humor at least some of the time. Although only one game received a high score for showing disrespect for life (*StarCraft*), 42% of violent games received nonzero scores. Over half (58%) of the games include at least some elements of gratuitous violence. Of those games that include gratuitous violence, 22% reward the gratuitous violence and 33% punish the gratuitous violence. Seventeen percent of violent games have some aspects of sexualized violence.

Characteristics of Game Characters

Across the top 20 games, the characters are predominantly White male adults. Across the violent games, the characters are also predominantly White male adults.

Main Characters

Across the top 20 games, the main characters (28%) are predominantly male. Only 10% of main characters are female, whereas 70% are male and 20% could be either. Over two thirds of the main characters (68%) are White, with 11% Black and 11% Latino. Of the specifically male main characters, 77% are White, 8% are Black, and 15% are Latino. Of the two specifically female main characters, one is Black and one is Israeli. Ninety-five percent of main characters are portrayed as adults, and 90% are humans.

Secondary Characters

Across the top 20 games, a majority of the secondary characters (48%) are male (55%). Thirty-one percent of secondary characters are female and 14% can be either male or female or are mixed groups of males and females. Over two thirds of the secondary characters (72%) are White, with 10% Black, and 0% Latino, although 9% include mixed-race groups. Of the specifically male secondary characters, 78% are White, 11% are Black, 0% are Latino, 6% are American Indian, and 5% are other races. Of the specifically female secondary characters, 87% are White and 13% are other races. Sixtynine percent of secondary characters are portrayed as adults, and 73% are humans.

The category of secondary characters tends to show the greatest flexibility in age. Although few characters are portrayed as children, adolescents, or seniors, when these age characters do appear in games, they are most likely to be secondary characters. Furthermore, although not many characters are portrayed as needing rescue or as highly sexualized characters overall, when they appear, they appear as secondary characters. Characters needing rescue are about equally likely to be males or females in this sample of games (43% male, 29% female, 28% both/mixed), although only females are portrayed as highly sexualized. Characters portrayed as comrades are much more likely to be male than female, regardless of whether they are main characters (76% male, 10% female, 14% both/mixed) or secondary characters (59% male, 30% female, 11% both/mixed).

Target Characters

Across the top 20 games, many of the characters who are portrayed as targets (24%) are also portrayed as aliens or animals. This makes discerning character sex, race, and age more difficult. Among the target characters whose sex is identifiable, 89% are male and 11% are groups comprising both males and females. Eighty percent of the targets whose races were identifiable are White and the other 20% are Middle Eastern. Of the specifically male target characters, 75% are White and the other 25% are Middle Eastern. Eighty-nine percent of targets are portrayed as adults. Twenty-seven percent of targets are humans, with 37% humanoid aliens, 26% animals, 5% robots, and 5% groups containing both humans and humanoid aliens.

DISCUSSION

As predicted, the world of video games is largely populated by aggressive, White, male adults in roles of power. Females, minorities, and older adults are grossly underrepresented as heroes in both violent games and games in general. Over 70% of main characters are male and 95% of main characters are younger adults. When diversity of age is represented, most of it occurs in the secondary characters. There are only two female minority main characters in all the games examined.

Of the target characters, the majority are White males, with Middle Eastern males being the next most common type of target. This finding bears further analysis. Even though these video games were created before September 11, 2001, Middle Eastern males are overrepresented as targets of violence. In the world of violent video games, Middle Eastern males are characterized as likely, and perhaps appropriate, targets of violence.

Also as predicted, most of the top-selling games are violent ones, with 60% having violence as the main theme. These games, taken as a group, rated close to the scale's endpoint of *extremely aggressive*. The games were also rated as very realistic and as having high-quality graphics. The characters and settings of the violent games were rated as very reality based. The weapons in the games are very realistic as well, with 92% being real, available weapons.

Most of the games portray instrumental aggression and about half portray a clear theme of retribution, a variable known to increase aggression in the viewer. In violent games, one fourth combine aggression with humor and all reward aggressive behavior. Over half of the games contain gratuitous violence and slightly less than half contain clear depictions of disrespect for life (in addition to the actual killing). Almost one fifth of the violent games include sexualized violence. Only six (30%) of the top-selling games include non-Whites. The majority of these (two thirds) are aggressive games. The typical role of the depicted minorities is soldiers.

It is interesting to note that much of what ethnic diversity there is in these games is shown either on the control screens, where players hear the story line and choose game settings, or in movie-like trailers or plot points that are scattered throughout some games. Both account for a relatively small percentage of actual time spent playing the games. For example, there are two versions of *Tom Clancy's Rainbow 6* game: *Rogue Spear* and *Gold* editions. In each of these versions, headshots of military personnel appear on a control screen, along with their nationality. When the player actually plays the video game, the hero's personal characteristics are not highlighted in the action, as the hero is a first-person shooter. In *Command & Conquer: Tiberian Sun*, the actual game play shows small, indistinguishable characters fighting from a distance. However, short movies are interspersed between the main action. Diversity is relatively heavy in these films, which star the actor James Earl Jones as the general and feature minorities as soldiers. This series of live action films also features a sexualized, scantily clad, White female character.

In sum, these popular games feature realistic depictions of aggression with high-quality graphics and realistic depictions of weapons, characters, and settings. Characters lack diversity with respect to sex, age, and race. Though this theme is in the minority, there is a consistent element of sexualized violence. Given the link between depictions of sexualized aggression and violence toward women, even smaller amounts of sexualized violence, if consistent, are a concern. When diversity of race is represented, Blacks, Latinos, and Middle Easterners are often the non-Whites depicted. Asian characters are virtually nonexistent. This is especially noteworthy given that Asians represent a large percentage of the world population and that Asian companies such as Nintendo are a major force in the video game industry.

It is important to note that the content and graphics of video games are rapidly changing. This makes it important to keep the research current, especially with regard to content analyses. The games examined here are not the most extreme available. Perhaps the most graphically violent of recently released video games is *Soldier of Fortune*. This game strives to depict violence with extremely graphic realism, so much so that the game was classified as an adult movie in Canada. The game developers hired an army consultant to help design extremely realistic depictions of physical trauma by different types of weapons. Killers dismember victims with guns and victims' bodies are destroyed beyond recognition. The game's horror includes victims who scream "Help me" as killers reply "Shut up," tossing their knives playfully in the air after a kill.

The Grand Theft Auto series of video games has topped sales lists throughout the last several years. Currently, *Grand Theft Auto: San Andreas* is one of the top selling games in the country (Reuters, 2005b). In the *Grand Theft Auto* series, the player can steal cars, kill enemies and bystanders, have sex with a prostitute, and kill the prostitute afterward to get his money back. These games exemplify a trend toward graphically violent games that focus on glamorizing crime and antisocial behavior (Walsh, Gentile, Gieske, Walsh, & Chasco (2003). The National Institute on Media and the Family (NIMF) currently suggests that parents also avoid a game called *Leisure Suit Larry: Magna Cum Laude*. In this game, the main character has "a distinct talent for getting slapped whenever he is around women." The game contains, "nudity, strong language, strong sexual content, [and] use of alcohol." (NIMF, n.d., p. 1)

Fantasy–Reality Distinction: Debunking the Myth

An often-held belief is that only the youngest consumers cannot differentiate between fantasy and reality; therefore if a person knows what he or she is seeing is not really happening, then he or she cannot be affected by the content. This line of reasoning is seductive, yet deceptive. It is true that, up until about the age of 7, children do not distinguish fantasy from reality in a reliable and adult-like manner (Cantor, 1998) and are, therefore, especially vulnerable to media exposure. However, it would be an error to assume that those who understand what they see in the media is not real are invulnerable to the messages being presented. This conclusion ignores the way human beings, as social creatures, learn lessons from depictions of human social interactions, even if these interactions are not portrayed as real. As Dietz (1998, p. 439) noted about video game violence exposure, "even if the child accepts the notion that video games are not real, he or she may still not challenge the ideas and characterizations presented in them."

Children learn what behaviors are appropriate from watching media. Given the violent nature of many popular video games, one lesson they learn is that aggression is an acceptable, even appropriate, way to solve conflict (e.g., Anderson & Dill, 2000). Another lesson learned is that women behave in stereotypical ways: Namely, they are generally unimportant, are inferior to men, and function many times as the objects of sex and violence (Dietz,

1998). Thus, negative concepts such as sex role stereotypes and aggression are reinforced in video games.

Signs of Change

In its annual Video Game Report Card, the NIMF noted that the popular games for 2002 showed a focus on extreme violence, particularly violence toward women. The institute warned that popular games such as *Grand Theft Auto: Vice City* portray "the brutal murder of women as entertainment" (NIMF, 2003, ¶ 9). For example, in that game, "the player is rewarded if he murders a prostitute after having sex with her" (NIMF, 2003, ¶ 7). These negative changes call for an update on the current investigation.

Only a Game?

Currently, a Web site (www.huntingforbambi.com) is selling videos that depict men hunting naked women and inflicting pain by shooting their bare flesh with paint-gun pellets. The Web site advertises: "Men hunting naked women. It's about f**k'n time. That's right, bitch . . . it's hunting season!" (*Men Hunting Naked Women*, 2005). This sad game brings to life the type of targeted, sexualized violence against women that has increased rapidly of late on video game screens. Practicing such violence on the video game screen has made the move to real violence that much easier. Some have argued that depictions of violence against women and other groups are harmless because they are for entertainment only. Yet, we contend that it is precisely because such violence is depicted as entertainment that we should be concerned. Mass media normalize and actively train behaviors (Anderson & Dill, 2000). If, as we have demonstrated here, video games are violent and depict White males as heroes and minorities as victims and commonly show sexualized images of women, those images will be accepted by the culture and acted on.

As we go to press, the mayor and city council members of Washington, DC are attempting to pass legislation that would ban the sale of violent and sexually explicit video games to minors (Reuters, 2005a). Council member Fenty is quoted as saying these video games perpetuate "the worst of our society," (Reuters, 2005a, p. 3) and contribute to youth violence. Entertainment Software Association president Douglas Lowenstein responded by invoking free speech rights and by calling the issue one of parental responsibility. Also, Lowenstein said that there is not objective scientific evidence that video game playing causes aggression. Four major health organizations disagree with Lowenstein. In a joint statement to Congress, the American Academy of Pediatrics, American Psychological Association, American Academy of Child and Adolescent Psychiatry, and the American Medical Association concluded that the accumulated scientific research "point[s] overwhelmingly to a causal connection between media violence and aggressive behavior in some children" (Joint Statement, 2000, p. 1). The Federal Trade Commission (Federal Trade Commission, 2000) investigated the video game industry for marketing Mature-rated games to children and found "Of the 118 electronic games with a Mature rating for violence, the Commission selected for its study, 83, or 70 percent, targeted children under 17." (Federal Trade Commission, 2000, ¶ 1). It is unfortunate that the video game industry lobbyists have been successful at shooting down legislation to restrict access of youth to video games with violent and sexual content. Anderson and Bushman (2001) explain that while there is strong evidence of a link between media violence exposure and aggression, that the media misinform the public about this research. Possible explanations offered by Anderson and Bushman (2001) include the fact that media have a vested interest in the entertainment industry and that media consumers are motivated to believe that their media diet is not harmful (see also Dill, in press). Media researchers such as ourselves struggle to inform the public of the scientific evidence. In the case of negative elements in video games, such as those described here, there is strong resistance from industry, media, and even the public who consume media, against believing the type of scientific research reported here.

REFERENCES

Anderson, C. A., & Bushman, B. J. (2001). Effects of violent video games on aggressive behavior, aggressive cognition, aggressive affect, physiological arousal, and prosocial behavior: A meta-analytic review of the scientific literature. *Psychological Science, 12,* 353–359.

Anderson, C. A., & Dill, K. E. (2000). Video games and aggressive thoughts, feelings, and behavior in the laboratory and in life. *Journal of Personality and Social Psychology, 78,* 772–790.

Berkowitz, L. (1993). *Aggression: Its causes, consequences, and control.* New York: McGraw-Hill.

Braun, C. & Giroux, J. (1989). Arcade video games: Proxemic, cognitive and content analyses. *Journal of Leisure Research, 21,* 92–105.

Buchman, D. D., & Funk, J. B. (1996). Video and computer games in the '90s: Children's time commitment and game preference. *Children Today, 24,* 12–16.

Cantor, J. (1998). *"Mommy, I'm scared."* San Diego, CA: Harcourt Brace.

Cohen, A. (2000). New game [Playstation 2]. *Time, 156,* 58–60.

Dietz, T. L. (1998). An examination of violence and gender role portrayals in video games: Implications for gender socialization and aggressive behavior. *Sex Roles, 38,* 425–442.

Dill, K. E. (in press). Children at play? An essay on *Kids and Media in America, Human Development.*

Dill, K. E., & Dill, J. C. (1998). Video game violence: A review of the empirical literature. *Aggression and Violent Behavior: A Review Journal, 3*, 407–428.

Federal Trade Commission (2000). *FTC releases report on the marketing of violent entertainment to children.* Retrieved February 28, 2005 from http://www.ftc.gov/opa/2000/09/youthviol.htm

Funk, J. B. (1993). Reevaluating the impact of video games. *Clinical Pediatrics, 32*, 86–90.

Geen, R. G. (2001). *Human aggression.* London: Open University Press.

Gentile, D.A., & Anderson, C.A. (2003). Violent video games: The newest media violence hazard. In D. Gentile (Ed.) *Media violence and children* (pp. 131–152), Westport, CT: Praeger.

Gentile, D. A., Lynch, P. J., Linder, J. R., & Walsh, D. A. (2004). The effects of violent video game habits on adolescent attitudes and behaviors. *Journal of Adolescence, 27*, 5–22.

Griffiths, M. D., & Hunt, N. (1998). Adolescents' computer game dependency. *Psychological Reports, 82*, 475–480.

Huntemann, N. (Executive Producer/Director). (2000). *Game over: Gender, race and violence in video games* [Video]. (Available from the Media Education Foundation, 26 Center Street, Northampton, MA 01060)

Joint statement on the impact of entertainment violence on children: Congressional public health summit. (2000, July 26). Retrieved February 10, 2005 from http://www.aap.org/advocacy/releases/jstmtevc.htm

Men hunting naked women. (2005). Retrieved April 24, 2005, from http://www.huntingforbambi.com

National Institute on Media and the Family. (n.d.) *Kidscore rating: Leisure suit Larry.* Retrieved March 1, 2005 from http://www.mediafamily.org/kidscore/chart.asp?ID=10871

National Institute on Media and the Family. (2003). *MediaWise video game report card.* Retrieved July 29, 2003, from http://www.mediafamily.org/research/report_vgrc_2002-2.shtm

Paik, H. (2001). The history of children's use of electronic media. In D. G. Singer and J. L. Singer (Eds.), *Handbook of children and the media* (pp. 7–27). Thousand Oaks, CA: Sage.

PC data top games of all time. (1999, November 1). Available at http://pc.ign.com/articles/071/071728p1.html

PC data top games of 1999. (2000, January 24). Available at http://pc.ign.com/articles/074/074263p1.html?framint=1

Phillips, D. P. (1986). Natural experiments on the effects of mass media violence on fatal aggression: Strengths and weaknesses of a new approach. In L. Berkowitz (Ed.), *Advances in experimental social psychology* (Vol. 19, pp. 207–250). Orlando, FL: Academic Press.

Provenzo, E. F. (1991). *Video kids: Making sense of Nintendo.* Cambridge, MA: Harvard University Press.

Reuters. (2005a). *U.S. capital seeks ban on graphic video games*. Retrieved February 28, 2005 from http://www.numberonenews.com/video-games/us-capital-seeks-ban-on-graphic-video-games.htm

Reuters. (2005b). *January US video game sales flat*. Retrieved February 28, 2005 from http://www.entertainment-news.org/breaking/20382/january-us-video-games-sales-flat---analysts.htm

Ryan, J., & Wentworth, W. M. (1999). *Media and society*. Boston: Allyn & Bacon.

Song, E. H., & Anderson, J. E.(2001). How violent video games may violate children's health. *Contemporary Pediatrics, 5*, 102.

Turner, C. W., & Goldsmith, D. (1976). Effects of toy guns and airplanes on childrens' antisocial free play behavior. *Journal of Experimental Child Psychology, 21*, 303–315.

Vasil, L., & Wass, W. (1993). Portrayal of the elderly in the media: A literature review and implications for educational gerontologists. *Educational Gerontology, 19*, 71–85.

Video game sales. (2001, January 19). Video game sales slide 5 percent in 2000. *Reuters*.

Walsh, D. A. (1997, December). Whoever tells the story defines the culture. *Cornerstones 1*(3), 4–7.

Walsh, D., Gentile, D. A., Gieske, J., Walsh, M., & Chasco, E. (2003, December). *MediaWise video game report card*. Minneapolis, MN: National Institute on Media and the Family.

9

MAMA BEARS, BITCHES, AND MONSTERS: MOTHERHOOD AND VIOLENCE IN POPULAR FILM

LYNN EDITH PAULSON

The film *Snow White: A Tale of Terror* (Cohn, 1997) presents a new spin on a classic fairy tale. Claudia, played by Sigourney Weaver, is a middle-aged woman—powerful, self-possessed, and sexually confident. At the beginning of the film, she is about to become the second wife of the widower Friedrich Hoffman and stepmother to his young daughter, Lilliana, whose mother died in childbirth. Claudia is the daughter of a sorceress with mysterious powers of her own. She hopes her marriage to the powerful Hoffman will bring her the love and social acceptance she desperately desires. She is delighted when she finds herself pregnant after several years of marriage to Hoffman. Like many stepmothers in real life, and like all stepmothers in fairy tales, her relationship with her step-daughter is uneasy at best, marred with a subtle competition for Friedrich's attentions. Yet it is not until she miscarries her own child and is told she will never bear another that Claudia's madness is unleashed. Insane with grief, Claudia becomes obsessed with aging and consumed by jealousy toward the recently betrothed Lilliana, whose womanly beauty and sexuality have just begun to flower. The inhuman sorceress in Claudia emerges, and she begins a violent campaign that leaves chaos and death in its wake. During a battle with Lilliana at the climax of the film, Claudia bursts into flames when her magic mirror explodes.

Snow White: A Tale of Terror highlights some of the many complex issues and questions embedded in popular imagery of women's violence. First, every popular image of women's aggression poses the question: What is women's nature? These images, regardless of the story in which they are embedded, assert definitions of femininity and take a position somewhere on the terrain of cultural expectations around doing and being female. Even within the individual text, these positions can be both multiple and contradictory.

Second, what functions and whose interests do these images of female violence serve? Many images of females committing violence in popular film

131

simultaneously issue two distinctly different warnings, or morals, if you will. On the one hand, as King and McCaughey (2001) state, these images "take the wind out of the sails of the culture in which sex differences seem unalterable" and issue a "challenge (to) smug oppressors" (p. 6). The image of a woman delivering a well-deserved beating is a thrilling spectacle. At the same time, viewers offended by these images can find comfort in them because at the end of the day patriarchal social order is usually somehow restored. "Bad" women meet a bad end, and "good" women put down the gun or drive off a cliff. Beyond their entertainment value, these images are cathartic and validating for viewers on both counts, allowing the audience to "exorcise certain psychological demons" (Chesler, 2001, p. 198).

Finally, images of women's violence in popular culture are shaped by the historical moment in which they are produced. They reflect changing conditions of and beliefs about women. In spite of being based on a classic and dated fairy tale, *Snow White: A Tale of Terror* is a distinctly modern story. This film hit the big screen when women's capacity for aggression and violence was the issue du jour among contemporary feminists.

The past few years have seen a spate of scholarly and popular articles and books written about women's direct and indirect aggression. Recent work by feminists across disciplines has examined women's physical and emotional abuse of one another (Chesler, 2001), their children (Meyer & Oberman, 2001), and their domestic partners (Jones, 1996; Pearson, 1997) in the home (Denfeld, 1997), on the streets (Baskin & Sommers, 1998), in the classroom (Simmons, 2002), and on the screen (King & McCaughey, 2001).

This chapter joins this growing body of feminist analyses of women's violence. Within this volume devoted to the topic(s) of women and the media from the perspective of psychology, I develop this chapter around the broad question of what psychologists can learn from a feminist analysis of images of women's violence depicted in popular film.

For this chapter, I focus my analysis specifically on film images of and issues around violence and motherhood. I begin by discussing the issue of women's nature and its relationship to violence, from the perspective of both patriarchal and feminist ideologies. Within this section, I address the phenomenon of violence committed by women and the gulf between cultural beliefs about women's violence and the violence perpetrated by women. The second section of this chapter addresses the role of popular culture in shaping cultural mythology about women's nature with respect to violence. Developing this chapter in broad strokes provides the context for the third section, in which I discuss selected images of women's violence in relation to the role of motherhood in popular film. Here I explore in more detail the relationships between these images and cultural mythology about women's nature. I conclude with a discussion of some general implications of this mythology for an understanding and treatment of women's violence toward their children.

WOMEN'S NATURE, WOMEN'S VIOLENCE

In spite of women's increasing social, economic, and political gains, in spite of women's greater visibility and successes in every traditionally male bastion, the one place where people remain reluctant to accept women's presence is the realm of violence. As boxer and journalist Rene Denfeld (1997) put it most simply, "for all the behaviors that fall under the umbrella of aggression . . . there is one stereotype that defines it: it is considered male" (p. 7). Consider the public outrage when, in the summer of 2001, Andrea Yates drowned her five children in the bathtub of her suburban Houston home, echoing the reactions to the crime of Susan Smith several years earlier. Vanessa Friedman (1996) captured the public response to women's violence thus:

> The first thought that probably comes to mind when people hear about a woman who has committed murder is that a crime against nature has occurred. That is, primarily a crime against *her* culturally prescribed nature. Somehow nothing would seem as horrible or perverse as a woman who can kill. Women, after all, give life—they are not supposed to take it away. (p. 62)

The feminine nature of patriarchal cultural ideology is rigidly reductionist: Women are the gentler, nurturing sex, earthy, most deeply fulfilled by hearth and home, monogamous heterosexual partnerships, and, of course, motherhood. Women who kill, women who harm their children, women who are turned off by childbirth or indifferent to children, women who embrace a motto of "Me first!" and who take serious pleasure in energetic sexual activity and exploration outside the safe haven of straight, monogamous marriage fall outside the boundaries of prescribed femininity. Within the sexist ideology of patriarchal culture, women who are elderly and ugly are Other. Where female violence does occur, Pearson (1997) argued that "we seek a pre-emptive cause for female aggression that preserves an emphasis on female victimization" (p. 57). Overlooked is the role of drugs and alcohol in women's violence, for example, or the fact that many of the women in prison for violent crimes have a history of prior offenses (Jones, 1996). Society turns away from the fact that the most common victims of women's violence are their own children (Denfeld, 1997, p. 50). Instead, the focus is on childhood trauma (particularly sexual abuse), abusive partners, hormonal imbalance, and male influence, for example, to explain the causes of physical aggression in females and to lessen their culpability so as to allay one's sense of profound unease. No such explanations for the phenomenon of male violence are needed, because it does not disrupt one's sense of the social order to the same degree.

Feminists have engaged in a pitched battle with the worst excesses of patriarchal definitions of the feminine. At the same time, feminists have until very recently been squeamish when it comes to the issue of women's capacity for violence. Feminists have historically shared the belief of main-stream patriarchal culture that women are the nicer sex, and the fact that females are responsible for between an estimated 10 to 15% (Jones, 1996) of all violent crimes seems to bear that out. The one type of violence that has received widespread feminist attention is the phenomenon of battered women who kill. Feminists Lenore Walker (1980) and Angela Browne (1987), for example, have written extensively about this phenomenon in an ongoing effort to bring public attention to the epidemic of domestic violence and violence against women. Walker's concept of battered woman's syndrome has become part of popular consciousness and has been used successfully to fight criminal charges brought against women who have killed the partners who were committing horrific violence against them. Feminist attention to the issue of battered women who kill has helped the public to under-stand why women do not leave violent relationships with men and how these situations are, in effect, a case of kill or be killed. Feminist attention in the early 1980s to domestic violence also led to what Poorman (2001) described as the "uneasy task of acknowledging the presence of abuse in lesbian domestic relationships" (p. 8). Denfeld (1997) and Pearson (1997) have more recently written about women who batter their partners within heterosexual relationships.

Women batter. Women kill their children and their partners. Women are serial killers operating for longer periods and claiming more victims be-fore being apprehended compared with their male counterparts. Women run their own gangs and engage in street violence. Women participate in terror-ism. But the low absolute number of reported violent crimes committed by women supports the widespread belief that violent women are the exception, the monstrous—that aggression is by nature male.

As Denfeld (1997) argued, the focus on nature or biology in studies and explanations of aggression "allows us to ignore the many ways men and women are socialized differently" (p. 33). She argued further that the equation of physical violence with aggression "doesn't allow for the enormous differences between one kind of aggression and another" (p. 7).

Recent work by feminist scholars indicates a shift in feminist thinking about women and aggression, toward acknowledging aggression as a more broadly human trait shaped differently in males and females. As Simmons (2002) stated simply, "aggression may be biological, but the face of anger is learned" (p. 11). Recent work by Simmons (2002) and Chesler (2001) has focused on the influence of patriarchal beliefs about women's nature on so-cialization practices that lead to expressions of aggression and anger in pri-marily covert forms in women and girls. It is easy to dismiss these strategies as victimless crimes because the consequences are not visible on the body. But the emotional damage is real, because these alternative aggressions can be easily denied by the perpetrator and because they often exist within intimate relationships, making the victim unsure of her own perceptions about what has occurred. As Pearson (1997) explained, indirect or psychological aggression "is no less aggressive than punching walls or picking a fight. The violence is equally willful, the consequences equally drastic for family and community, and the motive arises from a similar place" (p. 22). At the same time, she pointed out that "the capacity of women to use masculine violence emerges very clearly in those societies that sanction its expression" (p. 13).

bell hooks (2000) argued that "the fact that women may not commit violent acts as often as do men does not negate the reality of female violence" (p. 63). Meyer and Oberman (2001) explored the long history and varied types of infanticide committed by women across cultures. Curry and Allison (1996) examined the role of rage in female-perpetrated violence. Baskin and Sommers (1998) undertook an extensive study of the violence of women and girls living in disenfranchised, inner-city America. What is clear is that aggression in females exists, takes a multitude of forms, and varies in motivation, and the perpetrators themselves do not fit a neat profile. Women's aggression is, as Dunn (1997) wrote, a "rich, multi-faceted reality that flatly contradicts the myths" (p. xiii).

POPULAR CULTURE AND THE MYTH OF WOMEN'S NATURE

Whether film, television, or print media, popular culture does not serve the function of representing the real world so much as it reveals, reinforces, and shapes the cultural beliefs, values, and myths held about the "real world." Ferrell (2000) argued that "when an act, tradition, or rule of conduct requires sanction by the culture and it, for whatever reason, remains outside the scope of legislation, the manner in which that rule is communicated is in literary form" (p. 10). As Gitlin (1994) explained, "major social conflicts become transported into the social system [through media], where the hegemonic process frames them" (p. 532). Film, as a primary vehicle of contemporary cultural mythology, "transforms the ideology of patriarchy and renders it invisible (Johnston, 1999, p. 32). The images represented in film are seen as "natural" or "the way things are" (Thornham, 1999, p. 12).

Within popular culture, then, differences in the cultural expectations for and beliefs about the violent behavior of men and women are asserted. At the same time, the functions these images serve are often multiple and contradictory. This is contested terrain. On the one hand, popular images support patriarchal mythologies about women's kinder nature by the example they make of female perpetrators. In this way, these images serve "as reminders of the supreme social order of patriarchy" (Friedman, 1996, p. 67). At the same time these images of women's violence bump up against humankind's sacred beliefs about the essential nature of women, shining a light into the darkest corners of the cultural unconscious, they fascinate. They *sell*. Moreover, the secret thrill that images of women's violence give female spectators in particular cannot be overlooked. As Elizabeth Wurtzel, author of *Bitch: In Praise of Difficult Women* (1998), stated wryly, "we may not *do* it, but we *get* it" (p. 148).

Images of Motherhood and Violence in Popular Film

Although patriarchal mythology about women's nature paints the female sex as gentler than the male, the one arena in which this tenacious image finds exception is motherhood and reproduction. This makes sense given that within patriarchal mythologies, feminine nature is inextricably tied to the ability to conceive and bear young. Indeed, even popular explanations for women's ordinary aggression appeal to her menstrual cycle. Within essentialist definitions of the feminine, woman's madness is determined by her very biology. It is expected that women will instinctually defend their offspring at the cost of their own lives and suffer unbearable grief over childlessness. In the first case, women's violence is sanctioned and, in the second, it is understandable. The image of the human mother bear defending and protecting her cubs can be found throughout popular culture, right alongside images of women suffering mental torment and reduced to violence as a result of a barren womb.

So powerfully rooted is the figure of the Mama Bear in cultural mythology that she emerges in popular culture even in nonmothers and in nonhuman monsters. For example, the tough-talking, independent, and childless Ellen Ripley (Sigourney Weaver) of the science fiction film *Aliens* (Cameron, 1986) becomes a tender surrogate mother to a lone orphan girl stranded on the planet LB 40, where Ripley has gone with a company of U.S. marines to defeat the monsters who have killed off the rest of the colonists. The final showdown between Ripley and the alien queen is nothing less than the Battle Royale of two Almighty Mothers defending their young. In the horror films *Species* (Donaldson, 1995) and *Species 2* (Medak, 1998), the violence of the female monster is motivated in the first film purely by the quest for offspring, and in the second film by the desire to defend her baby.

Back on Earth, *Dolores Claiborne* (Hackford, 1995) presents a more realistic and complex story of a woman wrongfully under suspicion for having caused the death of her employer, Vera. Flashbacks in the film reveal that Dolores (Kathy Bates) killed her husband, Joe, when she learned he was sexually molesting their young daughter. Although Joe was violent toward Dolores, it was only when she discovered Joe's sexual abuse of their daughter that Dolores determined, with the help of Vera, to arrange his death through an "accident."

Whereas the landmark film *The Burning Bed* (Greenwald, 1985) portrayed Francine Hughes as a cowering, cringing battered wife, Dolores is a proud smart-ass, who gives as good as she gets. Dolores lives by the motto that "sometimes being a bitch is all a woman has to hold on to." Whereas

Francine Hughes found no help for her perilous circumstances when she reached out to family, friends, or the law, Dolores expects none. In terms of the issue of domestic violence, The Burning Bed, which was based on a true story, was released as feminists were only beginning to raise public consciousness of the dangers women and children face in the home. By the time Dolores Claiborne was released, the ineffectiveness of the law in protecting women from violent partners was well documented.

Dowdy, overweight, middle-aged, and sharp-tongued, Dolores Claiborne at once supports and subverts traditional definitions of feminine nature. She is heroic and unpleasant, triumphant and pitiful. Like any "normal" mother, she would kill to defend her child, yet her relationship with her daughter is damaged and uneasy. The primary tension in this film is not the abuse and horror that lead to her violence (though this is the narrative path of the film), but the isolation of Dolores within the community for her character. In the town's eyes, she is hard inside and ugly outside, and this, not her acquittal, defines her fate.

Both Snow White: A Tale of Terror (Cohn, 1997) and The Hand That Rocks the Cradle (Hanson, 1992) preserve straightforwardly sexist explanations for women's madness and violence. In both cases, a barren womb unleashes a madness that takes the form of jealousy toward women who are younger or mated but, above all, able to bear children. The objects of their jealousy are virtuous, traditionally feminine, and without guile. In The Hand That Rocks the Cradle, Rebecca De Mornay plays a seductive, barren widow driven to insanity and homicide by the suicide of her husband and the subsequent miscarriage that leaves her unable to bear children. She becomes nanny to the children of the woman (Anna Sciorra) who blew the whistle on her husband, an OB-GYN who sexually violated his patients. De Mornay seeks revenge by trying to murder the prim stay-at-home mom and lay claim to her children, her husband, and her comfortable suburban life. At the climax of the film, the virtuous real mother kills the attempted pretender to her throne, thereby saving the family and preserving the traditional home.

Even the comedy Raising Arizona (Cohen, 1987) portrays a female police officer (Holly Hunter) abandoning her oath to uphold the law and kidnapping a baby when she learns her own womb "is a rocky place." Though the focus of the blockbuster thriller Fatal Attraction (Lyne & Haagensen, 1987) was the terrorizing madness of a single, professional woman dumped after a brief affair with a married man, she justifies her harassment in part by her desperate fear that the child she is carrying from the affair might be her last and only chance to be a mother. Like Rebecca De Mornay in The Hand That Rocks the Cradle, she envies the conventional life of her lover and his wife (Anne Archer), a simpering icon of unambitious femininity who shoots her rival dead through the heart and restores order in the family and home.

Popular culture stubbornly maintains that all women, even female monsters, are humanized through their mothering instincts and that their greatest (and sometimes only) virtue derives from this role. Where motherhood is thwarted by biology or where a mother's offspring are endangered, mayhem results, even in the most dubious of mothers. This impulse is drawn as "common sense." In another sense, this maternal instinct is naturalized in popular images through a second sort of equation between motherhood, violence, and biology. In films such as *Snow White: A Tale of Terror* or *The Nanny*, a 1965 film starring Bette Davis as a murderous caretaker, only fake mothers are aggressive toward children. Real (biological) mothers do not even entertain the impulse.

Implications for Psychology

At the simplest level, women continue to be the dominant caretakers of their children, and their children are the targets which women unable to control their aggressive impulses have the easiest access to. But "the unfortunate and ugly truth," wrote Denfeld (1997), "is [that] child abuse is one of the most common forms of violence in our culture, and women are responsible for most of it. According to state agency reports on child abuse, women are involved in twice as many incidents as men" (p. 50), ranging from emotional abuse to neglect to punches and kicks and murder. Denfeld argued that statistics on maternal aggression contradict biological explanations of violence that claim women as possessing natural instincts against aggression that men lack (p. 54). At the same time, popular culture unswervingly paints and validates women's violence in the service of protecting their offspring as the only sort of aggression natural to women. Such images reproduce a powerful cultural mythology that good mothering is an instinct rooted in biology (particularly in the act of giving birth), rather than a skill, and that only women who are evil or insane harm their children. Because these images are rendered as "common sense" within a patriarchal ideology, women "inevitably see themselves through these representations" (Thornham, 1999, p. 10).

What can psychologists learn from these images? Obviously, from the point of view of understanding causes of and providing treatment for maternal aggression, they do not serve us well. Both Denfeld (1997) and Meyer and Oberman (2001) made the point that the persistent cultural mythology about women's natural aversion to violence ignores "the confluence of factors" that shape maternal violence, the reality of the oppressive social conditions in which mothering exists, and the relationship of these conditions to women's violence toward their children (Meyer & Oberman, p. 17). The mythology inhibits women from seeking treatment and helps keep maternal child abuse a dark secret hidden inside the home. Caring for children is an overwhelming occupation under the best of circumstances. Meyer and Oberman described it as "arguably the most difficult labor any human ever engages in" (p. 171) and were also quick to point out that there are not enough resources to help (p. 176). In the context of social isolation, depression, unwanted pregnancies, the breakdown of extended and nuclear families, substance abuse, domestic violence between partners, and a sexist social morality that both romanticizes and undermines motherhood, women's violence toward children is less unthinkable.

That social factors contribute heavily to women's violence toward their children in no way divests perpetrators of the responsibility for their crimes. Rather, it suggests that this serious social problem must be pulled out from behind the veil of pernicious mythologies such as those asserted in popular images, and be examined more aggressively under the careful scrutiny of feminist social science, especially psychology, which, in treating individuals, may ignore important social factors at work in maternal aggression. At an even more fundamental level, psychologists must ask how this powerful and compelling mythology surrounding motherhood has shaped the lens through which they view, research, and treat women's violence toward their children. To this day, research on maternal aggression has been and continues to be lacking and seeks reductive explanations, such as childhood abuse, hormonal imbalance, psychosis, or moral failure. Women's violence toward their children is a complex phenomenon that is shaped and perpetuated by the culture in which it exists as well as by individual history. It varies considerably in its expression and causes. Only when this is understood can it be prevented or treated effectively and with compassion.

REFERENCES

Baskin, D. R., & Sommers, I. B. (1998). *Casualties of community disorder: Women's careers in violent crime.* Boulder, CO: Westview Press.

Browne, A. (1987). *When battered women kill.* New York: Free Press.

Cameron, J. (Director). (1986). *Aliens* [Motion picture]. United States: Twentieth Century Fox.

Chesler, P. (2001). *Woman's inhumanity to woman.* New York: Thunder's Mouth Press/Nation Books.

Cohen, J. (Director). (1987). *Raising Arizona* [Motion picture]. United States: Twentieth Century Fox.

Cohn, M. (Director). (1997). *Snow White: A tale of terror* [Motion picture]. United States: USA Films.

Curry, R. R., & Allison, T. L. (Eds.).(1996). *States of rage: Emotional eruption, violence, and social change.* New York: New York University Press.

Denfeld, R. (1997). *Kill the body the head will fall: A closer look at women, violence, and aggression.* New York: Warner Books.

Donaldson, R. (Director). (1995). *Species* [Motion picture]. United States: MGM/ UA Studios.

Dunn, K. (1997). Foreword. In R. Denfeld, *Kill the body the head will fall: A closer look at women, violence, and aggression* (pp. xi–xvi). New York: Warner Books.

Ferrell, W. (2000). *Literature and film as modern mythology*. Westport, CT: Praeger Publishers.

Friedman, V. (1996). Over his dead body: Female murderers, female rage, and western culture. In R. R. Curry & T. L. Allison (Eds.), *States of rage: Emotional eruption, violence, and social change* (pp. 62–73). New York: New York University Press.

Gitlin, T. (1994). Prime time ideology: The hegemonic process in television entertainment. In H. Newcomb (Ed.), *Television: The critical view* (pp. 516–536). Oxford: Oxford University Press.

Greenwald, R. (Director). (1985). *The burning bed* [Motion picture]. United States:Anchor Bay Entertainment.

Hackford, T. (Director). (1995). *Dolores Claiborne* [Motion picture]. United States: Castle Rock Entertainment.

Hanson, C. (Director). (1992). *The hand that rocks the cradle* [Motion picture]. United States: Hollywood Pictures.

Holt, S. (Director). (1965). *The nanny* [Motion picture]. United States: Twentieth Century Fox.

hooks, b. (2000). *Feminism is for everybody: Passionate politics*. Cambridge, MA: South End Press.

Johnston, C. (1999). Women's cinema as counter-cinema. In S. Thornham (Ed.), *Feminist film theory: A reader* (pp. 31–40). New York: New York University Press.

Jones, A. (1996). *Women who kill*. Boston: Beacon Press.

King, N., & McCaughey, M. (2001). What's a mean woman like you doing in a movie like this? In M. McCaughey & M. King (Eds.), *Reel knockouts: Violent women in the movies* (pp. 1–24). Austin: University of Texas Press.

Lyne, A., & Haagensen, C. (Directors). (1987). *Fatal attraction* [Motion picture]. United States: Paramount Studios.

Medak, P. (Director). (1998). *Species 2* [Motion picture]. United States: MGM/UA Studios.

Meyer, C. L., & Oberman, M. (2001). *Women who kill their children: Understanding the acts of moms from Susan Smith to the "Prom Mom."* New York: New York University Press.

Pearson, P. (1997). *When she was bad: Violent women and the myth of innocence.*New York: Viking.

Poorman, P. B. (2001). Forging community links to address abuse in lesbian relationships. *Women and Therapy: A Feminist Quarterly, 23*(3), 2–24.

Simmons, R. (2002). *Odd girl out: The hidden culture of aggression in girls*. New York: Harcourt.

Thornham, S. (1999). Introduction. In S. Thornham (Ed.), *Feminist film theory: A reader* (pp. 9–13). New York: New York University Press.

Walker, L. (1980). *The battered woman*. New York: Harper and Row.

Wurtzel, E. (1998). *Bitch: In praise of difficult women*. New York: Doubleday.

10

VIOLENCE AND WOMEN: NEWS COVERAGE OF VICTIMS AND PERPETRATORS

ELIZABETH K. CARLL

It was a hot, steamy day in New York City's Central Park on June 11, 2000; the annual Puerto Rican Day parade was winding down. A group of men, estimated to be at least 60 in number, became increasingly aggressive. They began spraying female passers-by with water, then holding some down, stripping their clothes off, and sexually assaulting them.
—E. K. Carll (2003)

What was even more shocking was the initial reaction by the police and the media during the first few days following the incident. The incident made international headlines; news stories recounted police statements minimizing the violence (the incident involved "a few women and a small group of roving men") and exonerated the police department's handling of the situation. It was not until several victims came forward to describe their experiences, including how their cries for help were ignored by the police, and several videotapes taken by bystanders surfaced, that the full picture was seen by the public.

Police sources and reports typically minimized the incident until enough pressure was brought to bear on the mayor, who then issued statements of outrage at such an occurrence and launched an investigation into the incident. Police sources were quoted as blaming the incident on an "overdose of testosterone and stupidity," as if hormones rather than the men themselves were responsible for the sexual assaults. In a *Newsday* (Long Island's largest daily newspaper) report (Levitt, 2000), a police spokeswoman being interviewed about the Central Park attacks asked why none of the victims used their cell phones to call 911 while under mass assault. It is interesting that she did not ask why none of the male bystanders called 911, nor did she mention that a number of the victims who did go directly to police at the perimeter of the park encountered a "boys will be boys" attitude.

Throughout the world, an increasing number of incidents of violence against women are being reported by news outlets. This increased news coverage has resulted in a continual bombardment of news stories recounting murder, rape, assault, and other atrocities. The media not only reflect what is occurring in society but also reinforce stereotypes of how women are viewed, as both victims and perpetrators of violence. Therefore, how the news media cover this social problem is vitally important, as they play a major role in shaping public opinion and public policy as well as influencing the ways in which children view the world. Some of these children will grow up to control tomorrow's media outlets.

In recognition of the need to address the alarming problem of domestic violence, UN Secretary-General Kofi Annan, in his message on November 25, 2001, on the occasion of the International Day for the Elimination of Violence Against Women, stated,

> Violence against women is not a 'women's issue,' but one that concerns us all—especially men. Indeed, men must work to confront what should be described as *men's* violence against women, and recognize and respect the equal role and rights of women. When it comes to violence against women, there are no grounds for tolerance and no tolerable excuses. (United Nations, 2001)

The 1992 study *Rape in America: A Report to the Nation* concluded that 1.3 women are raped per minute in this country (National Victim Center, 1992). Intimate partner violence is pervasive, with nearly 25 percent of women surveyed reporting that they were raped or physically assaulted by a current or former spouse, cohabiting partner, or date at some point in their lifetime (Tjaden & Thoennes, 2000). According to the U.S. Department of Justice (1994), 4,936 women were murdered in 1992. Women are five to eight times more likely than men to be victimized by an intimate partner, according to a U.S. Department of Justice Report (1998). Women account for 84% of those treated for injuries by intimate partners (Rand, 1997).

The frequency of violence against women appears to be related to a number of variables. However, it has been suggested that the way women are portrayed in the media may be an important contributing factor. Various forms of media, including TV, films, video games, music, and music videos, include depictions of violence against women that result in desensitization, with males being more accepting of violence (Jhally, 1995; Linz, Donnerstein, & Penrod, 1988; Peterson & Pfost, 1989). Cyberstalking, a relatively new phenomenon arising from the development of the Internet, can be viewed as the electronic media doorway into the real world of violence against women. The newly developing media technologies are used not only to depict violence against women but to actually stalk and directly perpetrate violence.

Unfortunately, there appears to be a commonly held impression that rape and violence against women are less significant than are other forms of violence against women. Unlike films with larger-than-life villains, the news media reflect real life. Many people view the news as disseminating real and accurate information as opposed to fictionalized story lines as in movies and TV. Therefore, the distorted representation of women and violence is even more detrimental as it will mislead the public into viewing these distortions as fact (Carll, 1999).

Although there is a dearth of studies of media reports on the portrayal of women and violence, those that have been done seem to substantiate current and previous observations about news reporting. For example, a few studies (Lemert, 1989; Schwengels & Lemert, 1986) have examined newspaper rape coverage and concluded that rape stories have fewer details than do stories about murder or assault and do not provide information that puts the crime into perspective.

In an attempt to explain the reason for violence against women, news reports tend to blame either the victim or the assailant. According to Pagelow (1981), there is an interest in looking for the reasons why a woman was beaten or raped, whereas with other crimes, few people ask why a person was robbed. As a result, rape victims may be denigrated and their privacy invaded (Benedict, 1993).

According to a study by Meyers (1994), this portrayal is tied to an ideology that reflects cultural myths and patriarchal assumptions about the proper role and behavior of women. By presenting stories of violence against women as separate isolated events, the news media reinforce the idea that the violence was an isolated pathology or deviance. Maintaining this mirage of individual pathology, the news media deny the social roots of violence against women and absolve the larger society of any obligation to end it.

In their study of newspaper coverage of sex crimes in England, Soothill and Walby (1991) found that the media avoids depicting sex crimes as possibly relating to men's and women's position in society and prefer instead to focus on a few disturbed individuals who commit atrocities (Meyers, 1994).

What was also notable about the Central Park attacks was that they involved not one or two people, but a large group. This phenomenon of mob violence may be more common among males in general than among deviant individuals in particular (unlike what is implied by the reports of group- or mob-perpetrated violence by fans at sporting events.) It is interesting that the following year, extra security was assigned to the Puerto Rican Day event and to subsequent parades to prevent a reoccurrence. Yet the extra security was not the only change; there was also a change in attitude on the part of police in dealing with these problems, which may have been fostered by public pressure and criticism.

However, female perpetrators are viewed quite differently by the public. In June 1993, Lorena Bobbitt severed her husband's penis after he allegedly raped her. Not only was the violation sensationalized, making international headlines, but this one incident resulted in frequent comments and jokes on talk shows expressing males' fears of such castration becoming a worrisome social trend and that other women might resort to this kind of sadistic violence. Yet the epidemic of violence against women is not viewed as a major social problem and has only recently received significant media attention in the wake of the high-profile TV coverage of the O. J. Simpson trial (Carll, 1999) and other incidents such as the Central Park attacks in 2000.

The way in which the news media report domestic violence cases also reflects the different way in which female perpetrators are depicted. This is especially notable in domestic violence reports. Several cases illustrate how differently the news media covers and portrays female perpetrators in comparison to their male counterparts.

Take, for example, the media frenzy following the Toogood incident. The *New York Daily News* headline referred to Madelyne Toogood as "Monster Mom." Toogood attracted national attention when she was caught on videotape punching her daughter in the backseat of her car, outside a department store in Indiana. The incident became fodder for discussion on numerous evening news and talk shows as to what the appropriate consequences should be (Siemazsko, 2002). Yet, a similar offense occurring later that month involving a male as the perpetrator barely made the news. Michael Brandt was arrested for assaulting his nephews with a belt in the bathroom of a Kew Gardens, New York, courthouse. He was at the courthouse to be a witness at the trial of his sister's son for rape and murder. Hearing a child crying out, prosecutors ran into the bathroom and found Brandt with a belt in his hand. Brandt explained he was disciplining his two young nephews. Very few details were reported in the brief news story; not even the boys' ages were mentioned (Schifrel, 2002). In addition, on September 28, 2002, a crawler at the bottom of the TV screen during a News 12 Long Island telecast included "man accused of beating child in gas station in Elmont." The story apparently did not warrant any further coverage as further details were not discussed.

Another incident occurred in October 2002 concerning a Long Island man, Steven Murphy, who beat his 9-month-old son to death. The incident was reported in the November 5 issues of both *Newsday* (Kelleher, 2002) and the *Daily News* (Harmon, 2002). In the articles Murphy was referred to as "Dad" in the title, whereas the pejorative adjective "Monster" was used in the Toogood case. Both articles on Stephen Murphy were less than a third of a page and were published on page 7 in *Newsday* and on page 26 in the *Daily*

News—a far cry from the front-page headlines given to the Toogood incident. The inequitable treatment of these incidents by the news media is even more magnified when the severity of the crime is taken into account: Toogood assaulted her daughter, whereas Murphy murdered his son.

Although it is understandable that the availability of a videotape of the Toogood assault may have contributed to increased TV coverage, it does not account for the disparity in the amount and content of the print coverage. The national and international coverage of the Toogood incident is sharply contrasted to the local coverage of the Brandt and Murphy cases.

Another classic example involves reports of domestic violence that occurred in Long Island, New York, where I live, which were reported in *Newsday* between 1995 and 1996. The following details and an analysis of the incidents are described in the book *Violence in Our Lives: Impact on Workplace, Home, and Community* (Carll, 1999).

I cited these incidents as a classic example because it is very rare to be able to compare cases from the same area, reported in the same newspaper, and occurring relatively closely in time; thereby, these variables are controlled better than they could be in cases from different regions or newspapers. Two of the three cases involved a husband who shot his wife and the third case involved a wife who shot her husband. In the two reports of husbands shooting their wives, the headlines included a reason for the murder (i.e., rage, making good on a threat) that explained the shooting or killing. In the report of the wife shooting her husband, no extenuating reasons were given. The wife did not merely shoot or kill but "blasted spouse with shotgun," which stresses the nature of the crime, not the reason. Perhaps most revealing of the slant of the news report was the description of the woman perpetrator in the latter part of the story: "the woman, who police said is disabled and uses a walker, was also taken to the hospital . . . where she was treated and released. It was not clear if she was injured by her husband or what her injuries were."

The image conjured up by the headline of a woman "blasting" her spouse contrasts greatly with her physical description. The most revealing aspect of the bias in reporting was the fact that the reasons (anger, making good on a threat) for the male perpetrator's actions were stated in the headline, yet the possible reason (self-defense) for the woman's action was mentioned only several paragraphs down even though it may have been an appropriate reason in view of the circumstances.

Two recent cases of family violence also illustrate how differently the news media portray and cover female perpetrators in comparison with males. Female perpetrators still continue to make international headlines, as in the case of Andrea Yates, a Houston, Texas, mother who confessed to drowning her five children in the bathtub on June 21, 2001. Prosecutors stated that Yates had a mental illness but knew the difference between right and wrong at the time of the drownings. Yates's mother-in-law described her as catatonic and not herself for months before the children were killed (Brown, 2002). Andrea Yates's husband was reported to be upset with the doctors who he believed did not properly medicate his wife during that period, as well as the insurance company, which he viewed as limiting her medical care (Frey, 2002). Yates was subsequently convicted of first degree murder after 3 hours of deliberation by a jury and then sentenced to life imprisonment. Because violence by females is more rare than male violence is, it often receives more media coverage as the media perceive it as unusual and unique. It is unfortunate that this exaggerated coverage of the uncommon event gives the public the false impression that female-perpetrated violence occurs more frequently than it actually does.

Yet, how many can recall the case of John David Battaglia, the Houston accountant who was reported to have shot his two daughters on May 2, 2001 (one month prior to the Yates incident) while on the phone with his ex-wife, so she could hear the shots (Associated Press, 2001)? The apparent reason for the shootings was anger at his ex-wife. Battaglia called his ex-wife and had his daughter get on the phone and say to her mom, "Why are you trying to have daddy arrested and have him put in jail?" Before his ex-wife could respond, she heard her daughter screaming, "No daddy! No!" and then she heard several gunshots. News reports indicated that he had previously been convicted of an assault, allegedly on his daughter. The Battaglia incident was written up in a one-half-page report with little follow-up, yet the Yates case, which allegedly related to mental illness, received widespread coverage.

The epidemic of violence against women is of serious concern as the majority of women who are victims of violence are raped, assaulted, and murdered by men they know. When the woman has the misfortune of knowing her attacker, these crimes are viewed as misdemeanor murders and rapes. Misdemeanor murder is a term I originated 10 years ago to illustrate that these crimes are not considered serious by many people (Carll, 1994, 1999).

The media stereotypes of women as victims of misdemeanor murders or rapes or perpetrators of heinous crimes not only influence the court of public opinion but, unfortunately, also become embedded in our justice system. Imagine a judge ordering a woman who was abused by her boyfriend to marry him. In a July 15, 1995, Associated Press (1995) report, a Cincinnati judge ordered a man who pleaded no contest to having punched his girlfriend in the mouth to marry her within 9 months or risk being jailed. "I happen to believe in traditional American values," stated Municipal Court Judge Albert Mestemaker. The judge said that he wrote the requirement (even though he knew it would not stand up legally) after he learned that the couple had been living together for 5 years and had a 5-year-old girl.

In February 1994, a Maryland man shot and killed his wife because she was unfaithful. (I first reported this case at a presentation at the 1994 American Psychological Association Annual Convention.) The judge imposed the minimum sentence of 18 months' jail time for the murder and was reported to have stated, "I seriously wonder how many men married five, four years would have the strength to walk away without inflicting some corporal punishment. . . . I am forced to impose a sentence . . . only because I must do it to keep the system honest." This incident was first reported by an Associated Press (1994a, 1994b) story that appeared as a brief description in a few newspapers. However, letters to the editors from concerned citizens (including me) who had seen the reports were published by major newspapers and ignited a discussion of the issue on several radio news talk shows (Carll, 1999).

Violence against women and crimes of passion by men have a long record in the history of cultural tolerance. These misdemeanor murders and assaults rarely make front-page news or form the basis for television movies. Yet, when the perpetrator is female, the consequences are very different. For example, Amy Fisher (better known as the Long Island Lolita) received a prison term of 5 to 15 years for the attempted murder of Mary Jo Buttafuoco. This punishment was far more severe than the 18 months the Maryland man received for killing his wife. The Fisher story resulted in a media frenzy that continued for over a year and even resulted in three separate television movies.

With globalization of information and news coverage, it can be seen that biased news coverage is not unique to the United States. Although cross-cultural research on news coverage of violence and women is virtually nonexistent, observations by this author indicate similar trends in other parts of the world. With the increasing global influence of the news media, it is essential to become aware of these biases and promote objective media coverage. It is important that all cultures appropriately address the problem of violence against women and that the news media do not contribute further to the problem.

The impact of news coverage of violence and its implications for public policy are also very important. Increased media attention to violence and terrorism in the wake of the 9/11 World Trade Center disaster has focused the spotlight on the Middle East. As a result, stories about violence against women and honor killings have been appearing in the news. The publication of such atrocities has brought world attention to the problem, along with increased efforts to effect social, judicial, and legislative changes.

For clinicians, these biases can also affect the treatment of women who are or have been involved in violent relationships. It is not unusual for me to see a woman in therapy who has had a therapist, sometimes male, who advocated teaching the patient how to cope with violent situations, rather than supporting her if she should choose to leave. Often these women experience considerable feelings of guilt for taking the children away from their father figure; this guilt, combined with the potential reduced economic quality of life and fear of not being able to support themselves and their children, makes it difficult, if not impossible, to leave.

The treatment of abused women has also been affected by these biases. For example, more than 10 years ago (Carll, 1992), I spoke about violence against women at a conference for mental health professionals and members of a bar association. When I asked the audience how many treated women who were in abusive relationships or violent situations, all hands went up. When I asked how many treated individuals in such situations, again most of the hands went up. When I asked how many treated couples conjointly in such situations, the majority of hands went up. This was a surprising response, as it had been my experience and opinion that when dealing with violent relationships, conjoint therapy is at best ineffective and at worst dangerous. Often the woman pays dearly after the therapy session if she is honest during the session. The husband whose main objective is to control his wife also wants to control the therapy, which often is the motivation for the partner to agree to or desire couple or marital therapy. Women are also at most risk when attempting to leave a violent relationship. Discussing this option in therapy with the offending partner further increases risk of violence. Fortunately over the years, with the application of this knowledge, far fewer therapists advocate conjoint marital therapy for violent relationships.

The treatment of choice for the abused partner is individual treatment combined with a support group, if appropriate. For the abuser, group therapy focusing on anger management techniques, preferably with a male therapist, would be the treatment of choice. Group interventions, with cognitive behavioral techniques, have been reviewed in the research literature, with some reporting significant successful outcomes (Hamberger & Hastings, 1993; Tolman & Bennett, 1990). It should also be kept in mind that only a small percentage of violent and abusive persons are women; however, perpetrators are predominantly male, with 92% of all domestic violence incidents committed by men against women (U.S. Department of Justice, 1994). According to the National Institute of Justice and the Centers for Disease Control and Prevention Report (Tjaden & Thoennes, 2000), intimate partner violence is perpetrated primarily by men, whether against male or female intimates. Thus strategies for preventing intimate partner violence should focus on risks posed by men.

News coverage represents windows into the community and the world. There is a long history of cultural tolerance of violence against women. For this to change, it is imperative that news accounts about violence be reported in an accurate, unbiased manner regardless of the gender of the victim and perpetrator.

The following are recommendations to deal with the preceding issues:

- To help begin to change this pervasive bias, research is needed to document and publicize the often distorted news reports of violence against women.

- The news media can also be a very helpful tool to draw attention to the inequities in sentencing based on gender and to influence the court of public opinion and eventually public policy.
- Children are also exposed to TV news reports and incorporate this information into their perception of the world. Media literacy training for children should include not only critical evaluation of how violence is portrayed but also attention to gender-role stereotypes in the news.
- As a result of the epidemic nature of problems of violence against women, specialized training including sensitivity to bias in the treatment of victims of intimate relationship violence should be required as part of all clinical, judicial, and law enforcement training programs.

Objective news coverage and dissemination of information may be one of the most powerful tools in reducing the pervasive problem of violence against women. Merely reporting incidents and statistics is not sufficient and can even be misleading. Most important is how this information is crafted. The accuracy and objectivity of news reports is of great importance, as the news media legitimize subjective biases by appearing to report objective accounts of community and world events.

REFERENCES

Associated Press. (1994a, October 19). Furor on sentencing 1 1/2-year term for killing wife. *Newsday*, p. A4.

Associated Press. (1994b, October 19). Man kills wife for infidelity; gets 18 months. *New York Times*.

Associated Press. (1995, July 15). Marriage ordered in Ohio abuse case. *Newsday*, p. A4.

Associated Press. (2001, May 4). Man held in daughters' deaths—On phone with child, ex-wife heard shots. *Newsday*, p. A20.

Benedict, H. (1993). *Virgin or vamp: How the press covers sex crimes*. New York: Oxford University Press.

Brown, A. K. (2002, February 20). Mother-in-law says Andrea Yates was 'catatonic' weeks before she drowned her children. *Associated Press Worldstream*.

Carll, E. K. (1992, April). Violence against women: Psychological issues. In E. K. Carll (Chair), *Violence against women: Psychological, medical, and legal issues*. Nassau/Suffolk Law Services and Suffolk County Psychological Association Symposium, Adelphi University, Huntington, NY.

Carll, E. K. (1994). *Psychological perspective on the media's portrayal of women and violence*. Paper presented at the American Psychological Association Annual Convention, San Francisco, CA.

Carll, E. K. (1999). *Violence in our lives: Impact on workplace, home, and community*. Boston: Allyn & Bacon.

Carll, E. K. (2003). News portrayal of violence and women: Implications for public policy. *American Behavioral Scientist, 46*, 1601–1610.

Frey, J. (2002, March 16). A gray end to tragedy; In Houston, a sentence concludes the drama of Andrea Yates' story. *The Washington Post*, p. C1.

Hamberger, L. K., & Hastings, J. E. (1993). Court-mandated treatment of men who assault their partners: Issues, controversies, and outcomes. In N. Z. Hilton (Ed.), *Legal responses to wife assault: Current trends and evaluation* (pp. 188–229). Newbury Park, CA: Sage.

Harmon, B. (2002, November 5). Charge dad pummeled tot to death. *Daily News*, p. 26.

Jhally, S., (Ed.). (1995). *Dreamworlds II*. Northampton, MA: Media Education Foundation.

Kelleher, J. S. (2002, November 5). Dad beats infant to death, cops say. *Newsday*, p. A7.

Lemert, J. B. (1989). *Criticizing the media: Empirical approaches*. Newbury Park, CA: Sage.

Levitt, L. (2000, June 26). ONE POLICE PLAZA / Confidential / Ex-Chief: 'The Key Is Planning.' *Newsday*, p. A14.

Linz, D., Donnerstein, E., & Penrod, S. (1988). Effects of long-term exposure to violent and sexually degrading depictions of women. *Journal of Personality and Social Psychology, 55*, 758–768.

Meyers, M. (1994). News of battering. *Journal of Communication, 44*, 47–63.

National Victim Center and the Crime Research and Victim Center (1992). *Rape in America: A report to the nation*. Charleston, SC: Author.

Pagelow, M. D. (1981). *Women battering: Victims and their experiences*. Beverly Hills, CA: Sage.

Peterson, D. L., & Pfost, K. S. (1989, February). Influence of rock videos on attitudes of violence against women. *Psychological Reports, 64*(1), 319–322.

Rand, M. R. (1997, August). *Violence-related injuries treated in hospital emergency departments*. Bureau of Justice Statistics, Special Report. Washington, DC: U.S. Department of Justice.

Schifrel, S. (2002, September 26). Cops charge witness belted kid at court. *Daily News*, p. QLI1.

Schwengels, M., & Lemert, J. B. (1986, Spring). Fair warning: A comparison of police and newspaper reports of rape. *Newspaper Research Journal, 7*, 35–42.

Siemaszko, C. (2002, September 24). Monster mom will visit girl. *Daily News*, p. 4.

Soothill, K., & Walby, S. (1991). *Sex crime in the news*. London: Routledge.

Tjaden, P., & Thoennes, N. (2000, July). *Extent, nature, and consequences of intimate partner violence: Findings from the National Violence Against Women Survey*. Washington, DC: National Institute of Justice and Centers for Disease Control and Prevention.

Tolman, R. M., & Bennett, L. W. (1990). A review of quantitative research on men who batter. *Journal of Interpersonal Violence, 5,* 87–118.

United Nations. (2001, November 20). *"When it comes to violence against women, there are no grounds for tolerance," says Secretary-General in message for International Day* [Press Release SG/SM/8040 OBV/250]. Available at http://www.un.org/news/press/docs/2001/sgsm8040.doc.htm

U.S. Department of Justice. (1994, January). *Violence against women*. Bureau of Justice Statistics. Washington, DC: Author.

U.S. Department of Justice. (1998, March). *Violence by intimates: Analysis of data on crimes by current or former spouses, boyfriends, and girlfriends*. Washington, DC: Author.

11

GENDER AND THE PORTRAYAL OF DIRECT AND INDIRECT AGGRESSION ON TELEVISION

NORMA D. FESHBACH

A peaceful and sylvan setting. Five second-grade girls are playing jacks on the patio of Laura's house. Their voices are calm and the mood is pleasant. They stand up. The game is finished. Ellen rushes over to Leah and stands quite close to her and makes the following announcement: "Next Saturday is my birthday and I'm having a circus birthday party." A smile invades Leah's face as she inquires: "Am I invited?" A smile also invades Ellen's face as she responds and utters an emphatic "No!" Nicole, Laura, and Natasha stand by quietly awaiting the verdict. Psychologists today would label Ellen's behavior as an example of indirect aggression.

This type of behavior can also be observed on television. When Raymond's mother (in the program *Everybody Loves Raymond*) rolls her eyes in a social context whenever her daughter-in-law makes a suggestion or serves something she cooks, or when Elaine (in the program *Seinfeld*) makes a derogatory remark about a close friend who has just left the room, each is displaying indirect aggression. These behaviors are considered to be aggressive because, like direct aggression, their goal is to hurt or injure another. Although not appearing to be overtly aggressive, devaluing others, besmirching their reputation, or denigrating their efforts can be as destructive as a direct physical or verbal assault. Studies of aggression, whether carried out in the laboratory, naturalistic contexts, or the media, should include indirect forms of aggression. The focus of this chapter is on the portrayal of indirect aggression on TV, especially with regard to the gender of the TV character.

The investigation of aggression on TV and its effects on the behavior of children has a long and sometimes conflicting history. The general consen-

This project was partially supported by a research grant from the UCLA Academic Senate, 2002–2003.

sus is that television violence can cause children to engage in aggressive behavior and to develop values conducive to behaving aggressively in resolving
conflicts. This conclusion was reflected in the final report of the American
Psychological Association Task Force on Television and Society (Huston et
al., 1992) and is consonant with an earlier judgment reflected in the report
issued by the National Institute of Mental Health (Milavsky et al., 1982).
Also, according to Paik and Comstock (1994), the findings from a meta-
analysis they carried out firmly established the relationship between violence
and antisocial and aggressive behavior. They concluded that "whether one
examines laboratory experiments or surveys, simulated aggression, minor aggression, illegal and seriously harmful activities, or a narrow category of everyday interaction such as unconstrained interpersonal conflict, the pattern
is the same" (p. 536).

Most of the research on which these generalizations are based has focused on the physical, more direct manifestations of aggression both in the
viewer and as depicted on television (Comstock & Scharrer, 1999; Gerbner,
1972; Paik & Comstock, 1994). When measures of verbal aggression, defined as diminishing or hurtful statements, are included in the analysis, an
infrequent procedure, the rate of observed aggressive acts more than doubled
(Greenberg, 1980; Paik & Comstock, 1994). Also, when verbal indices are
involved, situation comedies match other programs in frequency of aggressive incidents. On television, females manifest more verbal aggression than
do males (Greenberg, 1980; Paik & Comstock, 1994). Although there have
been studies of verbal aggression, there have been no studies, as yet, of indirect aggression on television.

Indirect aggression refers to behaviors that deliberately inflict pain on
another person other than through direct physical or verbal attack. Examples
of indirect aggression include such behaviors as spreading malicious rumors
about another individual, deliberately rejecting another's overtures to hurt
him or her, and denigrating the contributions or attributes of another person
to devalue that person—that is, social actions that intentionally but indirectly hurt another person. Most psychological research on aggression, including aggression on television, has focused on physical aggression and, to a
lesser extent, has assessed direct verbal aggression. However, indirect aggressive behavior, until recent times, has received little attention in psychological writings.

The topic of indirect aggression, also referred to as relational or social
aggression, has been the object of considerable attention in recent years in
both the scientific literature (Björkqvist, Lagerspetz, & Kaukiainen, 1992;
Björkqvist, Österman, & Lagerspetz, 1994; Crick, 1996; Crick, Casas, &
Mosher, 1997; Crick et al., 1999; Lagerspetz, Björkqvist, & Peltonen, 1988;
Österman et al., 1998) and popular media. Examples of more popular treatments of indirect aggression are *Queen Bees and the Wannabees* (Wiseman,
2002), *Odd Girl Out: The Hidden Culture of Aggression in Girls* (Simmons,

2002), and *The Secret Lives of Girls* (Lamb, 2001) and segments on television programs such as *Oprah* and *48 Hours*. The theme of these popular treatments is that girls engage in destructive, hurtful behaviors to their peers that are nonphysical and most often not direct. This attention in the popular media to more covert forms of aggression is paralleled by systematic investigations of indirect aggression carried out by Björkqvist and Lagerspetz and by Crick and her colleagues.

This interest in indirect aggression reflects a recognition of the varied ways in which individuals can hurt or inflict injury on each other. The flavor of indirect aggression is conveyed in several studies that I conducted some three decades ago.

In my initial study, published in 1969 (Feshbach, 1969), I monitored 6- to 7-year-old children's modes of response to outsiders. Children's behavioral interactions during two experimental sessions were rated on three categories: direct aggression, indirect aggression, and approach behavior. Subcategories for indirect aggression were ignoring, avoiding, refusals, and exclusions—all behaviors that reflected active rejection of another child. In this study, I found that the initial response of girls, within a two-person dyad, to a new member, whether a boy or girl, was more likely to be one of exclusion and rejection compared with the responses of the boys. It is interesting that the results and implications of this first study were not well received by leading developmental researchers at that time. The findings of greater indirect aggression among females than males ran counter to the prevailing view of greater aggression among males.

A follow-up study (Feshbach & Sones, 1971) with adolescent males and females reflected developmental consistencies in the use of indirect aggressive behaviors. Adolescent junior high girls made less favorable judgments of the newcomer than did adolescent junior high boys. Also, on the behavior interaction measures obtained during a problem-solving task, females displayed more excluding behaviors than did males. The more recent work of Björkqvist et al. (1994) and of Crick (1996) and their associates has made use of questionnaire measures to assess indirect aggression in a number of different age groups and in a variety of social contexts. This research has yielded a number of important relationships and has reflected the cross-national generality of gender differences in indirect aggression. It has also established the salience of indirect aggression as a meaningful aspect of aggressive behavior (Österman et al., 1998).

Inasmuch as indirect aggression has been demonstrated to be a significant aspect of human aggressive behavior despite initial resistance to the concept, it should be included, along with physical aggression and direct verbal aggression, in the assessment of aggressive content on television, as well as in the analysis of aggressive behaviors in natural settings. Given the salience of the interest in aggressive content on television and given the social policy implications that have been drawn from the effects of witnessing aggressive content, it seems relevant to include a broad spectrum of aggressive behaviors as displayed on television.

I recently surveyed and analyzed the presence of indirect aggression on television programs. The method and findings of this study (Feshbach, 2002) are the primary foci of this chapter. Gender differences in the portrayal of indirect aggression are of special interest given the evidence of greater indirect aggression of females relative to males. The implications of the findings are evaluated in light of the attention being paid to the question of alleged female meanspiritedness (Wiseman, 2002).

This study had two objectives: (a) the determination of the frequency with which different types of aggressive behavior were depicted on popular television programs—including direct aggression (physical, verbal, gestural) and indirect aggression (social and relational)—and (b) the determination of gender differences in the degree to which different types of aggressive behavior are manifested by male and female TV characters.

OBSERVATION SCHEDULE

A detailed observation schedule assessing physical, verbal, gestural, and indirect aggression was developed. Physical aggression included any physical act of actual or intended harm (e.g., hitting, kicking, shoving) whereas verbal aggression referred to behaviors such as teasing, yelling, and threats aimed at an object who was present. Examples of gestural aggression included any nonverbal gesture, such as raising a fist, sticking out a tongue, or manifesting a dirty look, directed at an object who was present and aware of the gesture. Indirect aggression included such behaviors as excluding, ignoring, gossiping, and rejecting. These different categories of aggressive behaviors were comparable to the types of behaviors observed in social interactions in more naturalistic contexts. The observation schedule included a column listing the names of the characters in the observed programs, with their gender specified.

Reliability was established on a sample of similar programs before experimental observations began. Four different pairs of observers participated in the reliability phase of the study. Preliminary training was conducted until the observers approached satisfactory reliability. The final assessment of reliability entailed each pair observing a half-hour program and a one-hour program. The observation schedule was divided into 3-minute segments. Within each segment a particular category of aggression could be scored only once. However, several different categories of aggressive behavior could be scored within a single 3-minute segment. The gender of the television character carrying out the aggressive act was noted for each instance of aggressive behavior. Reliability was calculated by deriving a percentage of number of agreements divided by the total number of agreements plus disagreements for each observer pair. Reliability was greater than 75% between each pair of observers.

PROGRAMS

To help me select those television programs that are likely to be observed by older adolescents and young adults, a class of high school seniors and a class of college juniors were administered a brief questionnaire to determine their favorite television programs. Their responses were used as a major criterion in selecting programs for the study. In addition, the following criteria were also used: The programs should include central and significant supporting characters of both genders; the television programs should be aired between the hours of 7:00 and 11:00 p.m. on weekday evenings and aired on one of the major broadcast networks; and the programs should be listed in the top 100 most watched shows according to the Nielsen ratings (Nielsen Media Research, 2001). On the basis of these criteria the following 12 television programs were included in the observations: six 30-minute programs (*Friends, Seinfeld, Everybody Loves Raymond, Grounded for Life, Frasier,* and *Just Shoot Me*) and six 1-hour programs (*ER, Dawson's Creek, NYPD Blue, Ally McBeal, Malcolm in the Middle,* and *Gilmore Girls*).

METHOD

Observers watched the shows in pairs. Each instance of aggression manifested by a main character during a 3-minute interval was recorded. A main character was defined as any character who had a recurring role (i.e., appeared in multiple episodes) or any character who was on screen for at least one tenth of the episode. The scoring of each behavior was based on the mutual decision of the observer pairs. Two episodes of each program were observed.

FINDINGS

The frequency of physical, verbal, gestural, and indirect aggressive behaviors for each television character was determined by summing across 3-minute intervals used in scoring each of these behaviors. Many of the male and female television characters did not manifest any physical, gestural, or indirect aggression. As a result, for these categories of aggression it was inappropriate to use means, and chi-square was used instead. The number of males and females obtaining zero scores and the number obtaining greater than zero scores were determined for physical, gestural, and indirect aggression, respectively.

The data for physical aggression are presented in Table 11.1. It is evident from this table that the proportions of male and female TV characters who displayed physical aggression are quite similar. An incidental finding, but highly

TABLE 11.1
Frequency Differences in Depiction of Physical Aggression as a Function of Gender and Program Length

Program length	Frequency	Males	Females
1 hour	0	35	20
	>0	18	10
½ hour	0	15	11
	>0	0	3

relevant to the format in which aggression is depicted, is the data reflecting a very low incidence of physical aggression in the half-hour programs.

Verbal aggression was portrayed more frequently than was physical aggression and the distribution of verbal aggression scores permitted mean comparisons between genders. These data are presented in Table 11.2. For the 1-hour programs, the verbal aggression scores for females were significantly higher than those for males. Male and female verbal aggression scores for the half-hour programs were quite similar. Although half-hour programs do not depict much physical aggression, the degree of verbal aggression is quite high. The greater incidence of verbal aggression in half-hour programs as compared with hour programs is even larger than indicated. The scores for the half-hour programs should be doubled to make them comparable with the hour programs.

The data for gestural aggression are presented in Table 11.3. The only difference here of note is the greater proportion of males in the half hour as compared with the hour programs displaying gestural aggression. It is as if for half-hour programs that male physical aggression has been replaced by male gestural aggression.

Of special interest is the result for indirect aggression. The pertinent data are presented in Table 11.4. Overall, a greater proportion of females than males display some degree of indirect aggression. For the one-hour programs 32% of males displayed some form of indirect aggression. More female characters, however, manifested instances of indirect aggression during the hour programs. Fifty percent of female characters displayed one or more indirect aggressive behaviors in the hour-long presentations. The gender difference in this form of aggressive behavior is particularly striking for the half-hour programs. Almost every female character (93%) during the half-hour programs engaged in indirect aggression whereas less than half of the male characters (40%) did so. In half-hour shows indirect aggression has essentially been made normative for female characters.

IMPLICATIONS

Before inferences are drawn from the data that I have presented, I want to emphasize that the programs that have been analyzed are not a random or

TABLE 11.2
Means Differences in Depiction of Verbal Aggression as a Function of Gender and Program Length

Program length	Males	Females
1 hour	1.7	2.5
½ hour	3.3	3.1

Note. Distribution of scores permitted calculation of means.

representative sample. There would undoubtedly have been more instances of physical aggression if more crime dramas had been included. However, the viewed programs were all popular ones. They were selected because they aired in prime time as well as had many viewers. Although it is not surprising that there is more physical aggression in hour than in half-hour programs, it is of interest that the relative incidence of verbal, gestural, and indirect aggression is higher in the half-hour programs, which are primarily comedies. Although these comedies may be funny, they are not devoid of hostility. In fact, hostile barbs and malicious attributions (scored as verbal aggression) are among the primary sources of humor. Various forms of indirect aggression also loom large in situation comedy humor. Backbiting, negative rumors, exclusions, and sly rejections, all for the sake of humor, are used extensively in these half-hour comedies. The full import of these program format differences (half hour and hour) lies in the kind and degree of aggression displayed by the different genders.

Gender differences between males and females are most marked for verbal and indirect aggression. Females are portrayed on television as more verbally aggressive than males in the hour-long programs that were sampled in this study. Female characters are also portrayed as more indirectly aggressive than are male characters, particularly in the half-hour programs. In these programs, which are largely comedies, indirect aggression assumes the status of a character trait of females.

The gender differences in patterns of aggression manifested by television figures bear some correspondence to gender differences in modes of aggression that have been found in the literature on sex differences in aggression. With regard to physical aggression there was little correspondence (Coie & Dodge, 1998). In this sample of programs I found essentially no gender difference in the depiction of physical aggression. Also, in the empirical literature the findings for gender differences in verbal aggression are inconsistent (Coie & Dodge, 1998). The correspondence between the real world and the television is closer in the case of indirect aggression.

Even with respect to indirect aggression, there is some discrepancy between fantasy and reality. Although the empirical literature clearly reflects gender differences in indirect aggression (Crick, 1996), these gender differences are not as sharp and dramatic as conveyed in the half-hour television programs. The picture of females reflected in these programs is more of a

TABLE 11.3
Frequency Differences in Depiction of Gestural Aggression
as a Function of Gender and Program Length

Program length	Frequency	Males	Females
1 hour	0	36	22
	>0	17	8
½ hour	0	3	8
	>0	12	6

match with the more sensational image of females represented in the recent flurry of popular articles and books depicting females, especially preteen girls, as catty, mean, selfish, and exclusive (Lamb, 2001; Simmons, 2002; Tavris, 2002; Wiseman, 2002).

The question is then raised whether this portrait of female aggression has an influence on the development of girls. Most researchers have concluded that the depiction of physical aggression on television has increased the level of aggressive behavior, primarily physical aggression, in viewers. Given the research on indirect or social or relational aggression in females, it would appear reasonable to explore the possible effects of observing indirect aggression on television on viewers, particularly female viewers.

Further research assessing a wider sampling of programs is needed to confirm these findings regarding gender differences in television's depiction of indirect or social aggression. However, the research discussed here does indicate that indirect aggression displayed on television can be reliably assessed and investigated. From the perspective of social policy makers, the effects of the display of indirect aggression may be of little concern inasmuch as indirect aggression does not entail physical harm and property destruction. However, from a developmental perspective, it is important to determine whether television is among the socializing agencies that foster the development of indirect aggression. The more general issue of the factors implicated in the development of indirect or social aggression was not addressed extensively in this chapter. Although research on indirect aggression is a burgeoning field, many gaps remain in the field's understanding of the relevant variables. The presence of lacunae facilitates overgeneralization and exaggeration. What is required is research to help fill in the lacunae in the field's knowledge of the antecedents and patterns of indirect aggression as well as research investigating the display of indirect aggression on television and research addressing the effects of viewing indirect aggression.

Also required is an understanding of the social and developmental context in which gender differences in indirect aggression occur. Women are more socially oriented than are men (Block, 1973) and develop verbal skills at a younger age (Maccoby & Jacklin, 1974). They are less physically powerful than men and, perhaps more important, physical aggression is not consonant with their gender role. And, perhaps most important, assertive behav-

TABLE 11.4
Frequency Differences in Depiction of Indirect Aggression as a Function of Gender and Program Length

Program length	Frequency	Males	Females
1 hour	0	34	15
	>0	19	15
½ hour	0	9	1
	>0	6	13

ior by females is more likely to be labeled as aggressive and unacceptable than is comparable behavior by males (Freundl, 1977). As a result, women are more likely than men to engage in conversations in social settings in which dislikes of or anger toward some absent party is discussed—that is, indirect aggression.

Although women are more likely to engage in indirect aggression than are men, it is all too easy to exaggerate this difference and stereotype women as predominantly indirectly or socially aggressive. Many men also engage in indirect aggression. The depiction of women's aggressive behavior on television and the plethora of popular books and articles on women's social aggression may foster the distorted perception of indirect aggression as being a woman's trait that is rarely observed in males.

In one sense, both physical and indirect aggression have similar roots. If the socialization practices of a culture foster the direct expression of one's views and sentiments, whether by a male or female, then both direct aggression and indirect aggression should decline. Given that females in western culture have less freedom to assert themselves, this issue becomes a worthy topic for exploration in women's groups and in psychotherapy.

REFERENCES

Björkqvist, K., Lagerspetz, K. M. J., & Kaukiainen, A. (1992). Do girls manipulate and boys fight? Developmental trends in regard to direct and indirect aggression. *Aggressive Behavior, 18,* 117–127.

Björkqvist, K., Österman, K., & Lagerspetz, K. M. J. (1994). Sex differences in covert aggression among adults. *Aggressive Behavior, 20,* 27–33.

Block, J. H. (1973). Conceptions of sex role: Some cross-cultural and longitudinal perspectives. *American Psychologist, 28,* 512–529.

Coie, J. D., & Dodge, K. A. (1998). Aggression and antisocial behavior. In W. Damon (Series Ed.) & N. Eisenberg (Vol. Ed.), *Handbook of child psychology: Vol. 5. Social, emotional and personality development* (pp. 778–863). New York: Wiley.

Comstock, G., & Scharrer, E. (1999). *Television: What's on, who's watching, and what it means.* New York: Academic Press.

Crick, N. R. (1996). The role of overt aggression, relational aggression, and prosocial behavior in children's future social adjustment. *Child Development, 67,* 2317–2327.

Crick, N. R., Casas, J. F., & Mosher, M. (1997). Relational and overt aggression in preschool. *Developmental Psychology, 33,* 579–588.

Crick, N. R., Werner, N. E., Casas, J. T., O'Brien, K. M., Nelson, D. A., Grotpeter, J. K., & Markon, K. (1999). Childhood aggression and gender: A new look at an old problem. In D. Bernstein (Ed.), *Nebraska Symposium on Motivation: Vol. 45. Gender and motivation.* Lincoln: University of Nebraska Press.

Feshbach, N. (1969). Sex differences in children's modes of aggressive responses toward outsiders. *Merrill-Palmer Quarterly, 15,* 249–258.

Feshbach, N. (2002). *Gender and the depiction of direct and indirect aggression on television.* Paper presented at the meeting of the International Society for Research in Aggression, Montreal, Canada.

Feshbach, N., & Sones, G. (1971). Sex differences in adolescent reactions toward newcomers. *Developmental Psychology, 4*(3), 381–386.

Freundl, P. C. (1977). *When is assertion aggressive?* Unpublished doctoral dissertation, University of California, Los Angeles.

Gerbner, G. (1972). Violence in television drama: Trends and symbolic functions. In G. A. Comstock and E. A. Rubinstein (Eds.), *Television and social behavior: Vol. 1. Media content and control.* Washington, DC: U.S. Government Printing Office.

Greenberg, B. S. (1980). *Life on television.* Norwood, NJ: Ablex.

Huston, A. C., Donnertein, E., Fairchild, H., Feshbach, N. D., Katz, P. A., Murray, J. P., Rubenstein, E. A., Wilcox, B., & Zuckerman, D. (1992). *Big world, small screen: The role of television in American society.* Lincoln: University of Nebraska Press.

Lagerspetz, K. M. J., Björkqvist, K., & Peltonen, T. (1988). Is indirect aggression typical of females? Gender differences in aggressiveness in 11- to 12-year-old children. *Aggressive Behavior, 14,* 403–414.

Lamb, S. (2001). *The secret lives of girls.* New York: The True Press.

Maccoby, E. E., & Jacklin, C. N. (1974). *The psychology of sex differences.* Stanford, CA: Stanford University Press.

Milavsky, J. R., Kessler, R., Stipp, H., Rubens, W. S., Pearl, D., Bouthilet, L., & Lazar, J. (Eds.). (1982). *Television and behavior: Ten years of scientific progress and implications for the eighties. Vol. 2: Technical reviews* (DHHS Publication No. ADM 82-1196). Washington, DC: U.S. Government Printing Office.

Nielsen Media Research. (2001). *2001 Television Report.* New York: Author.

Österman, K., Björkqvist, K., Lagerspetz, K. J., Kaukiainen, A., Landau, S. F., Fräczek, A., & Caprara, G. V. (1998). Cross-cultural evidence of female indirect aggression. *Aggressive Behavior, 24,* 1–8.

Paik, H., & Comstock, G. (1994). The effects of television violence on anti-social behavior: A meta analysis. *Communication Research, 21*(4), 516–546.

Simmons, R. (2002). *Odd girl out: The hidden culture of aggression in girls.* New York: Harcourt.

Tavris, C. (2002, July 5). Are girls really as mean as books say they are? *The Chronicle of Higher Education,* pp. B7–B9.

Wiseman, R. (2002). *Queen bees and wannabees.* New York: Crown Publishers.

IV

GENDER IMAGES WITH A FOCUS ON RACE AND AGE

12

AFRICAN AMERICAN WOMEN IN SEARCH OF SCRIPTS

THEMA BRYANT-DAVIS

Ebony is a 14-year-old African American girl. She wakes up Saturday morning and plays video games with her brother. The games have no images that remind her of herself. Later she walks to the mall with her friends. The billboards on the streets and the mannequins in the store windows do not reflect her face. When she gets to the mall, she goes to the movies. The theater lights are turned off and the film begins. She scans the screen for glimpses of herself. She dreams about her future, considers her present, and rewrites the script to fulfill her fantasies. Simultaneously there are African American girls and women sitting in theaters all over the nation, hoping to finally see their reflection on the big screen.

African American women are in search of scripts—narratives that reflect their reality beyond the paths their mothers chose, covering ground their grandmothers did not travel. There is a search for scripts of a fulfilling womanhood—of models of role attainment that do not gloss over the embodiment of conflict but exemplify a resolution, a coming to terms with the self that is female, African-descended and unique. bell hooks (1990) reminds us that when films address issues of race, gender, and sexuality it actively confronts our conceptions and understanding of ourselves and others.

As African American adolescents and young adults seek out these scripts, there is a reminder of the clinical influence and clinical usefulness of media examination including film analysis. Bobo (1995) noted that African American females gain a clearer understanding of their social circumstances by viewing films. Film analysis can therefore serve as a coping strategy that enables African American women to recognize negative forces and then empowers them to change the negative conditions impeding their advancement (Bobo, 1995). Artistic representations of African American women recreate the texture of their lives and require that they be seen as whole people—rather than as familiar stereotypes that are within this society more commonly accessible than genuine images of African American women (Lorde, 2001).

IDENTITY DEVELOPMENT IN AFRICAN AMERICAN GIRLS

Erickson and Schlein (1987) noted that the primary role of adolescence is to forge an identity characterized by autonomy, achievement concerns, mastery, competency, and the development of an ideology. This pathway from adolescence to womanhood is complicated for African American girls by the realities of racism and the need to resolve varying identities (Harris, 1996). In moving toward womanhood, African American females attempt to define themselves outside of stereotypical images of mammies, welfare mothers, matriarchs, work mules, and sexually immoral women. Self-definition for African American females has been empirically found to include strength, gender identity, ethnic identity, spirituality, connection to others, family orientation, sexuality, independence, intelligence, compassion, assertiveness, career orientation, and political awareness (Bryant, 1997; Gay & Tate, 1998; Jackson, 1998; Kiely, 1997; Shorter-Gooden & Washington, 1996).

In developing their self-identity, youth develop strategies of attaining possible selves. Possible selves are both the dreams and ideals one seeks to attain and the perceptions and identities one seeks to avoid (Oyserman & Markus, 1993). These possibilities can create discrepancy strain, which, as described by Pleck (1995), is the difference between one's actual self and one's ideal self. The ideal self represents the self-concept one desires to attain; it is the hopes, wishes, and aspirations concerning different facets of one's life. The discrepancy between one's expectation for the self and one's perception of the actual current status of the self theoretically leads to negative psychological consequences because of negative social feedback as well as internalized negative self-judgments (Pleck, 1995). In fact, gender-role discrepancy has been found to create strain that is manifested in lower psychological well-being, higher distress, and higher anxiety (Bryant, 1997; Burris, Branscombe, & Klar, 1996; Grimmel & Stern, 1992).

CURRENT ANALYSIS

hooks (1990) stated that in the Black liberation struggle the media can be a tool for the decolonizing of Black minds. Even though the media have often been used as a tool that reinforces marginalization, it is imperative that psychologists determine ways of using the media to shed the weight of systematic oppression from the self-concept of African American women. This chapter is an analysis of African American gender-role attainment as embodied by the female main characters in four of Spike Lee's films. Lee was chosen because of the number of his films, their coverage of different periods, their portrayal of diverse women's roles, and the accessibility of his films to large audiences of African American females. The four Spike Lee films that are analyzed were chosen to get a range of Lee's work over the decades as well as to focus on his works that feature a central Black female character.

The main female characters for each selected film are framed in terms of actual self, ideal self, discrepancy strain, and resolution of strain. The actual self is composed of one's current identity as exemplified by one's attitudes, relationships, and behaviors. The ideal self is the person one desires to be. In this film analysis the actual self is coded by observing the behaviors and cognitions of the character. The ideal self is determined by the dreams and hopes of which the character speaks as well as the activities and relationships that the character prioritizes with her time, focus, and energy; the ideal self is determined by the goals one pursues, whether they are external rewards or relationships or internal values one seeks to embody. The guiding questions for this analysis follow:

1. What could an audience member conclude about the character's actual self on the basis of her activities, ways of thinking, and ways of relating with others?
2. What could an audience member conclude about the character's hopes, values, aspirations on the basis of her activities, ways of thinking, and ways of relating with others? Separate from her current status, what do we see her working toward?
3. How does the character manage the difference between her current status in life and where she hopes to be?

In addition, I provide commentary on the overall thematic moral of the film plot in terms of African American womanhood. Because of Spike Lee's common use of both satire and symbolism, I include both the surface moral of the film as well as a deeper message that is assumed to be the filmmaker's purpose in creating the film. As with all works of art, one cannot know the intent of the creator but it is important to determine the possible messages perceived by African American adolescent and young adult audience members.

The value of my voice as an African American psychologist is explained by Bobo (1995) who noted that "the task of the critic within the interpretive community is to give voice to those who are usually never considered in any analysis of cultural works." As an African American woman myself, it is imperative that I not distance myself from this work with the false stance of objectivity. It is more important for me to be authentically present and true to the investment I have in seeing African American stories told, honored, and examined with respect. I am a psychologist and artist who desires media images that contribute to the self-esteem and empowerment of African American girls and women. The interpretation of the scripts below represents my own reflections and analysis. It is likely that another woman or girl with a different life perspective will experience the films through a different lens.

Bamboozled

The first film is *Bamboozled*, which was released in the fall of 2000. In this film, which is a commentary on the relationship among media, power, privilege, and race, Sloan Hopkins is the main female character. In terms of her personal development, Sloan's actual self is educated, financially secure, successful, and culturally aware, and although in some ways isolated from the African American community, she feels a responsibility to the community. Sloan has read a lot about her culture and thinks critically about racial issues, yet we never see her connected to an African American community, either in the informal sense of friendship circles or in the formal sense of organizations. Sloan is clearly well read, articulate, and smart. She is an independent thinker but finds herself being the assistant producer of a television show that she finds culturally irresponsible and offensive. Yet she continues to suffer through the work, going against her own judgment and values.

As regards relationships, Sloan's actual self does not have any connection to or show any desire for female companionship. A network of sisterhood is blatantly absent in Sloan's work life, home life, and social life. In terms of relationships with males, her actual self is reduced to the actions of her sexualized past and present. She is falsely labeled by the men around her as one who seeks out sexual involvement as a way of bettering her professional status. One of her relationships was with her employer in the beginning of her career. This partner primarily dates White women, denigrates her in front of other Black males as a sexual object, and manipulates her into activities that run counter to her moral fiber. Her second partner is a Black male who appears to be younger than she, less educated, and less culturally aware. He too questions her sexual past as indicative of her character and assumes her career success is due to her sexual activity. Sloan's relationship with her White male boss is one of silent suffering. She disagrees with many of her boss's comments and behaviors but operates within the system by stifling her opinions. The closest male to Sloan in terms of longevity is her race-conscious brother. They have a conflictual relationship in which her brother accuses her of being a "house nigger," meaning she is an African American who associates primarily with Whites and values Whiteness over Blackness. Overall Sloan's actual self is educated, beautiful, successful, and culturally aware, yet professionally and relationally unsatisfied.

In terms of her ideals Sloan values her education and success but simultaneously her unfulfilled desires are (a) having a positive healthy romantic relationship; (b) being respected as a talented producer, not as someone who succeeded by using her sexuality or negating her Blackness; and (c) creating work that supports and empowers the African American community.

The question then becomes, How does she handle the discrepancy between her actual self and ideal self? Her desire for a romantic relationship results in her choosing a mate who is kind and talented but culturally unaware and susceptible to the belief that her worth is based on her sexual history. In essence, Sloan attempts to compromise the ideal. She holds on to the desire of romantic connection but fulfills this desire by selecting someone who does not stimulate her intellectually or emotionally. In terms of the second unfulfilled ideal of being respected, within certain parameters Sloan finds her voice by attempting to articulate the mislabeling to which she is subjected. When her respect is jeopardized by verbal attacks on her character regarding her sexuality she speaks up to both her current partner and her supervisor with whom she was previously involved. Sloan sees the bigger picture and names it in terms of her disrespect being specific not merely to her experience but also to the experience of successful, powerful women in general who she says are always assumed to have used their sexuality to gain their status. Although both men continue to doubt her credibility, Sloan finds the safety and self-assurance required to speak her truth. In terms of her brother's disrespect as translated in her statements about Sloan's success being related to her being less culturally committed or aware than she should be, Sloan again gives voice to her values and choices. In this way, Sloan addresses the role discrepancy by speaking up for herself and using confrontation to address the areas in which she felt misunderstood.

The third role discrepancy centers on Sloan's desire to positively impact the African American community. She ends up doing just the opposite because of interrole conflict. Her desire for the attainment of multiple ideals results in her making a morally imbalanced decision. Sloan simultaneously has the desires to build a successful career, support another Black person in her field who was also her supervisor and ex-partner, and promote a positive image of the African American community. These seemingly appropriate desires cannot co-occur and as a result she builds her career, supports her employer, and simultaneously participates in the destructive portrayals of African Americans in the media. Sloan resolves her conflict by initially surrendering one of her ideals. This causes her tremendous emotional strife and eventually leads to her killing the person she sees as responsible for destroying her opportunity to fulfill her ideals. This murder represents the ultimate abandonment of the quest for the ideal self.

Two main challenges to or critiques of Lee's portrayal are important for a counselor or parent to highlight in dissecting the film's depiction of gender roles with an adolescent. The first is the way in which Sloan's value is determined on the basis of her sexual past and present relationship. It is important for African American adolescent girls to develop full selves that are not limited to sexual roles or past relationships. The second issue is the relationship between Sloan's success and her disconnection from her community. It is important to consider the ways that academic and vocational success can be obtained and yet not result in isolation.

For audience members who are able to recognize and analyze the writer's use of satire, the message of the film for those experiencing role discrepancy strain or conflict is to avoid those who are dream killers because they will cost them everything, including their selves and their values. Unfortunately for those adolescents and young adults who attend only to the surface presentation of the film, the message becomes "surrender your ideals because striving for them will cost you everything, including yourself, your sanity, and those for whom you care." Through the character Sloan, Spike Lee masterfully displays the conflicts many African American females encounter around issues of racial commitment, romantic pursuits, professional and educational development, and fundamental drives for respect. The audience member is left with three choices in terms of resolving gender-role strain: giving up on dreams, giving up on those persons and things that jeopardize dreams, or compromising or revising the dream.

School Daze

Another Spike Lee film, *School Daze*, was released in 1988. In this comedic, musical drama, the plot centers on issues of identity development as they occur on a southern Black college campus. The two main female characters in this film are Jane Toussaint and Rachel Meadows. Jane represents the group of females referred to as the Wanna-be's. This group is known for being physically attractive as measured by their long hair and light skin. They are also the female organization that helps one of the primary male fraternities by paying for the males' parties, cleaning their rooms, and having sex with them. Rachel, on the other hand, represents the group of women referred to as the Jigga-bo's. This group of women does not receive as much attention or romantic overtures as a result of their darker skin complexion and their decision to wear their hair naturally or without a weave. Rachel is one of the darkest women in the group and is the girlfriend of the primary political activist on campus.

In terms of the actual selves of these characters, although they are positioned as opposite, in reality they have a lot in common. In terms of their own development, they value education and being within a predominately African American context. This is exemplified by their decision to attend a Black college. Although their attendance at this school is an indicator of some sociocultural commitment, these ladies have no political or cultural agenda outside of supporting the men in their lives. In terms of their relational dynamics both young ladies are judged by their outer appearance, have lives that center around the men they are dating, are vulnerable to manipulation by the men in their lives, and have female relationships that are shaped by male attention, competition, and perceived attractiveness. Just as Jane feels selected for her special girlfriend status because of her light complexion, long hair, and physical shape, Rachel wonders if her boyfriend has selected her because of her dark complexion and natural hair as opposed to her personhood. Whereas the men they are dating have important leadership roles and agendas that take precedence over everything else, it appears that Jane and Rachel's primary focus is being a good girlfriend. Both young ladies display a desire for the companionship of other females as exemplified by the quantity and quality of time spent with female friends. Unfortunately it appears these friendships are formed primarily on the basis of physical appearance and much of the women's time is spent competing and complaining about women who are not in their group.

The ideals that both women seem to hold are receiving an education, creating sisterhood connections, and having positive romantic relationships. They both handle the education discrepancy by choosing to attend college. They recognize the discrepancy between their actual and ideal and then work to reach the ideal. The more complicated discrepancy centers on the ideal of having a positive romantic relationship. To accomplish this, Jane gives this role priority in her life. In this regard her pursuit of the ideal leads to her willingness to have sex with another person at the request of her boyfriend and to work diligently to support his agenda, namely his fraternity. Within this framework, Jane confuses the ideal with the ideal person. It is not enough for her to attain a romantic relationship; she desires a romantic relationship that will give her status, fame, and recognition. She collapses the ideals of connection and status and thus concludes that the path to validation is through one man, a man who considers her dispensable. Rachel handles the discrepancy by attempting to create a fulfilling romantic relationship while still pursuing those ideals that will bring her fulfillment. Although Rachel sacrifices attending some social gatherings in support of her boyfriend's political agenda, toward the end of the film she reveals her decision to pursue one of her desires that runs counter to her boyfriend's politics (i.e., she decides to join a sorority). This decision brings into focus the discourse of sisterhood. Rachel attempts to manage the role conflict of pleasing her boyfriend and meeting her own needs for organized connection with other African American women. She does that by verbalizing her commitment to the romantic relationship but also by voicing her decision to make the choices outside of the relationship that she feels are right for her.

It is important to critically consider Lee's depiction of the role choices of the African American women in this film, particularly the lack of agency and power that the women have in comparison with the men in the film. It is essential for girls and women to claim their voices, power, and agency and not feel they have to surrender them for male approval.

A surface analysis of this film's message concerning role discrepancy resolution is that the pathway to role attainment for African American females is through their appearance. One could walk away from the film believing that one's worth is based in others' acceptance and approval and that the pathway for acceptance and approval is physical presentation and sexual availability. With this framework, education, spirituality, and leadership are not key in the shaping of a fulfilling African American womanhood. On the contrary, for those who look for a deeper message concerning role attainment and conflict resolution, the theme becomes making self-respect a primary ideal. This film shows how without self-respect as a part of the ideal self, the pursuit of all other ideals could lead to shame, regret, and dissatisfaction. In this film Spike Lee presents a few possibilities on the pathway to womanhood for African American females. These include the capacity to pursue multiple ideals, the significance of prioritizing ideals such as self-respect, and the time required for some roles to be attained, such as getting an education. The additional issue highlighted in this film is whose ideals one chooses to adopt: those of one's school, family, political leaders, or desired peer group, or those within one's own heart.

Crooklyn

The third film, *Crooklyn*, although released in 1994, is a depiction of African American urban family life in the 1970s. This semi-autobiographical comedic drama is the story of a family of seven living in Brooklyn, New York. This analysis focuses on the mother, Carolyn Carmichael. Carolyn's actual self is family oriented: She is in a loving relationship that on one occasion becomes physically violent, and is also the mother of four children who are respectful overall yet engage in normative childhood disruptions. She is also impoverished as manifested by the family's difficulty paying bills. Her actual self is also physically ill. Toward the end of the film the audience discovers the severity of Carolyn's illness. While healthy, Carolyn's actual self is creative, loving, outspoken, and connected to her community, as well as a disciplinarian.

Her ideal self is (a) a good mother who is able to provide moral guidance, economic resources, discipline, and love to her children; (b) a supportive loving wife who can maintain a healthy realistic relationship; (c) a woman with self-respect who is respected by others; and (d) one who is physically healthy.

In terms of the manner in which Carolyn handles the conflict between her actual self and ideal motherhood self, she uses creativity, love, discipline, and a gender, racial, and moral socialization process to strive toward her ideal. When economic barriers arise she uses candles for lighting and the extended family to help with child care. When conflicts arise within the family and within the community, she models confrontation and assertiveness for her children. The fulfillment of her ideal is shown by the end of the film, when Carolyn has died. Although the viewers don't see the children become adults, they do see their childhood attainment of a family connectedness as well as an emotional and moral development that is a testament to their mother's work. Although Carolyn's time to fulfill her ideal role is cut short by illness, she still exemplifies a striving toward ideals in the face of external barriers as well as her own human physical and emotional frailty.

In terms of her ideal to be a good wife, as with her ideal to be a mother, the path to this ideal is complicated by economic stress and domestic violence. She works toward the ideal of a healthy relationship by initially selecting a mate who is able to show love, compassion, discipline, and commitment. She also works on the relationship by being honest, affirming, and willing to address the conflicts but prepared to take time and space from the relationship when she feels the maintenance of her relationship pollutes her ability to feel respected. Carolyn, equally capable of expressing both her positive and negative affect, also shows her capacity for reconciliation.

The greatest ideal for Carolyn—being physically healthy and able to live to reach her other ideals—has become an unreachable reality. Given the disproportionate manner in which health problems impact African American women, this is an ideal that should not be taken for granted. Carolyn attempts to bring closure by expressing her feelings and thoughts to her family before she passes. The nonmaterial gifts that Carolyn gives her family are manifested in the way in which her children and husband are able to rally together even after her death.

There are two additional critical issues for African American female audience members to consider when thinking of applying the values portrayed in this film to their own lives. This first is the lighthearted treatment of the scene in which Carolyn's husband drags her down the stairs. The scene's design results in laughter from many audience members, when in fact this is one of the most serious issues that Carolyn faces. Physical violence by an intimate partner is an issue that many women, including African American women, face. It cannot be dismissed as mere comedic relief. Doing so only contributes to denial and minimization. The wounds of Black women have to be taken seriously and addressed by the entire community. Second, when Carolyn dies and her daughter takes on all of the domestic roles of her mother, a childhood has been prematurely ended. Many girls are forced to grow up before their time. The ability to fill, or better yet the necessity of filling, these adult roles should not merely be accepted as the norm or merely celebrated as strength. It is important to protect the experience of and demands on African American girls. They deserve a full childhood so they can develop into balanced women.

The messages Spike Lee presents in this film concerning gender-role attainment within the role of Carolyn are (a) the possibility of attaining ideals in the face of multiple external barriers, including poverty, racism, family violence, and death; (b) the importance of making self-care a priority in one's list of ideal selves; and (c) the necessity of allowing for multiple measures of one's role successes. Although the woman dies, the audience is able to see the fruit of her labor in her family's continued connectedness after her death. Those who do not analyze the numerous possible messages of the film may leave with the belief that tomorrow is not promised so ideals are distractions from simply enjoying today. Given the semi-autobiographical nature of this film, the validity of this argument is put into question when one looks at the works of Spike Lee, a product of a similar mothering that was grounded in the pursuit of an ideal self within the context of actual life circumstances called *barriers*.

She's Gotta Have It

In Spike Lee's first film, *She's Gotta Have It*, the main character is Lola Darling, an African American single woman. This movie demonstrates Lola's pursuit of romantic and sexual fulfillment. Lola's actual self is a woman who is juggling relationships with three men. One man makes her laugh, one man romances her with poetry and dance concerts, and one man has financial security and an athletic physique. Lola's actual self is up-front with the men she is dating and she lets them each know about the others, even going so far as to have them all over for dinner on the same night.

Lola's ideal self is a woman who is understood, respected, and free to express herself sexually with whomever she likes. These three themes create conflict for Lola because all three are not a part of her actual experience. In terms of being understood, Lola starts the movie by saying that some people consider her a freak but that she wants to clear her name. In terms of being respected, her economically affluent boyfriend verbally abuses her several times by reminding her that he is with her only because she is "fine" (beautiful). He also tells her if she gains any weight he will leave her. Her supposed romantic partner who attempts to express his love with poetry, dance concerts, and meals when she is sick eventually rapes her. He is angry with her because of her lack of commitment to him; he forcefully and painfully has sex with her and then says that he enjoyed it. As regards Lola's desire to be free sexually, she finds that her sexual choices bring on the judgment of others and increased conflict with others and within herself.

A critical issue for audience members to consider when reviewing the overall gender-role depiction in this film is power. Lola is portrayed as being the person in the story with power but in fact she is powerless. She is in relationships that do not honor or respect her and she is incapable of taking the steps necessary to honor and respect herself. Along with being emotionally and verbally abused, Lola is raped and then her rape is minimized and she is blamed for it. This is one of the greatest contradictions that exists in the role depiction of African American women. They are often portrayed as emasculating whores who are incapable of being raped. This depiction is damaging and is reflected in the experience of African American girls and women who are violated and shamed daily. It is crucial to challenge these roles to carve out a healthy perception of the self, especially in a society that devalues these women's worth and safety.

Lola manages her discrepancy strain by breaking up with all three men and deciding to take a break from sexual intimacy. Her actions give the message to women that sexual relationships with multiple men can lead to societal judgment; anger from the men themselves, possibly even resulting in sexual violence; and a sense of isolation. The audience can then decide that a healthy sexual choice would be (a) not to have sex, (b) to date only one person, (c) not to date anyone who disrespects them, or (d) to date multiple persons but not tell them about it. In the end, Lola is resolved to resist being controlled by any person or relationship. African American women, who have systematically been stereotyped as promiscuous, have to seek a balance in their identities that allows for understanding, respectful relationships that are not controlling or destructive to the self. It cannot be assumed that sexual freedom equals sexual or relational fulfillment. Freedom of sexual expression does not replace the need to be understood and respected.

DISCUSSION

This analysis has attempted to highlight the complexities involved in gender-role development for African American women. The characters discussed highlight the issues raised as a result of the intersection of racial and gender identity. They also exemplify the external circumstances that influence the development process for many African American women. Finally, and of most significance, these films model the multiple pathways and choice points available to African American women.

Intersection of Gender and Racial Identity

In terms of the intersection of racial and gender identiy, three of the major themes that emerged were politics, connection, and beauty myths. Political ideology and involvement have been key components of African American womanhood (Collins, 1991). Gay and Tate (1998) found that whereas African American women identify strongly with both their gender and their race, their racial identities more powerfully affected their political attitudes. As each behavior one chooses moves one closer to or further from one's ideal self (Oyserman, Terry, & Bybee, 2002), the choices made by the characters in these films indicate their political priorities. Some of the political choice points raised included perpetuating or protesting negative images of African Americans in the media, personal gain versus community gain, acceptance of or protest against the globlal maltreatment of Africans and diasporic persons, and silence versus community dialogue.

Connection also is repeatedly exemplified in the lives of these women. Connection has been recognized as both a cultural and gender-based value. These connections are sites of inspiration, education, support, and nurturance. Those that are based within and across gender and racial groups are shown. Exemplars of large-scale connection with the greater African American community and small-scale connections among families, peers, and institutions are shown in all of their important complexity. These films are true to the realities of the assistance and labor that can come from being a part of a support network, in terms of both the added help provided and additional demands (Greene, 1990).

In terms of beauty myths that are encountered for African American women, these works highlight the significance of complexion, hair texture, body type, and sexuality. One of the domains of self-esteem is body image. For African American women these issues of beauty, attractiveness, and sexuality are primary within both their historical and contemporary context. These issues are complicated by the objectification of African women's bodies, the assumption of African women's sexual availibility, and the continued presentation of White femaleness as ideal beauty. Lee's work shows both the external pressures presented by this schema as well as the manifestation of these internalized messages of self-doubt and self-loathing. To emerge with a healthy sense of body esteem and sexual esteem is a task that cannot be divorced from the racist, sexist society in which African American women develop.

Barriers to Identity Development

This work also demonstrates the ways in which African American females are bombarded with external barriers during their development. The nuances of these barriers as shown in Lee's films exemplify covert and overt racism, sexism, classism, and illness. Although the traumatizing effects of physical and sexual violence have been documented, less attention has been paid to the traumatizing effects of societal, institutional, and interpersonal oppression. Harrel (2000) has conducted groundbreaking work in this area by documenting the symptomatic responses to racism by African American men and women. These symptoms have included those traditionally associated with the posttraumatic stress of war veterans and abuse survivors. The characters in Lee's films demonstrate the sadness, anxiety, despair, and powerlessness often experienced by survivors of oppression, but there are also some examples of resilience and thriving. It is significant that Lee's character development allows the audience to recognize oppression as the fundamental problem not of the marginalized but of the privileged. The need for resistance to racism, sexism, and classism from persons in power so as to change systems, institutions, and individuals is appropriately located with those who passively or actively perpetuate inequality.

Multiple Pathways of Development

Finally, this work sheds light on the multiple pathways available to African American women. Though the barriers and stereotypes are named and acknowledged as powerful factors, there is nonetheless an array of possible selves among which African American girls and women can choose. These choices include many of the qualities presented in the theoretical and empirial work on African American gender-role development, including but not limited to being educated, compassionate, successful, connected, politically involved, sexual, spiritual, family oriented, respected, and strong (Greene, 1990; Shorter-Gooden & Washington, 1996).

Implications for Feminist Psychology

It is important that feminist psychologists in clinical practice become familiar with the popular scripts available and not available to their clients. When feminist psychologists refuse to learn the experiences, metaphors, and realities of their clients, they disempower and disserve them. In essence these psychologists force them to speak the language of traditional psychology without allowing space or acknowledgment for their voices and images. Learning about and using analysis of media products such as film provide a way for them to empower their clients to speak their truths. In addition, acknowledging the lack of images is crucial for feminist psychology that is based on the recognition of power, privilege, and oppression. Feminist psychologists have to see into the invisible and barely visible spaces where ethnic minority women are carving out their places in the world. This is also important for feminist research practice. Ethnic minority feminist psychologists need to be present beyond false objectivity as well as to be authentic in critiqing the media products that are supposed to represent their mothers, sisters, and personal selves. African American women's voices and the voices of our communities have to be qualitatively listened to as we continue to examine the mental health implications of dominant cinematic protrayals of ethnic minority women.

CONCLUSION

It should be acknowledged that Lee's work is not all-emcompassing in terms of the productive possibilities available to African American women's development. Some scholars may argue that many of his female characters are not productive or successful. One can only hope his future work will demonstrate even more of the possibilities available to and exemplified in the lives of African American women.

It is also hoped that the voices of more African American female film-makers, such as Julie Dash and Jacqueline Shearer, will be made accessible and available to wider audiences. Bobo (1995) noted that African American women are seeking out scripts that are produced by African American female filmmakers. African American female filmmakers are confronting and challenging negative portrayals of black women by recreating and expanding the images of black women in film (Bobo, 1995).The pathway to woman-hood is enhanced by the diversity of African American cultural strengths and simultaneously hindered by barriers of oppression. More work must be done to aid African American adolescent females in their search for scripts of identity.

REFERENCES

Bobo, J. (1995). *Black women as cultural readers*. New York: Columbia University Press.

Bryant, T. (1997). *Conceptions and correlates of manhood and womanhood: Gender identity role discrepancy for urban young adult African-Americans*. Unpublished manuscript.

Burris, C., Branscombe, N., & Klar, Y. (1996). Maladjustment implications of self and group gender-role discrepancy: An ordered-discrepancy model. *European Journal of Social Psychology, 27*, 75–95.

Collins, P. (1991). *Black feminist thought*. New York: Routledge.

Erickson, E., & Schlein, S. (1987). *A way at looking at things: Selected papers from 1930 to 1980*. New York: Norton.

Gay, C., & Tate, K. (1998). Doubly bound: The impact of gender and race on the politics of Black women. *Political Psychology, 19*, 169–184.

Greene, B. (1990). What has gone before: The legacy of racism and sexism in the lives of Black mothers and daughters. *Women and Therapy*, 207–230.

Grimmel, D., & Stern, G. (1992). The relationship between gender role ideals and psychological well-being. *Sex Roles, 27*, 487–497.

Harrell, S. (2000). A multidimensional conceptualization of racism-related stress: Implications for the well-being of people of color. *American Journal of Orthopsy-chiatry, 70*, 42–57

Harris, S. (1996). African-American and Anglo-American gender identities: An empirical study. *Journal of Black Psychology, 22*, 182–194.

hooks, b. (1990). *Yearning: Race, gender, and cultural politics*. Cambridge, MA: South End Press.

Jackson, L. (1998). The influence of both race and gender on the experiences of African American college women. *Review of Higher Education, 21*, 359–375.

Kiely, L. (1997). An exploratory analysis of the relationship of racial identity, social class, and family influences on womanist identity development. *Dissertation Abstracts International, 58*, 2086A, University of Maryland, College Park.

Lorde, A. (2001). Age, race, class, and sex: Women redefining difference. In P. Rothenberg (Ed.), *Race, class, and gender in the United States: An integrative study* (5th ed., pp. 588–601). New York: Worth Publishers.

Oyserman, D., & Markus, H. (1993). The sociocultural self. In J. M. Suls (Eds.), *Psychological perspectives on the self: Vol. 4. The self in social perspective* (pp. 187–220). Mahwah, NJ: Erlbaum.

Oyserman, D., Terry, K., & Bybee, D. (2002). A possible selves intervention to enhance school involvement. *Journal of Adolescence, 25*, 313–326.

Pleck, J. (1995). The gender role strain paradigm: An update. In R. Levant & W. Pollack (Eds.), *A new psychology of men* (pp. 11–32). New York: Basic Books.

Shorter-Gooden, K., & Washington, N. (1996). Young, Black, and females: The challenge of weaving and identity. *Journal of Adolescence, 19*, 465–475.

13

REFLECTION AND DISTORTION: WOMEN OF COLOR IN MAGAZINE ADVERTISEMENTS

JANIS SANCHEZ-HUCLES, PATRICK S. HUDGINS,
AND KIMBERLY GAMBLE

A White mother and daughter stare at a showcase featuring two Asian mannequins dressed in skin-tight, short, and provocative spandex outfits; Daisy Fuentes is featured with a caption explaining boldly that she is not pregnant but she takes multivitamins, as if it is novel for a Latina to be not pregnant when taking multivitamins; ads with African American women show them advertising oversized pantyhose and shopping at discount stores; Native American women are absent from all ads.

The media are active in both reflecting and distorting the lives of people of color. What is reflected is the United States' ongoing difficulty in dealing with race in inclusive and sensitive ways. Race and ethnicity issues are often distorted because the voice or perspective of the media typically represents a majority standpoint rather than the voices and perspectives of people of color. Media portrayals of people of color both reflect and shape social perceptions. Often these images are distorted because they reflect biased and limited views. Sometimes this distortion is accidental and innocuous, but in other cases it is purposeful and harmful. This chapter is designed to emphasize the importance the media play in supporting societal norms and standards. We demonstrate how magazine ads in particular continue to stereotype, limit, and distort women of color in ways that can be negative to how these women are perceived by themselves and others.

Women of color continue to be the most marginalized group in magazine ad representations despite changing attitudes about women and racial ethnic groups (Johnson & Kressen, 2002; Rhodes, 1993). This relative invisibility unfortunately reflects the low status they are accorded in the wider

185

society with respect to their economic, political, and social clout. Many majority theorists have ignored research aimed at women of color, and often too few women of color in academic circles are willing or able to advance this area of scholarship. Research suggests that the journalistic workforce is 87.5% European American (American Society of News Editors, 2003) and 69% male (Creedon, 2004).

Research has also repeatedly shown that the media have a profound impact on how individuals understand, relate, and code information. Media sources have the potential to offer effective and positive portrayals of the diverse individuals that comprise society in their role as potent socializing mechanisms. Ads can influence perceptions and create self-fulfilling prophecies by contributing to stereotypes, prejudices, and societal inequities. Specifically, advertisements have been identified as one of the most significant factors impacting society. It has been estimated that more than 184 billion ads are shown daily in newspapers and 6 billion ads appear in monthly magazines (Bogart, 1990). In magazines, ads comprise 52% of the content (Collins & Skover, 1993).

Content analyses of advertisements have historically focused on gender biases relating to the lives of middle-income White females. Advertisements stereotyped these women as housewives, incapable of decision making or responsibility, dependent, decorative, and in need of male attention (Courtney & Lockeretz, 1971).

The feminist movement has been credited with moving women out of the home and into the outside world of work. However, bias continues with regard to women being more likely than men to be portrayed in decorative and sexually provocative ads.

Content analyses that have focused on race and ethnicity have consistently shown underrepresentation of these groups relative to their population. Ads have historically portrayed people of color in subservient roles and jobs unless they were in athletics or entertainment. Scholars have found continued evidence of stereotypes for African Americans with these individuals depicted as athletes and entertainers and in need of charity from others (Green, 1991; Shuey, King, & Griffith, 1953). African Americans have been the focus of inquiry more so than other groups and have been seen in magazine ads in greater numbers than other groups.

It appears that just as the feminist movement led to some amelioration of bias for women, the civil rights movement helped increase the representation of minorities and decreased some of the racial biases. A host of researchers believe, however, that the battle to end racial bias was stalled in the 1990s. The obvious racism of icons such as Aunt Jemima and Frito Bandito ended, but advertising is still largely a segregated business (Green, 1991). Although the percentage of ethnic minorities portrayed in magazines has increased since the 1950s, there has never been accurate representation. This poor lack of representation is surprising because research has shown that using diverse ethnic minorities in ads does not have any adverse impact on majority members' use of advertised products (Green, 1991). It is also ironic that by not being more inclusive, magazine advertising may be limiting its potential markets in today's increasingly diverse society.

Techniques to investigate how ethnic minorities are portrayed in magazines have varied. In general, research has focused on the frequency of ethnic minority portrayals, whether the depictions were positive or negative, and how these ads have changed over time. It has been difficult to arrive at firm conclusions about minority representation because representation frequencies vary across studies as different magazines are used, there is subjectivity in assessing how positive or negative ads are, and finally many studies examine only one ethnic minority group at a time, making cross-minority comparisons impossible (Taylor, Lee, & Stern, 1996).

Only recently have researchers looked at the intersection of race and gender for individuals of color. Plous and Neptune, in their 1997 study of racial and gender bias for Whites and African Americans in magazine ads, examined fashion-oriented ads from six magazines from 1985 to 1994. During this period, they found an increase from past levels in the number of African American females featured in fashion ads in women's magazines. African American women, however, were significantly more likely to be portrayed as exotic, as predatory, and in animal prints, and both races of females were more likely than men to be shown in sexually provocative and revealing attire such as lingerie or bathing suits.

For the purpose of our research, we have adapted Plous and Neptune's 1997 methodology to look at portrayals of women of color in female and family-oriented magazines. Plous and Neptune's 1997 methodology was used because it was the only other study that had a similar focus of inquiry. Like Plous and Neptune, we examined the content and possible messages of magazine ads. We developed a typology of categories based on content that emerged from the data and that in many cases overlapped with the categories of Plous and Neptune. We wished to explore basic questions about the representation of women of color in majority versus ethnic magazines. Our specific goals were to investigate the following research questions:

1. What are the percentages of women of color ads in majority versus ethnic magazines?
2. Are there differences in the ad focus for majority versus ethnic magazines?
3. Are there differences in how women of color are portrayed in majority ads versus ethnic magazine ads?

METHOD

We conducted a content analysis of six female or family-oriented magazines: *Family Circle, Cosmopolitan, Filipinas, Ebony, Essence,* and *Latin Girl.*

These publications were selected because of their high readership (based on consumer rankings of readership), their use in previous research, and their availability. All ads in the chosen magazines were coded. The time period selected was from July 2000 to July 2001, with three issues selected from each publication by means of a random number table. Hence the research findings reflect 18 periodicals over a span of 1 year. The monthly circulations for the magazines are as follows: *Essence*, 7.6 million; *Ebony*, 10.7 million; *Family Circle*, 21 million; *Filipina*, 120,000; *Cosmopolitan*, 16 million; and *Latin Girl*, 110,000 (*Essence: About Us*, 2003; *Family Circle*, 2003; *Filipinas Magazine*, 2001; Johnson Publishing Company, 2003; Standard Rate and Data Service, 2001; *United States of America World Magazine Trends*, 2003).

An African American male, a multiethnic female, and a White female conducted the coding. The biggest challenge and area of subjectivity related to determining ethnicity/race by examining a picture. It is impossible to know with certainty racial or ethnic affiliation unless a person is asked. High interrater reliability was achieved by using the category of *indeterminate* when it appeared that an individual was of mixed racial background or otherwise racially ambiguous. Only in the case of coding for Latinas were there a number of racially indeterminate women, as women of Latin descent can also be coded as White, Black, or multiethnic. The interrater agreement on race category was 99% with the use of the indeterminate category.

RESULTS AND DISCUSSION

To conduct the content analysis, copies of all ads were made and reviewed by the three raters. Each rater independently determined responses to the content issues of race, ad focus, and how women of color were portayed with respect to sexualization of ads and ethnic exoticism.

Descriptive Data

Examination of three issues of the six magazines revealed a total of 453 ads. *Cosmopolitan* accounted for 154 ads; *Ebony*, 91; *Essence*, 114; *Family Circle*, 39; *Filipina*, 22; and *Latin Girl* 33. The total numbers of people pictured in these 453 ads were 830 people with 588 female (71 %) and 242 (29%) male. Of the total ads, 43% depicted women of color; 23%, men of color; 27%, female European Americans; 7%, male European Americans; and 0.7%, racially ambiguous females that the coders could not agree on and therefore were coded as "indeterminate female."

Table 13.1 shows the gender by race by magazine distribution of the sample. As some of these magazines obviously target female readers, many of these magazines have high percentages of female ads (ads that feature fe-

TABLE 13.1
Gender by Race by Magazine

Title	LAF	LAM	AAF	AAM	WF	WM	AF	AM	NAF	NAM
Cosmopolitan	4	1	8	1	72	10	4	1	—	1
Family Circle	3	2	8	—	61	26	—	—	—	—
Ebony	2	1	49	42	4	2	—	1	—	—
Essence	3	2	63	22	6	3	1	—	—	—
Latin Girl	56	16	5	—	9	4	2	—	—	9
Filipina	—	—	1	—	5	3	48	44	—	—

Note. All data are percentages. AAF = African American female; AAM = African American male; AF = Asian female; AM = Asian male; LAF = Latin American female; LAM = Latin American male; NAF = Native American female; NAM = Native American male; WF = White female; WM = White male.

males). The two exceptions are *Filipina* and *Ebony*. In *Filipina*, the majority of ads include both males and females. In *Ebony*, there is a more diverse distribution across ad categories, and this publication features the highest percentage of men in its ads. It is striking that no Native American women were depicted in any of the ads and only one Native American male was observed.

Ads by Racial Background

The percentages of women by racial background for each of the magazines are displayed in Table 13.2. Each magazine reflects a clear racial focus with one racial group accounting for the majority of ads. In the two majority magazines, only African Americans are reflected at a level that is comparable to their percentage in the population; all the other racial groups are underrepresented.

Ad Focus

Table 13.3 displays the ad focus across magazines. Overall, the primary foci for ads were cosmetics/cologne/beauty, medicine/health, food, and clothing. Differences were also apparent across ethnic groups. It is difficult to make accurate comparisons between these magazines because their readership and focus are somewhat different.

Filipinas actually appears to be a family-oriented publication with ads that focus on technology (45%), medicine/health (32%), and food (18%). Previous research (Taylor et al., 1996) has shown that some Asian magazines focus more on technical and business content and less on traditional feminine and domestic ads for both genders. This ad focus reinforces stereotypes of Asians as being interested in technical areas such as computers, mathematics, and the sciences. These ads can subtly suggest messages about the unsuitability of the arts, humanities, and nontechnical areas for Filipinas. We must note that in addition to the technical and business stereotypes that

TABLE 13.2
Percentages of Women of Color in Ads in Majority and Ethnic Magazines

Ethnicity	Cosmopolitan	Family Circle	Latin Girl	Filipina	Essence	Ebony
European American	82	84	5	9	8	7
African American	10	11	7	2	86	90
Latin American	4	6	64	0	4	3
Asian American	3	0	0	89	2	0
Native American	0	0	0	0	0	0
Indeterminate	1	0	24	0	0	0

can affect both Asian males and females, there is also a larger cultural stereotype of Asian females as submissive and sexual. It appears that Asian females can be stereotyped at the extreme ends of being scientific and unfeminine or passive and provocative. These stereotypes offer very limited perspectives for how majority members and members of other ethnic groups view Asians and especially Asian women.

With the exception of *Filipinas*, there are similarities across ads and ethnic groups. The category of cosmetics is first for all other magazines except *Family Circle* where it ranks second. Medicine/health is in the top two categories for all but *Latin Girl* where it is third and *Ebony* where it is seventh. Although medicine/health is the second highest category for *Essence*, it is somewhat disturbing to see the paucity of these types of ads in the two African American magazines and in *Latin Girl* compared with the other magazines, given the major health risks that these population groups have.

Clothes are among the top five categories for all magazines except *Filipinas* where this category is not included and *Ebony* where the percentage is only 3%. Both *Cosmopolitan* and *Essence*, which are aimed at younger female audiences, show the greatest diversity of products. *Latin Girl* is unique in having 12% of its ads focusing on education and careers; other publications do not emphasize these areas.

There were some interesting gender differences in ad portrayals as depicted in Table 13.4. As to be expected, the vast majority of beauty ads featured women. Differences across gender were seen in ads for cigarettes, alcohol, automobiles, and clothing. In the ads portraying cigarettes, alcohol, and automobiles, there was more use of ads featuring both males and females. In the ads featuring cigarettes, half were of women only and half were of both men and women with no ads of men only. Of the alcohol ads, 27% featured women, 17% featured men, and 56% had both men and women. In the category of automobile ads, 35% featured men only, versus 24% with females only and 41% with males and females. In contrast, clothing ads focused heavily on women.

In what appears to be a continuation of a historical theme, all of the ethnic magazines except *Filipina* included entertainment ads whereas only

TABLE 13.3
Ad Type for Majority Versus Ethnic Magazines (Percentages)

Ad Type	Latin Girl	Family Circle	Filipina	Cosmopolitan	Essence	Ebony
Alcohol/beverages	0	0	0	6	2	8
Cigarettes	0	5	0	1	2	2
Entertainment	12	0	0	1	3	6
Automobile	0	0	0	1	6	10
Feminine products	6	3	0	3	1	0
Nonprofit groups	3	0	0	0	0	1
Cosmetics/cologne/beauty	36	18	0	60	45	28
Institutional	0	3	5	1	8	11
Clothing	6	8	0	9	7	3
Medicine/health	9	30	32	10	9	7
Technology	3	3	45	1	3	2
Education	12	3	0	1	3	3
Travel	0	0	0	0	1	0
Food	9	18	18	3	6	10
Investment	0	0	0	1	4	8
Cleaning products	3	0	0	1	1	0

TABLE 13.4
Ad Types by Race and Gender (Percentages)

Ad type	LF	LM	AAF	AAM	WF	WM	AF	AM	IF	NAM
Alcohol/beverages	3	0	4	10	5	0	0	0	0	0
Cigarettes	0	0	2	5	1	0	4	0	0	0
Entertainment	8	14	1	14	1	0	0	0	50	0
Automobile	0	14	3	17	0	0	0	0	0	0
Feminine products	8	0	1	0	2	0	0	0	0	0
Nonprofit groups	0	0	<1	0	1	0	0	0	25	0
Cosmetics/cologne/ beauty	45	0	27	12	49	22	11	0	0	100
Institutional	3	0	5	10	2	0	4	6	0	0
Clothing	8	0	4	0	9	6	4	0	0	0
Medicine/health	8	0	4	7	17	28	11	28	0	0
Technology	3	0	1	3	2	17	36	0	0	0
Education	5	43	2	5	2	6	4	44	0	0
Travel	0	0	1	0	0	6	0	0	0	0
Food	11	14	7	8	4	11	11	22	0	0
Investment	0	0	3	9	1	6	0	0	0	0
Cleaning products	3	0	4	0	1	0	0	0	25	0

Note. AAF = African American female; AAM = African American male; AF = Asian female; AM = Asian male; IF = Indeterminate female; LF = Latin female; LM = Latin male; NAM = Native American male; WF = White female; WM = White male.

TABLE 13.5
Minimal Versus Suggestive Body Exposure by Race by Magazine

Title	Minimal or no body exposure	Latin American female	African American female	White female	Asian female
Latin Girl	79	21	0	0	0
Family Circle	74	0	0	13	0
Filipina	100	0	0	0	0
Cosmopolitan	58	0	0	14	0
Essence	68	1	6	2	0
Ebony	87	0	2	0	0

one of the two majority magazines included this category and at a lower percentage than the ethnic magazines. A racial difference can also be seen in the distribution of ads for cigarettes and alcohol. Two of the three magazines that advertised both cigarettes and alcohol were the African American magazines and Blacks were featured in the majority ads as well. Perhaps it is not surprising to observe that the two African American magazines also had the lowest percentage of medical and health ads.

Sexualization of Ads

In an attempt to assess the potential sexualization of ads, body exposure, body positioning, and clothing were also documented. The majority of ads had no or minimal body exposure. *Essence* and *Cosmopolitan* depicted the highest percentages of body exposure and *Filipina* showed the least body exposure. Table 13.5 contrasts minimal body exposure with suggestive body exposure by race and magazine. For the purposes of this study, *suggestive* was defined as depicting bare bodies, cleavage, or some combination of upper legs, bare shoulders, and bare stomach.

The majority of women (66.2%) were depicted in a standing position, 20% were sitting, 6% were reclining, and the remainder were depicted exercising, crouching, or being held in the air. In terms of clothing worn, 49% were attired in casual clothes, 16% were shown in head shots with no clothes visible, 11% were in evening attire, 8% were in business dress, 5% were in athletic outfits, 4% were in lingerie or sleepwear, and 2% were in bathing suits. The remaining women wore wedding or other ceremonial dress. These findings are inconsistent with Plous and Neptune's 1997 finding that indicated a high percentage of females were attired in sexually provocative clothing such as lingerie and bathing suits.

There were 10 examples of women who were portrayed as ethnically exotic. *Ethnically exotic* was defined as focusing on ethnic features of the face, ethnic clothing, or ethnic stereotypes. Two of these women were Latina and were featured in *Latin Girl*. Six ethnically exotic women were Black women: Two were shown in *Cosmopolitan*, one in *Family Circle*, and three in *Essence*.

There were also two Asian mannequins featured in *Family Circle* that were deemed ethnically exotic.

There were a total of 23 sexually provocative ads. *Sexually provocative* was defined by a combination of suggestive clothing, postures, and facial expressions. Four were of Latinas and were featured in *Latin Girl*, one Black female and one White female were featured in *Ebony*, one Black female was in *Essence*, one White female and two mannequins were shown in *Family Circle*, and 13 White females were featured in *Cosmopolitan*. There were no ads depicting women in animal prints. These findings suggest that there is still some use of ethnically exotic women of color and that women of color accounted for about 35% of the sexually provocative ads. These results offer at least some support of Plous and Neptune's study (1997) with respect to sexually provocative and ethnic exotic ads. There was no support of their finding that women of color tend to be depicted in animal prints.

How Women of Color Are Portrayed in Majority Magazines

Despite the fact that women of color are typically underrepresented in majority magazines, images of these women still function to disproportionately portray them as exotic and in stereotyped ways, and they are used to advertise less socially desirable products. For example, although the European American magazine *Family Circle* did not use any ads featuring Asian women, it featured an ad with a mother and child staring at two Asian mannequins in a store window who were dressed in revealing and provocative dressy spandex outfits. This portrayal fits the all-too-familiar stereotype of sexuality, passivity, and availability that Asian American women are often placed in, and it also fetishes them as objects. Other examples of how women of color were portrayed in majority magazines include the following:

- One magazine shows an African American female cooking a turkey with a European American female offering help or instruction by proffering a baking bag;
- In one majority magazine, an African American woman is used to advertise plus-size pantyhose;
- An African American female is used in one majority magazine ad to promote shopping at Wal-Mart because "the everyday low prices are very affordable";
- Women of color are more frequently featured in majority magazines to advertise beauty products for damaged hair;
- Individual women of color and groups of individuals of color feature disproportionately in cigarette and alcohol ads;
- There is only one ad on birth control in all the ads studied, and it features women of color; and
- There were no ads featuring Native Americans.

How Women of Color Are Portrayed in Ethnic Magazines

Ethnic magazines focus on one group of ethnic women and underrrepresent majority women and ethnic women who are not in their group. Women of color are more likely to be portrayed with men in ethnic magazines than in majority magazines, and there are higher percentages of males in these magazines. Part of the explanation for this may relate to the fact that both *Filipina* and *Ebony* target more of a family readership, whereas the other magazines have more of a female focus. Despite the fact that more men and couples are seen in ethnic ads, only one interracial couple was shown in all of the ads, and this occurred in one of the Black magazines. This suggests some continuing discomfort with portraying interracial relationships.

Ethnic magazines, like majority magazines, feature women of color in ads for alcohol and cigarettes and show low percentages of ads for health and medicine. Given the long-term health problems in many ethnic communities, it is disturbing to see ads devoted to products that can impair health rather than promote wellness. A similarity is found in ethnic magazines, which, like majority magazines, use women in provocative and sexualized ads to promote products unrelated to sex.

There appeared to be some competing themes in ethnic magazines. On the one hand, models showed somewhat more diversity in size, especially in African American magazines. This appears to suggest some healthy resistance to using only super-thin models as is often seen in majority publications. It also appears that minority magazines show a diversity of appearances and no longer focus only on lighter skinned and more anglicized-looking models. However, there also seems to be a very subtle but intransigent adherence to White beauty standards as well. In ethnic magazines women are exhorted to change their appearance by straightening or texturing their apparently unruly hair, lightening or covering up their skin, and generally conforming to the flawless appearance of models. The fact that ethnic magazines show a diversity of colors but also pay allegiance to White beauty standards suggests ambivalence in advertising messages from a racial identity development perspective. It is positive that magazine ads feature more Afrocentric-looking models but there are vestiges of perhaps a realistic reminder that White females continue to epitomize what society deems to be beautiful.

In contrast to majority magazines, there were fewer sexually provocative ads in ethnic magazines. Majority individuals also seemed to occupy a different role in ethnic magazine ads than did ethnic individuals in majority ads. For example, European American women were not reverse-stereotyped as exotic or sexually provocative in ethnic magazines. White individuals were not used to advertise less desirable products such as alcohol or cigarettes. In fact several ads appeared somewhat paternalistic by showing White individuals offering words of support or encouragement to people of color in work settings.

CONCLUSIONS

Bias, stereotypes, and mixed messages appear to be alive and well in magazine ads. Ethnic women are still underrepresented based on their population in majority publications. Only African American females have come close to achieving proportionate representation in the majority magazines examined. It is striking to note that Native American females were not depicted at all in any of the ads. It appears that the paucity of this population group and their broad dispersion across the United States makes them an insignificant consumer market to advertisers. Hence, they are ignored.

Despite the low representation of women of color in majority magazines, they are still portrayed in ads that are sexual or exotic or that show them advertising less socially desirable products. It is stunning to see that magazine ads still show such biases toward women of color. The goal of advertising is to appeal to consumers, and yet advertisers are insensitive to the increasing numbers of ethnic women and the expanded financial markets that these women represent. Some researchers have noted that many ethnic minority women should be considered prime consumers because they make major financial decisions in their families (Dates, 1993).

Because ethnic women also buy and are exposed to the ads of majority magazines, it is long overdue for these publications to make more accurate representations of these women. Given the power of the media, men, women, and children of all races should not be exposed to ethnic women in ads that disproportionately associate them with less socially desirable products such as alcohol, in need of help for damaged hair, or dependent on advice for cooking or finding low-budget stores. These images reinforce negative stereotypes. Furthermore, researchers have consistently noted that because of the widespread segregation of people's social lives, most of what people learn about other races comes from the media and not personal experiences (Entman & Rojecki, 2000).

In ethnic magazines, there are also mixed messages. It is positive to see some diversity in body sizes and that not all ads feature anglicized models. But ethnic magazines do reflect subtle messages reinforcing majority beauty standards that can be damaging to the self-esteem of ethnic minority women. This reinforcement of majority beauty standards also has a major impact on what partners of ethnic women come to value as beautiful and can lead partners to feel that they are forced to settle for what is less than ideal in terms of societal standards of attractiveness.

It is also of concern that the two African American magazines focus more on cigarettes and alcohol than do most of the other magazines and less on health and medicine. These magazines could play an important public service by attempting to raise the health awareness of their readership and decrease negative stereotyping.

This present study is limited in scope by highlighting only 18 magazines over three frames within a year. Future research should expand on the number of magazine issues studied and the range of magazines used and include a longitudinal focus. Research should also document the racial and gender breakdown of the gatekeepers in journalism and advertising and hold these individuals accountable for doing a better job to increase the proportions of ethnic women of color in more positive and less stereotyped ad representations. The intransigence of stereotypes of women of color indicates that feminist psychology must continue to monitor and research the biases and distortions in how society treats all women.

Consumers across race need to let magazine publishers know that they will no longer buy magazines or advertised products in publications that practice stereotyping and marginalization. The world is shrinking in size as people become increasingly linked to one another through communication networks. People continue to rely heavily on the media for information. A collective effort must be made to ensure that magazines do a better job of reflecting society's rich multicultural population. Prejudice, bias, and distortion toward women of color in society cannot be fostered. The economic, political, and social costs are too great.

REFERENCES

American Society of Newspaper Editors. (2003, April 8). *Minority newsroom employment inches up in 2003*. News release. Retrieved March 1, 2003, from http://www.asne.org/index.cfm?ID=4446

Bogart, L. (1990). *Strategy in advertising: Matching media and messages to markets and motivations* (2nd ed.). Lincolnwood, IL: NTC Business Books.

Collins, R. K. L., & Skover, D. M. (1993). Commerce and communication. *Texas Law Review, 71*, 697–746.

Courtney, A. E., & Lockeretz, S. W. (1971). A woman's place: An analysis of the roles portrayed by women in magazine advertisements. *Journal of Marketing Research, 8*, 92–95.

Creedon, P. (2004). Introduction: We've come a long way, maybe. In R. Rush, C. Oukrop, & P. Creedon (Eds.) *Seeking equity for women in journalism and mass communication education: A 30 year update* (pp. xv–xvii). Mahwah, NJ: Erlbaum.

Dates, J. L. (1993). Advertising. In J. L. Dates & W. Barlow (Eds.), *Split image: African Americans in the mass media* (pp. 461–493). Washington, DC: Howard University Press.

Entman, R. M., & Rojecki, A. (2000). *The Black image in the White mind: Media and race in America*. Chicago: The University of Chicago Press.

Essence: About us. (2003). Retrieved January 28, 2003, from http://www.essence.com/

Family Circle. (2003). Retrieved January 28, 2003, from http://www.familycircle.com/info/readers.jsp

Filipinas Magazine. (2001, June 30). Retrieved January 28, 2003, from http://www.filipinasmag.com/Advertising/circ.htm

Green, M. (1991). *Invisible people: The depiction of minorities in magazine ads and catalogs*. New York: City of New York Department of Consumer Affairs.

Johnson, S., & Kressin, L. (2002, October). *The face on the cover: Racial diversity in fashion magazines 1996–2000*. Paper presented at the annual Association for Women in Communication Professional Conference, Denver, Colorado.

Johnson Publishing Company. (2003). Retrieved January 28, 2003, from http://www.johnsonpublishing.com/me2/dirsect.asp?sid=0dbc492d47324d88af77f382aeb79f63&nm=magazines

Plous, S., & Neptune, D. (1997). Racial and gender bias in magazine advertising: A content analytic study. *Psychology of Women Quarterly, 21,* 627–644.

Rhodes, J. (1993). Falling through the cracks: Studying women of color in mass communication. In P. J. Creedon (Ed.), *Women in mass communication* (2nd ed., pp. 24–31). Thousand Oaks, CA: Sage.

Shuey, A. M., King, N., & Griffith, B. (1953). Stereotypes of Negroes and Whites: An analysis of magazine pictures. *Public Opinion Quarterly, 17,* 281–287.

Standard Rate and Data Service. (2001). *Standard rate and data service, consumer magazine advertising source*. Des Plaines, IL: Serial Publications.

Taylor, C. R., Lee, J. Y., & Stern, B. B. (1996). Portrayals of African, Hispanic, and Asian Americans in magazine advertising. In R. P. Hill (Ed.), *Marketing and consumer research in the public interest* (pp. 133–150). Thousand Oaks, CA: Sage.

United States of America world magazine trends 2001/2002. (2003). Retrieved January 28, 2003, from http://www.magazineworld.org/members/wmt/pdfs/usawmt01.pdf

14

AGING TO PERFECTION OR PERFECTLY AGED? THE IMAGE OF WOMEN GROWING OLDER ON TELEVISION

KIM S. KJAERSGAARD

After a hard day's work, a middle-aged woman settles down for an evening of prime-time television. Sitcoms and dramas alike sport slim young actors, often wearing sexy outfits. Of the few older women shown, one is an overweight, overbearing, meddling mother, and another is a passive, sedentary wife. Still another is an insensitive businesswoman who contributes to the comedy by endeavoring to be sexy but apparently doesn't realize that she is past her prime. Commercials promise that "priceless youth" is affordable through special cosmetics or workout machines and encourage women to "fight aging every step of the way." Other ads offer medicines to help older people with aches and pains feel young and alive again. After an evening of television, the woman goes to bed feeling depressed.

Aging is still primarily a woman's issue (Cohen, 2002; Hurd, 1999). And television is a powerful means for shaping attitudes and beliefs about aging and gender (Cohen, 2002; Eschholz, Bufkin, & Long, 2002; Signorielli, 2001). Recent research indicates that images on television continue to celebrate youth and reflect a double standard of aging, with women being more negatively portrayed in the aging process than men (Cohen, 2002; Eschholz et al., 2002; Gerbner, 1998; Hurd, 1999). What can be done to foster more accurate and positive images of older women on television? Although there is no simple solution to this problem, increased effort is needed to change the vision of aging on television and ultimately shift the conceptual paradigm to enhance the journey through life for everyone.

ISSUES IN CONCEPTUALIZING WOMEN'S AGING

A variety of interrelated issues militate against a unified vision regarding women's aging. One issue is the paucity of theories. It is amazing that although women have long comprised the majority of the elderly, there are few adequate theories of aging for women (Clarke, 2001; Lippert, 1997; Scharlach & Fuller-Thomson, n.d.). Further, definitions of aging are continually changing (Bradley & Longino, 2001; Cohen, 2002; Maddox, 1996). Traditionally based solely on chronological age, current definitions of aging have broadened to include various facets of life, such as psychological, cultural, spiritual, and gender differences (Cohen, 2002). Hence, aging is now viewed as a more complex and diverse process than originally conceived.

In addition, although much research has focused on the similarities involved in the aging process, relatively little has focused on the diversity of the aging process, especially for women (Bradley & Longino, 2001; Lippert, 1997). Neugarten (1996), a leading pioneer in fighting the stereotype that old age is homogenous, stated that "not only do people grow old in very different ways, but the range of individual differences becomes greater with the passage of life time" (p. 11). More research is needed to highlight the web of cultural, social, and individual characteristics, traits, and factors that contribute to the diverse experiences of women growing older.

A correlated issue historically impeding research on the diversity of women's aging has been the dominance of male developmental norms as universal. Indeed, the assumption that women develop in a similar fashion as men went unchallenged for decades (Tavris, 1992). There is now a growing body of literature that fosters a new perspective on women's development, emphasizing that women have their own norms and rhythm for change and growth across the life span. For example, Gilligan (1993) proposed that whereas men's moral development is based on principles of justice and independence, women's moral development tends to be based on an ethic of caring, relationships, and interdependence.

All of these issues combine to contribute remarkable gaps in knowledge regarding women's development and aging. And this leads to the current situation: Many commonly held images and beliefs about older women are based on negative stereotypes and myths (Cohen, 2002; Hurd, 1999; Scharlach & Fuller-Thomson, n.d.; Troll, 1984). What makes this situation alarming is that recent research has discovered that older people with a positive self-perception of aging live an average of seven and a half years longer than do those with a more negative self-perception of aging (Levy, Slade, Kunkel, & Kasl, 2002). Thus, one's images of aging may have a very profound impact on one's life. Hence, there is a need for accurate information and images of women's aging not only for informative purposes (to more fully understand the nature of women's current issues regarding aging) but also for reparative and preventive action (to help foster optimal growth for both women and men). Although numerous avenues could be taken to address these issues, the focus here is on the social construction of images of aging and how television is a significant vehicle for perpetuating or changing those images.

THE SOCIAL CONSTRUCTION OF AGING
AND THE ROLE OF TELEVISION

Reality is, to a large extent, socially constructed (Berger & Luckmann, 1966; see also Gergen & Gergen, 2001; Rodkin, 1993). This is a simple fact, but it is easily overlooked at this time when the influence of one's genes on thought and behavior is the rave topic of the day. From a personal constructivist approach (Viney, 1992; see also Belenky, Clinchy, Goldberger, & Tarule, 1986), people are both observers and creators of reality; that is, to a certain extent people build their own reality. By acknowledging the dialectical relationship between the various factors and processes involved in construing reality, this theoretical framework views people as dynamically engaged with life rather than as purely objective observers (Hare-Mustin & Marecek, 1990). From this theoretical perspective, people create their own meanings and notions about what it means to grow older. That means that images of aging can be rich, diverse, multifaceted, and, most important, fairly mutable. This is a potent perspective for helping to change current concepts of women aging (Hare-Mustin & Marecek, 1990).

"It is not news that age-related norms are socially constructed. What is news is that such norms are, under conditions of social change, continually reconstructed. Societies, not just individuals, age and develop as populations age" (Maddox, 1996, p. 22). Indeed, broad social trends are helping to form a new tapestry of aging for both women and men. Over the past few decades, the demographic landscape of the United States has changed tremendously. In particular, three trends have merged to create a unique phenomenon that is popularly termed "the greying of America": (a) the average life expectancy has significantly increased, (b) there has been a substantial decrease in birth rates, and (c) the baby boom generation is now reaching retirement age (Dychtwald & Flower, 1990). These trends, along with other movements, such as the Women's Rights Movement, have helped to instigate a shift in the quality, pattern, and texture of people's lives, especially regarding age- and gender-related roles and activities.

In this context of change, Bateson (1990) proposed a dynamic image of women growing older. She conveyed that the context of people's lives is constantly changing and hence, they are continually adapting to life while at the same time actively creating their lives. The image is one of passionate engagement with living, a "dance of intimacy" (borrowing the relationship metaphor of Lerner, 1989)—only the dance is with each person's own life. Within this dance is an ongoing need for a new and more flexible vision of the future, especially given a continually changing society. As aptly portrayed by Bateson (1990),

> Fluidity and discontinuity are central to the reality in which we live.
> Women have always lived discontinuous and contingent lives. . . . [We]

need to look at multiple lives to test and shape our own. . . . [There is a] need for multiple models, so that it is possible to weave something new from many different threads. (pp. 13–16)

Indeed, as the bulk of the baby boomers approach retirement, they are redefining what it means to grow older, such as changes in work and retirement options, revisions in family composition, differences in activities and projects pursued by older people, shifts in attitudes toward growing older, and more openness about relationships in older age (Dychtwald & Flower, 1990; Moen, 1998; Wattenberg, 1986;). As optimistically proposed by Sherman (1996), "As America ages, we are witnessing an altered concept of age, one that includes surprising possibilities and uncharted territories—'a landscape without a map.' Adventure has become a new metaphor for age" (p. 1). The problem inherent in this change is that there are few good models to help guide people through the complexities of this transition in living and relating.

If each person is responsible for crafting his or her own life (Bateson, 1990), then what is helping us to formulate our journey through such shifting sands of change? More important, who or what is helping youth to formulate their foundational images for launching them into the adult world? The not-surpising answer is that the media—television, movies, magazines, and newspapers—play an extremely powerful role in shaping constructions of reality and, hence, people's model of what their journey through life will be like (Cohen, 2002; Eschholz et al., 2002; Signorielli, 2001). Television in particular has been identified as an extremely powerful educational force in society. As Signorielli (2001) stated, "Television is the central and most pervasive mass medium in the culture of the United States. In the past fifty years it has come to play a distinctive and historically unprecedented role as our nation's most common, constant, and vivid learning environment" (p. 34).

Exposure to television's influence is fairly substantial. Americans tend to watch television an average of 3 to 4 hours per day (Eschholz et al., 2002; Woodard & Gridina, 2000); viewing television thus comprises a large portion of Americans' leisure time. As poignantly stated by Kilbourne (2001),

The average American will spend one and one half years of his or her life watching television commercials. The ads sell a great deal more than products. They sell values, images, and concepts of success and worth, love and sexuality, popularity and normalcy. *They tell us who we are and who we should be* [italics added]. (p. 1)

Research has lent support to this notion that television influences the formation of people's identities and values by indicating that television is a powerful social force influencing concepts of gender and aging (Cohen, 2002; Eschholz et al., 2002; Signorielli, 2001) as well as behavior toward the elderly (Ross, 2000; Signorielli, 2001). The influence of television on concepts of gender has been suggested to begin at a very early age (Smith, 1994). It is logical to assume that perhaps the same thing happens for learning the concepts associated with age and aging. Adults should therefore be concerned about what children are learning from television regarding adult life. What, then, does the most prominent form of media—television—currently convey regarding images of aging for women?

RESEARCH REGARDING IMAGES OF WOMEN GROWING OLDER ON TELEVISION

A substantive amount of research has focused on how television programs depict women. Television images of women tend to vary somewhat between the types of programs (documentaries, soap operas, movies, etc.) and time of airing (prime-time television versus late-night or daytime shows). However, research results are broadly consistent across both program types and time of airing. These findings can be clustered into the following categories: (a) demographic profiles of female television characters, (b) demographic profiles of older characters, (c) types of roles, and (d) age-related changes in these demographic profiles and types of roles. Although this is not an exhaustive review of the literature, it highlights recent and relevant findings that are extremely poignant in their consistency regarding television's negative images of older women.

Demographic Profiles of Female Television Characters

Recent research indicates that in general, women are underrepresented on television (Greenberg & Collette, 1997; Lauzen, 2002; Signorielli, 2001). Contrary to current demographics, there are twice as many men as women on television (Gerbner, 1998; Greenberg & Collette, 1997), and in particular, women over 40 years of age are underrepresented (Lauzen, 2002; see also Elasmar, Hasegawa, & Brain, 1999). In addition, characters of the young age group (from 25 to 44 years of age) appear twice as frequently (61%) as they do in the real world (30%) (Cumberbatch, Gauntlett, Littlejohns, Woods, & Stephenson, 1999; Gerbner, 1998). Furthermore, the characters portrayed by women are younger than in previous years (Gerbner, 1998). Hence, the focus in television remains on young women.

Demographic Profiles of Older Television Characters

In general, older people are underrepresented on television (Greenberg & Collette, 1997; Signorielli, 2001). Approximately 7% of the characters are 60 years or older whereas 21% of the current population are 60 years or older (Cumberbatch et al., 1999). Older men also outnumber older women on television (Lauzen, 2002), with more women than men over 50 being portrayed as elderly in character (Signorielli, 2001). What is worse, the proportion of older people on television has actually decreased over the past few years instead of reflecting the increase in the older population (Gerbner, 1998). Overall, these results indicate an increasing emphasis on youth, along with a continued predominance of male over female characters.

Types of Roles

In general, women tend to be cast in less serious or supporting roles than do men (Elasmar et al., 1999; Kilbourne, 2001), and women tend to be cast primarily in domestic or romantic type roles (Greenberg & Collette, 1997; Kilbourne, 2001). Overall, men are better represented than women in every single genre on television.

Furthermore, older people—especially women—are presented in a negative light or in a stereotypical fashion (Cumberbatch et al., 1999; Greenberg & Collette, 1997; Scharlach & Fuller-Thomson, n.d.; Signorielli, 2001). Older women are likely to be portrayed as victims, asexual, dependent, frail, vulnerable, poor, grumpy, antiquated, passive, invisible, and so on. Rarely are older women represented in prominent roles or featured as strong leading characters. In essence, it is apparent that older women's roles on television still tend to be negatively stereotyped and do not provide diverse and positive images of aging.

Age-Related Changes in Demographic Profiles and Types of Roles

Perhaps most alarming is the research finding that the presence of women on television after the age of 30 decreases more rapidly than does the presence of men after the age of 40 (Gerbner, 1998, see also Signorielli, 2001). Men have a relatively slow and later exit from the television screen compared with women, who tend to just vanish from the stage and at an earlier age. Moreover, Gerbner (1998) indicated that as women characters age on television, they are more likely to be portrayed as both sexless and evil. This age-related trend was noted to be exclusive to female characters. Gerbner also found that "as characters age, they lose importance, value, and effectiveness" (p. 11). This seems to hold true especially for women characters. Overall, older women on television portray a disproportionate number of negative characterizations, and all compacted into fewer television roles than for male characters. This paints a rather bleak picture of women growing older.

IMPACT AND IMPLICATIONS

What these findings indicate is rather alarming: Television is providing a significantly distorted and negative view not only of what being a woman is all about but especially of what growing older is and means for women. As eloquently voiced by Gerbner (1998), "the world of television is frozen in a time-warp of obsolete and damaging representations" (p. 3). In particular, television portrays women, regardless of age, the same as it always has: focusing on the external (physical body) with little diversity in roles. These obsolete and damaging representations have profound implications for both men and women, as well as for society in general.

A highly negative consequence of these images is that many women internalize these stereotypes, which potentially limits their lives and contributions to society (Eschholz et al., 2002; Kilbourne, 2001). Adolescents, who are in the process of forming their identities, may be particularly vulnerable to incorporating these images into their self-concepts, and thus run the risk of constricting their options not only for how they live their youth but also for how they live their adult lives. How much potential is unknowingly being squelched or misdirected in this process?

In addition, these images perpetuate the myth that beauty is only skin deep—that one's worth is based on one's physical body. On television, rarely is anyone in a leading role overweight, homely, deformed, or disabled (Kilbourne, 2001). This is a particularly powerful message. Women continue to perceive aging as "the relentless enemy," and the consequential "culturally promoted self-hatred" is evident by the multi-billion-dollar cosmetics and beauty industries (Scharlach & Fuller-Thomson, n.d., p. 1). More alarming is the statement made by Kilbourne (2001), who indicated that for television, "Growing older is the great taboo. Women are encouraged to remain little girls ('because innocence is sexier than you think'), to be passive and dependent, never to mature" (p. 2). Many women seem to have taken this to heart and go to great lengths to look young (plastic surgery is a billion-dollar business). After all, who wants to be considered old or asexual?

It is common knowledge that American society has long valued youth and beauty. As expressed by Kubler-Ross and Kessler (2000): "We don't value age in Western culture. We don't see wrinkles as part of life; they're something to be prevented, hidden, removed" (p. 120). This fear of wrinkles is deeply ingrained in our society and is reinforced by television, and the impact of this fear is far reaching. For example, recent research (Ross, 2000; Signorielli, 2001) has indicated that the negative stereotyping of older people on television contributes to how they are disrespectfully treated in their own lives, especially by younger people. This disrespect is shown by behavior conveying the belief that old people are antiquated and therefore have little, if anything, of relevance to offer young adults, and by the use of pejorative terms (e.g., "old geezer" or "old hag").

With older women being portrayed on television from a negative perspective and in less than prominent roles, it is no wonder that many women (old and young alike) have fears about growing old. Indeed, society has been noted to be "deeply gerontophobic" (Dychtwald & Flower, 1990, p. 30; see also Cohen, 2002). Such deeply rooted fears and prejudices are not easily dismissed or eliminated, and serve only to muddy visions of what it means to grow old. Yet if these fears are not uprooted, the full potential of people's lives will remain dormant and unknown. Further, such fears constrict fullness of living for both the elderly (as stereotypes become self-fulfilling prophecies) and the youth (by encouraging the focus on external beauty instead of on living and relating). In addition, these fears help create an orientation to life that makes it more difficult to transition into and accept older age as well as to live life fully and age with integrity, precisely because this orientation blinds people to the opportunities of old age.

Overall, the relative absence of older women as well as positive images of women growing older on television provide a distorted view of reality—a warped perspective of growing older—and promote ageism along with sexism. How can these negative images of aging be changed and accurate and healthy visions of growing older be promoted?

POSITIVE STEPS TOWARD THE FUTURE

The first step in change is always awareness. If the profound impact of television on one's life is ignored, also ignored will be "one of the most powerful 'educational' forces in the culture—one that greatly affects our self-images, our ability to relate to each other, and effectively destroys any awareness and action that might help to change that climate" (Kilbourne, 2001, p. 3). Hence, more effort is needed to help raise awareness of the impact of television on people's lives. At the same time, research is needed to provide an ongoing and truthful assessment of television's impact (to avoid throwing the baby out with the bathwater).

Television needs to help debunk the myths about growing old, to demystify the aging process. The truth about aging needs to be portrayed; images are needed that help people look forward to and value growing older. These images need to portray growing older as a process of filling one's glass (aging to perfection) as opposed to depleting one's glass (becoming perfectly aged and decrepit). Such a positive image would help enrich everyone's lives, both young and old. Indeed, it has been suggested that helping youth to foster positive yet realistic images of one's aging self may promote later life satisfaction (Cross & Markus, 1991).

The central imperative regarding images of women growing older is diversity and depth. To dispel myths and stereotypes about women growing older, people need to see and experience the diversity of lives across the life span reflecting both individuality and common transformations (Troll, 1984). Because television is such a potent influence on people's lives, it needs to provide a diversity of images about growing older that will help both women and men. And these images need to include ethnic diversity, as ethnic minorities also remain significantly underrepresented on prime-time television (Elasmar et al., 1999). Moreover, emphasis needs to be given to the real essence of life (the internal) as opposed to beauty and youth (the external).

Television also needs to engender new ways of thinking about old age and the process of growing old. This includes thinking outside the lines of current mainstream psychological theories that advocate healthy development as a process of moving toward autonomy and independence (male-based goals). Instead, fresh visions and theories are needed that embody healthy development as also involving growth toward positive interdependence (female-based goals). Hence, television needs to foster positive connections between people, especially between those of different ages, to make society a truly solid fabric of intergenerational ties.

In addition, more women need to be involved in the creation and production of television programs. Overall, women comprised approximately 23% of the creators, writers, editors, and producers for the 2001–2002 prime-time television season. At the same time, however, there was also a dramatic decrease from the previous 2000–2001 season in the percentage of women writers (from 27% to 19%) and women directors (from 12% to 8%) (Lauzen, 2002). This severe imbalance of male and female perspectives behind the scenes needs to be remedied to help achieve greater visibility and realistic images of older women on television.

Also, the (young) television writers need to be more accurate in their portrayal of older individuals. Older actors and actresses need to be used along with older people behind the camera. Prime examples of older actresses are Ann-Margret, who portrayed a vibrant and exciting older female character in *Grumpy Old Men*, and Sophia Loren, who successfully portrayed a sexy older woman in *Grumpier Old Men*.

In addition, older women need to be portrayed in prominent roles, such as main contributors to society and positive characters leading active and meaningful lives. However, as Ross (2000) indicated, the real issue is not about portraying old age in glowing terms. After all, older women do have health problems and other difficulties unique to their age. The core issue facing television is to reflect the inner beauty and diversity of all people, particularly that of older people's lives and experiences.

Television could also take a more active (and proactive) role in educating the public regarding the aging process, such as through documentaries or educational programs. Recent efforts to incorporate curriculum on aging into K–12 programs seem promising, such as those that present aging as a diversity issue (Wircenski & Walker, 1999) and promote aging appreciation (Chowdhary, 2002; see also Langer, 1999). Perhaps television could follow suit by supporting various educational programs on aging, thereby sowing seeds across several generations to help eradicate ageism.

Amid the sea of criticisms, however, it must be noted that some progress has been made regarding the images of older women on television. For example, the gap between the proportion of men and women on prime-time television is decreasing (Elasmar et al., 1999). And there are now more realistic portrayals of older women on television; consider the middle-aged female characters of Carmela Soprano and Dr. Jennifer Melfi on *The Sopranos* and the senior doctor character of Harriett Lanning on *Presidio Med*.

It must also be noted that perhaps the greatest challenge lies not with making changes in television, but with transforming society's own conceptual paradigms about aging. Although television may be a powerful social force in society, one cannot wait for television to broadcast better models of aging. People must begin reforming their own thoughts and living. These individual efforts in tandem with revised programming on television can create a stronger and more dynamic process of change that will more likely achieve a paradigm shift than either one could achieve separately.

In summary, to promote aging to perfection, television needs to portray growing older as continual and dynamic, as a creative dance of intimacy, thus encouraging a passionate engagement in living, as proposed by Bateson (1990). Television also needs to portray aging as filled with opportunities, using such techniques as the positive metaphors of adventure and creativity offered by Sherman (1996). At the core of both of these perspectives is the need to be flexible. Young women (and young men) need to be given a sense that they create their own lives—that they have choices and flexibility to live their lives—and that aging is not to be feared. Life is not something that passively happens to people; rather, it is something to be actively shaped. Television needs to provide a greater diversity of images of women (and men) growing older, thus offering choices and possibilities.

"To know how to grow old is the master-work of wisdom, and one of the most difficult chapters in the great art of living" (Henri Amiel, 1874, as cited in Vaillant, 2002, p. 3). From this perspective, we need all the help that we can get to navigate this most difficult part of our journey. Everyone needs to have models, mentors, and heroes to inspire them and to compel them to make the best of their lives. But most important, people need rich images of diverse possibilities from which to imagine and weave their own tapestry of life.

REFERENCES

Bateson, M. C. (1990). *Composing a life*. New York: Plume/Penguin Books.

Belenky, M. F., Clinchy, B. M., Goldberger, N. R., & Tarule, J. M. (1986). *Women's ways of knowing: The development of self, voice, and mind*. New York: Basic Books.

Berger, P. L., & Luckmann, T. (1966). *The social construction of reality*. Garden City, NY: Doubleday & Co.

Bradley, D. E., & Longino, C. F. (2001). How older people think about images of aging on advertising and the media. *Generations, 25*(3), 17–21.

Chowdhary, U. (2002). An intergenerational curricular module for teaching aging appreciation to seventh-graders. *Educational Gerontology, 28,* 553–560.

Clarke, L. H. (2001). Older women's bodies and the self: The construction of identity in later life. *Canadian Review of Sociology & Anthropology, 38,* 441–464.

Cohen, H. L. (2002). Developing media literacy skills to challenge television's portrayal of older women. *Educational Gerontology, 28,* 599–620.

Cross, S., & Markus, H. (1991). Possible selves across the life span. *Human Development, 34,* 230–255.

Cumberbatch, G., Gauntlett, S., Littlejohns, V., Woods, S., & Stephenson, C. (1999, July). *Too old for TV? The portrayal of older people on television: Executive summary.* Retrieved April 5, 2002, from http://members.netscapeonline.co.uk/crghq/olderpeople.htm

Dychtwald, K., & Flower, J. (1990). *Age wave.* New York: Bantam Books.

Elasmar, M., Hasegawa, K., & Brain, M. (1999). The portrayal of women in U.S. prime time television. *Journal of Broadcasting & Electronic Media, 43,* 20–34.

Eschholz, S., Bufkin, J., & Long, J. (2002). Symbolic reality bites: Women and racial/ethnic minorities in modern film. *Sociological Spectrum, 22,* 299–331.

Gerbner, G. (1998). *Casting the American scene: A look at the characters on prime time and daytime television from 1994-1997.* Retrieved April 5, 2002, from http://www.media-awareness.ca/eng/issues/minrep/resource/reports/gerbner.htm

Gergen, M., & Gergen, K. J. (2001). Positive aging: New images for a new age. *Ageing International, 27,* 3–21.

Gilligan, C. (1993). *In a different voice: Psychological theory and women's development.* Cambridge, MA: Harvard University Press.

Greenberg, B. S., & Collette, L. (1997). The changing faces on TV: A demographic analysis of network television's new seasons, 1966-1992. *Journal of Broadcasting & Electronic Media, 41,* 1–13.

Hare-Mustin, R. T., & Marecek, J. (1990). Gender and the meaning of difference: Postmodernism and psychology. In R. T. Hare-Mustin & J. Marecek (Eds.), *Making a difference: Psychology and the construction of gender* (pp. 22–64). New Haven, CT: Yale University Press.

Hurd, L. C. (1999). We're not old!: Older women's negotiation of aging and oldness. *Journal of Aging Studies, 13,* 419–439.

Kilbourne, J. (2001). *Beauty . . . and the beast of advertising.* Retrieved April 7, 2002, from http://www.medialit.org/ReadingRoom/Media&Values/beautynbeast.html

Kubler-Ross, E., & Kessler, D. (2000). *Life lessons.* New York: Scribner.

Langer, M. (1999). Changing youngster's perceptions of aging: Aging education's role. *Educational Gerontology, 25,* 549–554.

Lauzen, M. M. (2002). *Boxed in: Women on screen and behind the scenes in the 2001-2002 prime-time season: Executive Summary.* Retrieved January 16, 2003, from http://www.nywift.org/resources/status_lauzen2.html

Lerner, H. (1989). *The dance of intimacy.* New York: HarperPerennial.

Levy, B. R., Slade, M. D., Kunkel, S. R., & Kasl, S. V. (2002). Longevity increased by positive self-perceptions of aging. *Journal of Personality and Social Psychology, 83*, 261–270.

Lippert, L. (1997). Women at midlife: Implications for theories of women's adult development. *Journal of Counseling & Development, 76*, 16–22.

Maddox, G. L. (1996). Definitions and descriptions of age. In D. A. Neugarten (Ed.), *The meanings of age: Selected papers of Bernice L. Neugarten* (pp. 19–23). Chicago: The University of Chicago Press.

Moen, P. (1998). Recasting careers: Changing reference groups, risks, and realities. *Generations, 22*(1), 40–45.

Neugarten, B. L. (1996). The aging society and my academic life. In D. A. Neugarten (Ed.), *The meanings of age: Selected papers of Bernice L. Neugarten* (pp. 1–16). Chicago: The University of Chicago Press.

Rodkin, P. C. (1993). The psychological reality of social constructions. *Ethnic and Racial Studies, 16*, 633–656.

Ross, K. (2000, May). *Growing old invisibly: Third agers and television.* Retrieved April 7, 2002, from http//www.coventry.ac.uk/ccmr/publish2/Invisibly.pdf

Scharlach, A. E., & Fuller-Thomson, E. (n.d.). *Images of older women: Curriculum module on women and aging.* Retrieved April 8, 2002, from http://socrates.berkeley.edu/~aging/ModuleWomen.html

Sherman, A. (1996). *Arts participation: The greying of America.* Retrieved January 5, 2003, from http://www.nea.gov/partner/Accessibility/Monograph/Sherman.html

Signorielli, N. (2001). Aging on television: The picture in the nineties. *Generations, 25*(3), 34–38.

Smith, L. J. (1994). A content analysis of gender differences in children's advertising. *Journal of Broadcasting & Electronic Media, 38*, 323–337.

Tavris, C. (1992). *The mismeasure of woman.* New York: Touchstone.

Troll, L. E. (1984, August). *Poor, dumb and ugly: The older women in contemporary society.* Paper presented at the meeting of the American Psychological Association, Toronto, Ontario, Canada.

Vaillant, G. (2002). *Aging well.* Boston: Little, Brown.

Viney, L. L. (1992). Can we see ourselves changing? Toward a personal construct model of adult development. *Human Development, 35*, 65–75.

Wattenberg, E. (1986). The fate of baby boomers and their children. *Social Work, 31*, 20–28.

Wircenski, M., & Walker, M. (1999). Age as a diversity issue in grades K-12 and in higher education. *Educational Gerontology, 25*, 491–500.

Woodard, E. H., & Gridina, N. (2000). *Media in the home 2000: The fifth annual survey of parents and children.* Philadelphia: The Annenberg Public Policy Center of the University of Pennsylvania.

AFTERWORD

After reading this book, one can conclude that media are an integral part of the daily lives of children, women, and men in the United States. Media are everywhere and present every day. Media matter. This volume is a call for psychologists who are so inclined to become involved with reshaping and shaping the images that mold human behavior.

Psychologists who are practitioners, scientists, public policy advocates, and educators may consider ways to work with the media. Although psychologists share the role of consumers with the general population, their potential media-related roles are as varied as the numerous constituencies in the discipline.

Media can be used to distribute information to the public about mental health and mental illness. The Practice Directorate of the American Psychological Association (APA) assumed this role after September 11, 2001. The information on the APA Web site was user friendly and easily accessible, with a focus on developmental stages of reactions to the unfolding events. In addition to print information, the Practice Directorate also produced, with the Discovery Health Channel, a documentary entitled *Aftermath: The Road to Resilience.* It was shown on television and has been distributed to many psychologists for use in their respective communities. Psychology may continue a proactive stance by producing documentaries that address life issues.

On a larger scale, psychology alone or with other mental health disciplines could contract with cable channels to produce talk shows, documentaries, and news programming to keep the general public current on developments in the field.

News shows with a focus on psychological implications can include analyses across the developmental spectrum or focus on targeted groups of persons. Such programming could increase the psychological awareness of viewers. Talk shows could feature research findings and effective interventions at both the individual and community levels. Documentaries can be excellent resources for instruction and training. Psychologists with an interest in media may become consultants on documentary projects or produce documentaries that can advance learning in the field. This form of media is especially powerful as a way to introduce marginalized groups to the general population, offering alternative images and contextual information.

Media can play a role in the development of girls in terms of their gender roles, body image, and sexuality. Psychologists may create ways to address the gender and sexual development of girls that are proactive and expansive rather than reactive and restrictive. It may mean working in the entertainment industry, perhaps producing comic books, video games, and cartoon shows. The identification of subtle and not-so-subtle shifts could lead to changes in how girls experience the development of multiple identities. This volume is a call for psychologists to become consultants on television programs. Psychologists who consult to television shows by reviewing scripts can focus on strengthening the story while not interfering with the creativity of the writers (Alvin Poussaint, personal communication, 2005). The idea is to develop a story that is psychologically believable. Demeaning storylines, stereotypes in their many forms, and gratuitous violence can be brought to the attention of the writers as points for discussion. They can suggest themes that can educate the viewer and possibly promote healthy interactions. The psychologist can be presented as a resource whose input can add to the cohesion of the script as the story is being developed. The highly successful *Cosby Show* in the 1980s, for example, employed Alvin Poussaint, MD, as a consultant.

The portrayal of psychologists in films has been extremely problematic. The discipline may campaign for a healthier presentation of psychologists, especially female psychologists. Psychologists can be proactive in offering their services as consultants for film and television programming that cast female and male actors as psychologists. Even if the biased presentations continue, psychologists can produce empirical documents that lend credence to the position that the images are inaccurate and misleading. One effect of these distorted images is that they may discourage individuals from seeking needed mental health services. These distortions are not benign in their influence and effect.

Some state psychological associations participate in the Healthy Workplace Program, a project endorsed by the APA Practice Directorate. In addition to assessing the psychological health of the organization, the criteria may be expanded to include a review of job advertisements, especially those involving technical tasks and skills. The focus would be on the inclusion of women in the ads.

"If it bleeds, it leads" is one statement that drives both the print and electronic media. Women as perpetrators appear to receive especially negative treatment in the media. Psychologists may present an annual report of women in the print media, just as there is an annual report of children in the media. The report could document biases in the media as well as any progress that may have taken place after such reports have been published over time.

Psychologists also could write op-ed articles for their local and regional newspapers, commenting on news coverage involving women as victims and perpetrators. The topic of women and violence can also include reviews of films, television programs, and video games. Articles distributed for printing in-state psychological association newsletters are a way to alert psychologists across the country about media images of women in violent contexts. They can be the awareness foundation that may generate more op-ed pieces in newspapers.

Psychologists who focus on community psychology may lobby for effective intervention programs for girls and women to be featured in the *Living* sections of newspapers. Psychology as a source of hope and good news for girls and women would be the goal of such a series.

Women who belong to the emerging majority groups are too often portrayed in stereotypical roles and contexts. Given the changing demographics in the United States and the persistence of stereotypes about women, working with the media to reduce the pervasiveness of such assaults on the self-esteem of these girls and women could be a source of affirmation. Advertisements for products appear to have racial or ethnic overtones. The collection and dissemination of such data in newspapers may alert the companies to this damaging pattern of advertising.

We recognize that every chapter in this book will not have been of interest to every psychologist. But whether our readers are practitioners, scientists, educators, or public policy advocates, we hope that this has been, for them, a call to action. The message we hoped to impart is that psychologists can collect data and disseminate the findings in the popular media. They can consult with the media. These activities will require an active and concerted effort to make psychology an integral part of mass media in the United States. It is time.

INDEX

AAUW. *See* American Association of University Women

ABC television network, 63

Abused women, therapeutic treatment of, 149–150

Actors, character traits of characters vs., 72

Adolescent Femininity Ideology Scale (AFIS), 30, 31, 33

Adolescent Masculinity Ideology in Relationships Scale (AMIRS), 30, 31, 34, 35

Adolescents

    aggressive behaviors in, 157

    aggressive responses to outsiders in, 157

    effect of television on. *See* Television, effect of, on sexual behavior of adolescent girls

    identity development in African American, 170, 174

    and images of older people on television, 205

Adult themes, 63

Advertising

    and body dissatisfaction, 43

    depiction of women in television, 63

    and internalization of thin ideal, 46

    profound impact of, 186

    and social comparison, 44

    women of color in magazine. *See* Women of color in magazine advertisements

AFIS. *See* Adolescent Femininity Ideology Scale

African American women, 11. *See also* Women of color

African American women, film portrayal of, 169–182

    and actual vs. ideal self, 176–177

    and adolescent identity development, 170, 174

    in *Bamboozled,* 172–174

    and barriers to identity development, 178, 180

    beauty myths in, 180

    and character selection, 171

    connection as value in, 180

    in *Crooklyn,* 176–178

    and female companionship, 174–175

    and feminist psychology, 181

    ideals of character in, 172–173, 176–178

    and lack of agency, 175

    partner violence in, 177

    and pathways to development, 181

    and political priorities, 179

    and power, 178–179

    in *School Daze,* 174–176

    and self-respect, 176

    and sexual past of characters, 172, 173

    in *She's Gotta Have It,* 178–179

African American women, in reality TV shows, 79–80

African American women, suggestive videos featuring, 13

Aftermath: The Road to Resilience (documentary), 211

Age, treatment of, in video games, 117

Age of Empires II: The Age of Kings (video game), 119

Aggression

    effect of televised, on children, 155–156

    and exposure to violence in video games, 118

    indirect, on television. *See* Indirect aggression, television portrayal of

Aging women, as portrayed on television, 199–208

    and beauty myths, 205

    and diversity of aging, 200

    and dynamic image of aging women, 200–202

    efforts to change, 206–208

    and fears of growing old, 205–206

    and female character profiles, 203

    and male developmental norms, 200

    and older character profiles, 203–204

    and paucity of theories of aging, 199–200

    reality TV shows, 79

    and role types of characters, 204

    and self-image, 205

    significance of, 200

215

and social construction of aging, 201–203

Agnes of God (film), 108

Alda, Alan, 102

Aliens (film), 136

Ally McBeal (television program), 159

The Amazing Race (television program), 73–80

American Academy of Child and Adolescent Psychiatry, 127

American Academy of Pediatrics, 127

American Association of University Women (AAUW), 95–97

An American Family (television program), 74, 75

American Medical Association, 127

American Psychological Association (APA), 104, 105, 110, 111, 127, 211

American Psychological Association Media Watch Committee, 110–111

American Psychological Association Task Force on Television and Society, 156

Amiel, Henri, 208

AMIRS. *See* Adolescent Masculinity Ideology in Relationships Scale

Analyze That (film), 105, 106

Analyze This (film), 102, 111

Anderson, C. A., 118, 128

Aniston, Jennifer, 60

Annan, Kofi, 144

Ann-Margret, 207

Antwone Fisher (film), 105

APA. *See* American Psychological Association

Archer, Anne, 137

Asian descent, women of
    and *Filipinas* magazine, 189, 190
    in reality TV shows, 79

The Bachelor (television program), 66, 74, 79

The Bachelorette (television program), 66

Baldur's Gate (video game), 119

Bamboozled (film), 172–174

Barriers, developmental, 178, 180

Basic Instinct (film), 106, 107

Bateson, M. C., 201–202

Battaglia, John David, 148

Battered woman's syndrome, 134

Beauty myths, 180, 205

Becker, Anne, 41, 43

Bergen, Candace, 65

Bergman, Ingrid, 103

Bewitched (television program), 61

Big Brother (television program), 74–76

Bischoff, R. J., 104, 109

Bitch: In Praise of Difficult Women (Elizabeth Wurtzel), 136

Bitches, strong women as, 77–78, 80

Blind Date, 74

Bobbitt, Lorena, 146

Bobo, J., 169, 171, 182

Body Chemistry 3 (film), 106, 108

Body dissatisfaction
    influence of media on, 8–9
    and internalization of thin ideal, 45–46
    and social comparison, 44–45

Body ideal, feminine, 41–42

Body image
    in African American women, 180
    and depiction of women on television, 63–64

Body image, effect of media on girls' and women's, 41–51
    dissonance-based prevention, 48–49
    and eating disorders, 49–50
    and female television characters, 63–64
    and internalization of thin ideal, 45–46
    media literacy programs, 47–48
    prevention studies, 47–49
    and previous studies of media exposure, 42–43
    and social comparison, 44–45

Boston Legal (television program), 65

Boy Meets World (television program), 63, 66

Brandt, Michael, 146

Bravo Network, 76–77

Brooks, Mel, 102

Brosnan, Pierce, 61

Browne, Angela, 134

Buffy the Vampire Slayer (television program), 31, 33–36

Bulimia, 46

The Burning Bed (film), 136–137

Bushman, B. J., 118, 128

Buttafuoco, Mary Jo, 148

Cabela's Big Game Hunter 2 (video game), 119

Cable television, 62, 64, 77

Carmela Soprano (character in *The Sopranos*), 208

Carolyn Carmichael (character in *Crooklyn*), 176–178

Carroll, Diahann, 61

Catfights, 80
CBS television network, 63
Charlie's Angels (television program), 61
Chicago Hope (television program), 111
Child abuse, by women, 138–139
Children. *See also* Adolescents
    aggressive responses to outsiders in, 157
    effect of aggression on television on, 155–156
Christianity, 78
Color of Night (film), 106–108
Command & Conquer: Tiberian Sun (video game), 119, 125
Commercials, depiction of women on television, 63
Computer advertisements in magazines, gender narratives in, 85–97
    content analysis, 88–89
    discourse analysis, 89–93
    and ethnicity in ads, 88–89
    and gender gap in computer science, 95–96
    and gender stereotypes, 94
    and influence of advertising, 94
    intervention strategies, 96–97
    methodology, 87
    previous studies, 86
    and readership of magazines, 94
    study results, 87–93
    themes of advertisements, 95
Computer science, 93
Comstock, G., 156
Conjoint therapy, 150
Connection (as value), 180
Conspiracy Theory (film), 102
Constructivism, 201
Content analysis, 86
COPS (television program), 75
Copycat (film), 106, 108
Cornett, J., 104
Cory (television character from *Boy Meets World*), 67
Cosby Show, 212
Cosmopolitan magazine, 87, 89, 187–194
Crews, television, 73
Criminal justice system, 148–149
Crooklyn (film), 176–178
Crouse, Lindsay, 108
Crystal, Billy, 102
CSI (television program), 63
Cuban American women, 11
Cusack, Ami, 77

Cybertalking, 144–145

Daniels, Jeff, 107
Dating shows, 74, 79, 80
Davis, Bette, 138
Dawson's Creek (television program), 159
Dean, Loren, 107
Deer Hunter III (video game), 119
Demetrulias, D. M., 86
De Mornay, Rebecca, 108, 137
Denfeld, Rene, 133, 134, 138
Dieting, 42
Dietz, Tracy, 116, 118, 120
Discourse analysis, 86
Discovery Health Channel, 211
Dissonance-based interventions, 48–49
Documentaries, 211, 212
Dolores Claiborne (film), 136, 137
Don Juan de Marco (film), 106–107
Don't Talk to Anyone (film), 105, 106
Dr. Phil (television program), 66
Dreyfuss, Richard, 102
Duke Nukem 3D (video game), 115

Eating behaviors, influence of media on, 10–11
Eating disorders, 11, 41, 42, 44, 46
Ebony magazine, 187–195
8 Simple Rules for Dating My Teenage Daughter (television program), 68
Eleanor Frutt (television character from *The Practice*), 64–65
Elimidate (television program), 74
Ellen Ripley (character in *Aliens*), 136
Entertainment magazine, 87, 89
Entertainment Software Association, 127
ER (television program), 63, 159
Essence magazine, 187–194
Ethnic diversity, of characters in video games, 125
Everybody Loves Raymond (television program), 66, 155, 159
Extreme Dating (television program), 66

Family Circle magazine, 87, 89, 187–194
Family PC magazine, 87
Fantasy, reality vs.
    in television portrayal of indirect aggression, 161–162
    and video games, 126–127
Fashion magazines, 42
Fatal Attraction (film), 110, 137

PC Magazine, 87, 89, 91
Pearson, P., 135
Peck, Gregory, 103
People magazine, 87, 89
Perfect Dark (video game), 117
Perpetrators, news coverage of. See News coverage, of victims and perpetrators
Phoebe (television character from Friends), 67
Physical aggression, 158
    indirect vs. direct, 155–156
    in television programs, 159–161
Playboy magazine, 82, 87, 89
Plous, S., 187
Police, 143–144
Poussaint, Alvin, 212
Power, in Spike Lee's She's Gotta Have It, 178–179
The Practice (television program), 64–65
Practice Directorate (American Psychological Association), 211
Presidio Med (television program), 208
Primal Fear (film), 106
Prince of Tides (film), 102, 106, 108
Propaganda, advertising as, 93
Pseudodocumentaries, 75
PsycINFO, 4
Psychology, ix, 213
    feminist, 82–83, 181
Psychology professionals, portrayal of, in film, 101–111
    and APA Media Watch Committee, 110–111
    stereotypes, 102–104
    survey results, 105–110
    and underrepresentation of psychologists, 104–105
Puerto Rican Day parade (New York City), 143, 145–146
Putnam, A., 78

Race, treatment of, in video games, 117
Rachel (television character from Friends), 31, 33–36, 67
Rachel Meadows (character in School Daze), 174–175
Racial identity, 179
Racism, responses to, 180
Raising Arizona (film), 137
Raising Cain (film), 106–108
Rand, K., 104
Rape, 144, 145, 178
Rape in America: A Report to the Nation, 144

Reality TV shows, depiction of women in, 71–83
    and character traits of characters vs. actors, 72
    clearly fictional portrayals of women, 82
    and gender stereotypes, 72–73, 80
    and genres of reality shows, 74–75
    and "hyper-masculine ethos," 79
    lesbians, 76–77
    minority women, 79–80
    older women, 79
    and production crew, 73
    significance of, 80–83
    strong women, 77–79
    viewers' perception of, 81
The Real World (television program), 66, 67–68, 74, 75, 77
Reiter, A. D., 104, 109
Relationship-challenge shows, 74
Role discrepancy, 172–175, 179
Role models for girls and women, and depiction of women on television, 64–66
RollerCoaster Tycoon (video game), 119
Rory (television character from Gilmore Girls), 65–66, 67
Rosenthal, N. R., 86
Ross, K., 207
Russell, Kurt, 107
Russo, Rene, 107

Samuels, L., 110
Sassler, M., 104
SATAQ. See Sociocultural Attitudes Towards Appearance Questionnaire
Satellite television, 62
Saving Silverman (film), 105, 106, 108
Schneider, I., 102
School Daze (film), 174–176
Sciorra, Annabella, 108, 137
Sega, 116
Seinfeld (television program), 155, 159
Self-consciousness, 9–10
Self-image, 205
Self-judgments, 170
Self-respect, 176
September 11, 2001, terrorist attacks, 149
Seventeen magazine, 11
Sex, in television programs, 62
Sex in the City (television program), 63, 64
Sexism, 6
Sexual behavior, in film portrayals of African American women, 172, 178–179

ABOUT THE CONTRIBUTORS

EDITORS

Ellen Cole, PhD, is professor of psychology at Alaska Pacific University in Anchorage and a former editor of the journal *Women & Therapy* and of the Haworth Press book program, Innovations in Feminist Studies. She is the president-elect of the Alaska Psychological Association. She has received a Distinguished Publication Award from the Association for Women in Psychology (AWP), was twice the recipient of the Jewish Scholarship Award from AWP's Jewish Caucus, and has hosted a mental health call-in radio show. Dr. Cole is a fellow of two American Psychological Association (APA) divisions—Society for the Psychology of Women and Media Psychology—and chaired APA's Committee on Women in Psychology.

Jessica Henderson Daniel, PhD, ABPP, is director of training in psychology and associate director of training in adolescent medicine at Children's Hospital, Boston. She is an assistant professor of psychology in the Department of Psychiatry at Harvard Medical School and adjunct associate professor in the Clinical Psychology Program at Boston University. Dr. Daniel is a member of the American Psychological Association (APA) Board of Directors and is a recipient of the 2002 APA Award for Distinguished Contributions to Education and Training in Psychology. She is past president of the Society for the Psychology of Women of the APA. Her teaching and presentations have focused on the impact of media images on people of color, especially women.

CONTRIBUTORS

Laura S. Brown, PhD, is professor of psychology in the Washington School of Professional Psychology at Argosy University, Seattle, and maintains a

225

private feminist therapy practice specializing in treating survivors of trauma. She has published widely on feminist practice theory, diagnosis and assessment, trauma treatment, psychotherapy with lesbians, and issues of diversity in feminist therapy. She began her career as a media psychologist in 1980 as the host of a weekend call-in self-help show and has appeared as a guest commentator on issues of women and violence on local and national TV and radio shows. She is past president of American Psychological Association Division 35 (Society for the Psychology of Women) and 44 (Society for the Psychological Study of Lesbian, Gay, and Bisexual Issues) and twice winner of the Distinguished Publication Award of the Association for Women in Psychology.

Thema Bryant-Davis, PhD, earned her doctorate in clinical psychology from Duke University, with a focus on trauma recovery and the intersection of racial and gender identity. She completed her postdoctoral fellowship at Harvard Medical Center's Victims of Violence Program and served for 3 years as S.H.A.R.E. Program Coordinator at Princeton University. She was appointed as an American Psychological Association representative to the United Nations and was recently elected to the Committee on International Relations in Psychology. Dr. Bryant-Davis resides in Los Angeles and is the author of the book *Thriving in the Wake of Trauma: A Multicultural Guide* (2005).

Laura J. Burlingame-Lee, MS, is currently a doctoral candidate in counseling psychology at Colorado State University. While researching information about advertisements for a class project, she became intrigued by the ways in which computers are marketed to the public. She is very interested in continuing to research diversity issues related to marketing and use of computer technology. This is her first publication in that area. While an undergraduate, Ms. Burlingame-Lee also aided in research concerning the psychology of peace and violence, especially as it relates to sustainable development.

Silvia Sara Canetto, PhD, is associate professor of psychology at Colorado State University in Fort Collins. She has published on various topics relating to gender and culture. She is best known for her research on gender, culture, and suicidal behavior. She is a recipient of the Shneidman Award of the American Association of Suicidology and is an elected member of the International Academy for Suicide Research. Dr. Canetto is on the editorial board of five national and international professional journals and has served as program chair for the Society for the Psychology of Women. Dr. Canetto is a fellow of two American Psychological Association divisions, the Society for the Psychology of Women and International Psychology.

Elizabeth K. Carll, PhD, is a clinical and consulting psychologist in private practice in Long Island, New York, with interests in stress and posttraumatic stress management; crisis, disaster, and violence intervention; health psychology; family conflict and relationships; and mass media. Dr. Carll is the author of *Violence in Our Lives: Impact on Workplace, Home, and Community* (1991) and frequently writes and speaks on topics impacting the community. Dr. Carll is a pioneer in working with the news media to help the public cope with the psychological aftermath of disaster and violence. She is president of the Media Psychology division of the American Psychological Association and is the founder and chair of the division's News Media, Public Education, Public Policy Committee. She is also the representative to the United Nations from the International Society for Traumatic Stress Studies and chairs the Media/ICT Working Group of the United Nations NGO Committee on Mental Health.

Jody C. Dill, PhD, is assistant professor of psychology at Lenoir-Rhyne College in Hickory, North Carolina. He received his PhD in social psychology at the University of Missouri—Columbia in 1997 and has published extensively in the areas of aggression, attribution, and social inference and in his primary interest of motivation and emotion. He has given numerous presentations and seminars to professional societies in these areas.

Karen E. Dill, PhD, received her doctorate in social psychology from the University of Missouri—Columbia. Her work on the effects of violent video games on aggression has received wide interest from the media, including *Time Magazine*, CNN, *USA Today*, and the BBC. Dr. Dill has testified before the United States Congress about media violence effects and has led media literacy workshops in her community. She is currently an associate professor of psychology at Lenoir-Rhyne College in Hickory, North Carolina.

Nicole Dubowitz is a junior at Bethesda–Chevy Chase High School in Maryland and a part-time intern at the National Research Center for Women & Families. As an intern, she provides a teen perspective for various articles and projects, conducts Internet research, and helps with graphic image editing for the center's newsletter.

Norma D. Feshbach, PhD, ABPP, is professor emerita and former dean and chair in the Graduate School of Education, University of California, Los Angeles. Her research, teaching, and policy activities reflect her multidisciplinary interests and training in developmental, clinical, and educational psychology. Empathic behavior in children, gender differences, chronic stress in parents, children's rights, and television have been the subject of many of her more than 100 publications. Her past awards include Distinguished Alumnus, City College of New York; Fulbright; Hayton Foundation for Outstanding Research; Distinguished Psychologist, California Psychological Association; Cattell Sabbatical Award; Who's Who in America; and a Distinguished Contribution to Psychology and Media Award, Division

42 of the American Psychological Association. She is a frequent consultant on television programs for children and adolescents.

Kimberly Gamble is a doctoral student at the Virginia Consortium Program in Clinical Psychology. She received a master's degree in clinical/community psychology in May 2003. Ms. Gamble's research interests include the HIV/AIDS epidemic in minority communities, aggression and violence among adolescents, and the psychological well-being of youth at risk. Ms. Gamble plans to pursue a clinical career working with children and adolescents.

Douglas A. Gentile, PhD, is a developmental psychologist, an assistant professor of psychology at Iowa State University, and the director of research for the National Institute on Media and the Family. He directs the Media Research Lab at Iowa State University where he conducts research on media's impact on children and adults (both positive and negative). Dr. Gentile has authored numerous studies and is the editor of the recent book *Media Violence and Children: A Complete Guide for Parents and Professionals* (2003). His research has been reported on National Public Radio's *Morning Edition* and NBC's *Today Show* as well as in the *New York Times*, *Washington Post*, *Los Angeles Times*, and *USA Today*. He received his doctorate in child psychology from the Institute of Child Development at the University of Minnesota.

Stefanie C. Gilbert, PhD, is assistant professor of psychology at Howard University in Washington, DC, and a licensed clinical psychologist in Maryland. She is president of the Washington Society for the Study of Eating Disorders and Obesity and a member of the governance board for the Women's Studies Program at Howard University.

Kristen Harrison, PhD, is an associate professor in the Department of Speech Communication at the University of Illinois at Urbana–Champaign. In 2002 she received a W.T. Grant Scholars Award from the William T. Grant Foundation to study the effects of mass media exposure on body image, self-perceptions, and disordered eating in preadolescents. Her interest in media effects on children dates back to her involvement as a coauthor on the National Television Violence Study. Professor Harrison has also studied children's fright reactions to scary media and children's understanding of television content ratings and advisories.

Patrick S. Hudgins is a recent graduate of the Virginia Consortium Program in Clinical Psychology. He completed a predoctoral internship with the University of Arkansas for Medical Sciences Child Study Center located at Arkansas Children's Hospital in Little Rock. Mr. Hudgins's interests include child and family therapy, parenting training, and the development of prevention programs to promote resiliency in children.

Helene Keery, PhD, is a postdoctoral fellow in the Leadership Education in Adolescent Health Program at the University of Minnesota Division of General Pediatrics and Adolescent Health. She completed her doctoral studies at the University of South Florida and her clinical internship in the Department of Clinical and Health Psychology at the University of Florida Health Sciences Center. Her research interests are in the developmental psychopathology of body image and eating disturbance as well as prevention of child and adolescent eating disorders and obesity.

Kim S. Kjaersgaard, PhD, is professor of psychology at Alaska Pacific University in Anchorage. She received her PhD in developmental psychology from the University of Chicago, with an emphasis on adult development and aging. She has conducted evaluation research regarding a variety of mental health, educational, and community development issues. She has a particular interest in how people create meaning in their lives, with a recent focus on worldviews and the terrorist events of September 11.

Lynn Edith Paulson, PhD, is a professor in the Liberal Studies Department at Alaska Pacific University, where she teaches communication and women's studies. She researches women's violence and representations of women's violence in popular culture.

Michelle V. Porche, EdD, is a research scientist at the Center for Research on Women at Wellesley College. She is also a research analyst at Harvard University Graduate School of Education, working on a longitudinal project investigating language and literacy development related to motivation and academic achievement for children and adolescents. She has focused most recently on the relationship between masculine role expectations and boys' engagement and achievement in language arts.

William A. Richter, PhD, is chair of the School of Communication and Literature at Lenoir-Rhyne College in Hickory, North Carolina. He also has a secondary specialty in early childhood education. His research interests include children and television and communication history.

Janis Sanchez-Hucles, PhD, is professor of psychology at Old Dominion University and the Virginia Consortium Program in Clinical Psychology. She became interested in the power of media images through her teaching, clinical, training, and research activities and collects and uses examples of how the media both reflect and distort societal images of the lives of people of color. Dr. Sanchez-Hucles is active in the American Psychological Association's Society for the Psychology of Women, Society for the Study of Ethnic Minorities, and Society for Independent Practice. She is the author of numerous publications, including *The First Session With African Americans: A Step-by-Step Guide* (2000).

Harriet T. Schultz, PhD, received her AB from Barnard College, her MEd from Harvard University Graduate School of Education, and her PhD in clinical psychology from the University of Pittsburgh. She is in independent practice in Houston, Texas. She was recently president of the Houston Psychological Association (2001–2002) and is the current chair of the Media Watch Committee of the Division of Media Psychology (Division 46) of the American Psychological Association (APA). This committee monitors the portrayal of fictional mental health professionals in television and film. She has conducted research in this area and presented papers at local and state psychological associations as well as at annual conventions of the APA.

C. Lynn Sorsoli, EdD, is a research scientist on the Television Consumption and Adolescent Sexual Activity Project at the Center for Research on Women at Wellesley College. She received her doctorate in human behavior and psychology from Harvard University's Graduate School of Education, where she studied women's experiences of personal disclosure and the effects of trauma on relationships and development. Her recent work has explored the intersection of race, class, and complex posttraumatic stress, and she is currently exploring men's experiences of disclosing a history of sexual abuse.

J. Kevin Thompson, PhD, is professor of psychology in the Department of Psychology at the University of South Florida. He is on the editorial boards of three eating disorder journals (*International Journal of Eating Disorders, Eating Disorders,* and *Eating and Weight Disorders*). He has authored, coauthored, or edited four books on body image, eating disorders, and obesity, including *Exacting Beauty: Theory, Assessment, and Treatment of Body Image Disturbance* (1999, American Psychological Association). His current research interests are in the assessment of risk factors for the development of body image and eating problems in adolescence.

Deborah L. Tolman, EdD, is senior research scientist and associate director at the Center for Research on Women at Wellesley College. In 1995, she founded the Gender and Sexuality Project, which she continues to direct. She has been involved in research pertaining to adolescent development and women's sexuality for over a decade. Her current research focuses on the development of sexuality for girls and boys over the course of adolescence. Her new book *Dilemmas of Desire: Teenage Girls Talk about Sexuality* was published in 2002. Dr. Tolman is a fellow of the American Psychological Association (APA), the Society for the Psychological Study of Social Issues (Division 9), and the Society for the Psychology of Women (Division 35). She received a Committee on Women in Psychology Leadership Award from the APA in 2002.

L. Monique Ward, PhD, is an associate professor of psychology (developmental) at the University of Michigan. Her research examines the dynamics of gender and sexual socialization, focusing on the nature and impact of messages received from parents, peers, and the media about male–female relations. Much of her current work has examined the contributions of television to the sexual socialization of American youth. She has been invited to present findings from this work at several national conferences and venues, including the U.S. Senate. Her current research also explores the intersections between gender roles, body image, and sexuality for White and Black women.

Diana Zuckerman, PhD, is president of the National Research Center for Women & Families, a Washington, DC-based think tank that uses research to advocate for programs and policies that improve the health and safety of women, children, and families (www.center4research.org). She started her career working in psychology and public health at Vassar, Yale, and Harvard before moving to Washington, DC, to work on domestic social policy issues in the U.S. Congress, the U.S. Department of Health and Human Services, the White House, and several nonprofit organizations. She is the coauthor of four books and several articles on the impact of the media on children and society. She has also written numerous congressional reports and articles for academic journals, medical journals, and national newspapers and magazines on public policy issues involving health and social programs and has been interviewed on all the major TV networks, many radio programs, and national newspapers and magazines.